MW01230890

What's New in Visual FoxPro® 8.0

Tamar E. Granor
Doug Hennig

Hentzenwerke Publishing

Published by:
Hentzenwerke Publishing
980 East Circle Drive
Whitefish Bay, WI 53217 USA

Hentzenwerke Publishing books are available through booksellers and directly from the publisher. Contact Hentzenwerke Publishing at:
414.332.9876
414.332.9463 (fax)
www.hentzenwerke.com
books@hentzenwerke.com

What's New in Visual FoxPro® 8.0
   By Tamar E. Granor and Doug Hennig
   Technical Editor: Jim Slater
   Copy Editor: Nicole McNeish
   Cover Art: "Riviera" by Todd Gnacinski, Milwaukee, WI

ISBN: 1-930919-40-9

Manufactured in the United States of America.

Our Contract with You, The Reader

In which we, the folks who make up Hentzenwerke Publishing, describe what you, the reader, can expect from this book and from us.

Hi there!

I've been writing professionally (in other words, eventually getting a paycheck for my scribbles) since 1974, and writing about software development since 1992. As an author, I've worked with a half-dozen different publishers and corresponded with thousands of readers over the years. As a software developer and all-around geek, I've also acquired a library of more than 100 computer and software-related books.

Thus, when I donned the publisher's cap five years ago to produce the *1997 Developer's Guide,* I had some pretty good ideas of what I liked (and didn't like) from publishers, what readers liked and didn't like, and what I, as a reader, liked and didn't like.

Now, with our new titles for 2003, we're entering our sixth season. (For those who are keeping track, the '97 DevGuide was our first, albeit abbreviated, season, the batch of six "Essentials" for Visual FoxPro 6.0 in 1999 was our second, and, in keeping with the sports analogy, the books we published in 2000 and 2001 comprised our third and fourth.)

John Wooden, the famed UCLA basketball coach, posited that teams aren't consistent; they're always getting better—or worse. We'd like to get better…

One of my goals for this season is to build a closer relationship with you, the reader. In order for us to do this, you've got to know what you should expect from us.

- You have the right to expect that your order will be processed quickly and correctly, and that your book will be delivered to you in new condition.

- You have the right to expect that the content of your book is technically accurate and up-to-date, that the explanations are clear, and that the layout is easy to read and follow without a lot of fluff or nonsense.

- You have the right to expect access to source code, errata, FAQs, and other information that's relevant to the book via our Web site.

- You have the right to expect an electronic version of your printed book to be available via our Web site.

- You have the right to expect that, if you report errors to us, your report will be responded to promptly, and that the appropriate notice will be included in the errata and/or FAQs for the book.

Naturally, there are some limits that we bump up against. There are humans involved, and they make mistakes. A book of 500 pages contains, on average, 150,000 words and several megabytes of source code. It's not possible to edit and re-edit multiple times to catch every last misspelling and typo, nor is it possible to test the source code on every permutation of development environment and operating system—and still price the book affordably.

Once printed, bindings break, ink gets smeared, signatures get missed during binding. On the delivery side, Web sites go down, packages get lost in the mail.

Nonetheless, we'll make our best effort to correct these problems—once you let us know about them.

In return, when you have a question or run into a problem, we ask that you first consult the errata/FAQs for your book on our Web site. If you don't find the answer there, please e-mail us at books@hentzenwerke.com with as much information and detail as possible, including 1) the steps to reproduce the problem, 2) what happened, and 3) what you expected to happen, together with 4) any other relevant information.

I'd like to stress that we need you to communicate questions and problems clearly. For example…

- "Your downloads don't work" isn't enough information for us to help you. "I get a 404 error when I click on the **Download Source Code** link on **www.hentzenwerke.com/book/downloads.html**" is something we can help you with.

- "The code in Chapter 10 caused an error" again isn't enough information. "I performed the following steps to run the source code program DisplayTest.PRG in Chapter 10, and I received an error that said 'Variable m.liCounter not found'" is something we can help you with.

We'll do our best to get back to you within a couple of days, either with an answer or at least an acknowledgment that we've received your inquiry and that we're working on it.

On behalf of the authors, technical editors, copy editors, layout artists, graphical artists, indexers, and all the other folks who have worked to put this book in your hands, I'd like to thank you for purchasing this book, and I hope that it will prove to be a valuable addition to your technical library. Please let us know what you think about this book—we're looking forward to hearing from you.

As Groucho Marx once observed, "Outside of a dog, a book is a man's best friend. Inside of a dog, it's too dark to read."

Whil Hentzen
Hentzenwerke Publishing
February 2003

List of Chapters

Table of Contents

Chapter 10: COM and Web Services Enhancements   195

Chapter 11: Event Binding   213

Acknowledgements

A number of people contributed to this book in both tangible and intangible ways. Our thanks to all of them for making it a better book.

Particular thanks to our publisher and friend, Whil Hentzen, who gives us the opportunity to write. Our technical editor, Jim Slater, did a terrific job in checking our work, pointing out what we had missed, and generally keeping us on the straight and narrow. Copy editor, Nicole McNeish, cleaned up after our messes, ensuring that what's left is clean, readable prose.

Once again, the Visual FoxPro team at Microsoft handed us a new version worth writing about. We believe VFP 8 is the most significant upgrade to FoxPro since VFP 3. A few members of the team were particularly helpful in deepening our understanding of the new features. Our thanks to Randy Brown, Gene Goldhammer, Aleksey Tsingauz, Fabian Winternitz, and especially Beta newsgroup sysops Jim Saunders and Brad Peterson, and documentation writer Esther Fan.

The Visual FoxPro beta testers are the greatest. They pound on the product, ask good questions, write examples, argue about features, and sometimes it seems contribute nearly as much as the VFP team. They've helped us understand the purpose and uses for many of the new features.

Now, on to our individual thanks.

My family continues to support my work in all kinds of ways. My husband, Marshal, and sons, Solomon and Nathaniel, let me ramble on about things they don't understand and don't get too glassy-eyed when I come to dinner raving about an exciting new feature or a chapter I'm really proud of. Without them, it wouldn't be anywhere near as much fun.

Tamar

My wife Peggy and son Nick, who had to put up Halloween and Christmas decorations without me this year, light my life with love, joy, laughter, and adventure. I feel especially lucky because I actually realize how blessed I am to share my life with them.

Doug

About the Authors

Tamar E. Granor

Tamar E. Granor, Ph.D, is the owner of Tomorrow's Solutions, LLC. She has developed and enhanced numerous FoxPro and Visual FoxPro applications for businesses and other organizations. She currently focuses on working with other developers through consulting and subcontracting. Tamar served as Editor of FoxPro Advisor magazine from 1994 to 2000. She is currently the magazine's Technical Editor and co-author of the popular Advisor Answers column.

Tamar is co-author of the *Hacker's Guide to Visual FoxPro 7.0* (and its award-winning predecessor), *What's New in Visual FoxPro 7.0*, and *Microsoft Office Automation with Visual FoxPro*. She is the Technical Editor of *Visual FoxPro Certification Exams Study Guide*. All of these books are available from Hentzenwerke Publishing (**www.hentzenwerke.com**). Tamar is also co-author of the *Hacker's Guide to Visual FoxPro 3.0* (Addison-Wesley) and she contributed to John Hawkins' *FoxPro 2.5 Programmer's Reference* (Que).

Tamar is a Microsoft Certified Professional and a Microsoft Support Most Valuable Professional. Tamar speaks frequently about Visual FoxPro at conferences and user groups in Europe and North America, including every FoxPro DevCon since 1993. She served as Technical Content Manager for the 1997-1999 Visual FoxPro DevCons and was part of the coordination team for the Visual FoxPro Excellence Awards.

Tamar earned her doctorate in Computer and Information Science at the University of Pennsylvania, where her research focused on implementation of user interfaces. She lives in suburban Philadelphia with her husband and two teenage sons. Tamar's website is **www.tomorrowssolutionsllc.com**; she can be reached at tamar@tomorrowssolutionsllc.com.

Doug Hennig

Doug Hennig is a partner with Stonefield Systems Group Inc. He is the author of the award-winning Stonefield Database Toolkit (SDT), the award-winning Stonefield Query, and the CursorAdapter and DataEnvironment builders that come with Microsoft Visual FoxPro 8. Doug is co-author of *The Hacker's Guide to Visual FoxPro 7.0* and *What's New in Visual FoxPro 7.0*. He was the technical editor of *The Hacker's Guide to Visual FoxPro 6.0* and *The Fundamentals*. All of these books are from Hentzenwerke Publishing. Doug writes the monthly *Reusable Tools* column in FoxTalk. He has spoken at every Microsoft FoxPro Developers Conference (DevCon) since 1997 and at user groups and developer conferences all over North America. He is a Microsoft Most Valuable Professional (MVP) and Certified Professional (MCP). His Web sites are **www.stonefield.com** and **www.stonefieldquery.com**, and he can be reached at dhennig@stonefield.com.

Jim Slater

Jim Slater is an independent developer specializing in Visual FoxPro client/server applications and .Net web applications. He has extensive experience with every version of Foxbase, FoxPro and Visual Foxpro, as well as with SQL Server and Sybase databases.

Jim is a Microsoft Certified Professional and past Microsoft Most Valuable Professional. His articles and tips have appeared in several publications including FoxPro Advisor. He is vice president of the Rocky Mountain FoxPro User Group and a frequent presenter at user group meetings.

Jim lives in Denver, CO, and enjoys hiking, fly fishing, and snowshoeing in those rare moments away from the computer. He can be reached at jim@jslater.com.

How to Download the Files

Hentzenwerke Publishing generally provides two sets of files to accompany its books. The first is the source code referenced throughout the text. Note that some books do not have source code; in those cases, a placeholder file is provided in lieu of the source code in order to alert you of the fact. The second is the e-book version (or versions) of the book. Depending on the book, we provide e-books in either the compiled HTML Help (.CHM) format, Adobe Acrobat (.PDF) format, or both. Here's how to get them.

Both the source code and e-book file(s) are available for download from the Hentzenwerke Web site. In order to obtain them, follow these instructions:

1. Point your Web browser to **www.hentzenwerke.com**.

2. Look for "Downloads" link and follow the link to book downloads.

3. A page describing the download process will appear. This page has two sections:

   - **Section 1:** If you were issued a username/password directly from Hentzenwerke Publishing, you can enter them into this page.

   - **Section 2:** If you did not receive a username/password from Hentzenwerke Publishing, don't worry! You'll need to register with us. After doing so, look for the question about your book. Note that you'll need your physical book when you answer the question.

4. A page that lists the books we have associated with you will appear.

5. An e-mail with hyperlinks for your downloads will be sent to the e-mail address we have on file for you.

Note that the e-book file(s) are covered by the same copyright laws as the printed book. Reproduction and/or distribution of these files is against the law.

If you have questions or problems, the fastest way to get a response is to e-mail us at books@hentzenwerke.com.

Introduction

Here we are again with a book discussing new features in the latest version of Visual FoxPro.

The first question someone asks when they hear about a new version of Visual FoxPro is "what's new?" To help answer that question, we wrote *What's New in Visual FoxPro 7.0*, along with co-author Kevin McNeish. That book was a concise guide to all the new features, language elements, and functionality in VFP 7. Unlike the *Hacker's Guide to Visual FoxPro* (also available from Hentzenwerke Publishing), it wasn't intended to be an exhaustive look at the new features, but instead to give the reader an idea why they were added or what they might be used for.

As we went over the list of new and improved features in VFP 8, we realized there was an even bigger need for a "what's new" book for VFP 8 than there was for VFP 7. Although VFP 7 provided enhancements to many areas of the product, it was largely viewed as a developer productivity upgrade because of the huge impact of IntelliSense. VFP 8, on the other hand, has improvements in nearly every aspect: the database engine, OOP, COM, Web Services, xBase language, and so forth. Although the documentation received a major overhaul in version 8, it still doesn't gather all of the new features in a single, well-organized place, nor does it give practical examples of when you might use these features. Thus, this book is intended to be your tour guide to what's new in VFP 8, explaining not only the "what", but also the "why" and the "when." It also points out potential drawbacks for some of the new features and steers you around the pitfalls.

Organization

This book has three major sections. Chapters 1 through 5 cover changes related to developer productivity. The changes include enhancements to the interactive development environment (IDE) and existing tools, as well as three major new components: the Toolbox, Task Pane Manager, and Code References tools.

Chapters 6, 7, and 8 cover improvements to VFP's powerful database engine. The most exciting changes provide new and easier ways to access non-VFP data, such as SQL Server, and better support for XML, including the ability to consume hierarchical XML and ADO.NET DataSets. Changes in the SQL engine may break existing code, so be sure to check out the details (and workarounds) in Chapter 8.

The final six chapters cover enhancements related to application development. Included here are such features as new base classes, improvements to existing base classes, structured error handling, event binding, and language enhancements.

As with our previous book, because many new and changed items could logically fit into more than one place, we've provided lots of cross-references, pointing you to other sections or chapters where a topic is discussed more fully.

Get the picture

We used a few icons in this book to highlight important information.

 *This symbol is your clue that there's example code available. All the code for this book can be downloaded from **www.hentzenwerke.com**. See page xvii for details.*

Some items just need to be pointed out or don't fit very well into the flow of the text. This icon identifies notes of that sort.

What about the code?

The code for this book is organized by chapter, with a separate zip file for each chapter that has code. Each zip file should be self-contained, with everything you need to run it.

Thrill ride

VFP 8 is the most significant new version of Visual FoxPro since VFP 3. We are very excited about this version, and are certain that once you've read this book and spent some time working with the product, you'll be as excited as we are.

Chapter 1
Interactive Development Environment (IDE)

Life has gotten easier for developers in each version of Visual FoxPro. VFP 8 is no exception. It brings improvements in window docking, adds IntelliSense to the Watch window, and more.

Visual FoxPro 8 doesn't have any revolutionary changes in the IDE like IntelliSense (introduced in VFP 7), or color-coded syntax (introduced in VFP 5). But it does include a number of changes that make it easier to focus on what you need to get done rather than on how to do it.

Window docking

VFP 7 introduced docking for a number of IDE windows, such as the Command window and the Property Sheet. But the docking capabilities in that version had a number of weaknesses that made it difficult to use docked windows productively. VFP 8 addresses those weaknesses in several ways.

Perhaps the most important change is that window docking is now persistent. If windows are docked (whether together or to a border of the VFP desktop) when you close VFP, they'll still be docked when you open it again. This makes it possible to find your own optimal arrangement of the IDE windows, set it up once, and use it forever.

Docking windows programmatically

Of course, different window arrangements work best for different situations. So, the VFP team went farther and gave developers the ability to manage window docking programmatically. The new DOCK WINDOW command lets you dock windows to the VFP borders, as well as tab-dock and link-dock groups of windows. The ADOCKSTATE() function lets you determine the current arrangement.

As with interactive docking, DOCK WINDOW applies only to IDE windows and toolbars. See the topic "Docking Windows" in the VFP Help for a list of windows and toolbars that can be docked. Also, be aware that the window or toolbar mentioned in the command must be open or you get an error.

The syntax for DOCK WINDOW is a little confusing, so rather than provide the complete syntax diagram, we'll show you three ways to use it:

```
DOCK WINDOW WindowName POSITION nPosition
DOCK WINDOW WindowName WINDOW TargetWindowName
DOCK WINDOW WindowName POSITION nPosition WINDOW TargetWindowName
```

The first form of the command lets you dock a window along the borders of the VFP desktop. If you have the Debugger running in the Debug frame, you can also use this version of DOCK WINDOW to dock any of the Debugger windows along the borders of the Debug frame; tab-docking and link-docking aren't supported in this case. The value you specify for nPosition determines where it's docked; use 0 for the top border, 1 for the left border, 2 for the right border, and 3 for the bottom border. For example, issuing this command:

```
DOCK WINDOW Command POSITION 3
```

docks the Command window at the bottom of the VFP desktop.

> *Issuing DOCK WINDOW on any window that supports docking makes the window dockable. That is, even if the dockable attribute is turned off for that window (interactively or with WDOCKABLE()), issuing DOCK WINDOW turns it on.*

The second form of the command tab-docks the specified window with the specified target window, placing the specified window (the one named first) on top and having the left-most tab. For example, the following command produces the configuration shown in **Figure 1**. Once a pair of windows is tab-docked, you can add additional windows to the tab-docked group by specifying any window in the group as the target window.

```
DOCK WINDOW View WINDOW Command
```

> *For historical reasons, the name of the Data Session window is View.*

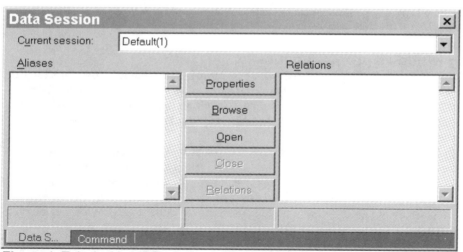

Figure 1. *Tab-docking IDE windows. Two forms of the DOCK WINDOW command let you tab-dock windows.*

The third form of the command does two different things. If nPosition is between 0 and 3, the specified window is link-docked with the target window, putting the specified window in the position indicated by nPosition (again, 0 for top, and so forth). The following command results in the arrangement shown in **Figure 2**.

```
DOCK WINDOW View POSITION 1 WINDOW Command
```

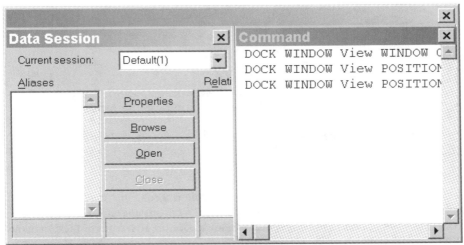

Figure 2. *Link-docking. Specifying both a position (between 0 and 3) and another window in DOCK WINDOW results in link-docking.*

If nPosition is 4, the two windows are tab-docked. The following command shows another way to produce the result in **Figure 1**.

```
DOCK WINDOW View POSITION 4 WINDOW Command
```

Once two or more windows are docked together, whether tab-docked or link-docked, you can dock the entire group by issuing DOCK WINDOW for any window in the group. For example, given the configuration shown in **Figure 2**, issue either of the following commands to dock the group at the bottom, with the result shown in **Figure 3**.

```
DOCK WINDOW View POSITION 3
DOCK WINDOW Command POSITION 3
```

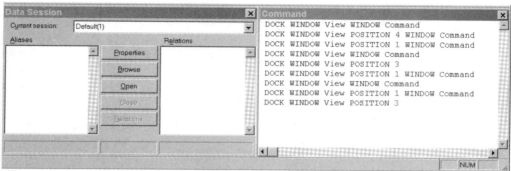

Figure 3. *Docking docked groups. Once windows are docked together, you can dock the whole group by issuing DOCK WINDOW for any window in the group.*

> *In VFP 8, when link-docked windows are docked to the VFP desktop, the border surrounding the group is removed. This is a (good) change from VFP 7's behavior.*

VFP lets you create some extremely complex combinations through tab-docking, link-docking, and docking to borders. Fortunately, DOCK WINDOW provides a way to undock just what you want without interfering with other windows. Use the first form of the command (DOCK WINDOW WindowName POSITION nPosition) for undocking.

Specify –1 for nPosition to totally undock the specified window, both from any VFP border and from any other windows with which it's either tab-docked or link-docked. For example, given the configuration in **Figure 3**, the following command undocks the Command window, leaving it free-floating, while the Data Session window ("View") remains docked at the bottom of the desktop.

```
DOCK WINDOW Command POSITION -1
```

Specify –2 for nPosition to undock an entire tab-docked or link-docked group from the VFP border. Doing so leaves the group tab-docked or link-docked. For example, starting with the configuration shown in **Figure 3**, issue either of the following commands to restore the configuration shown in **Figure 2**.

```
DOCK WINDOW Command POSITION -2
DOCK WINDOW View POSITION -2
```

If the window you specify when you indicate POSITION –2 isn't part of a tab-docked or link-docked group, but is docked to the VFP desktop, DOCK WINDOW treats it as POSITION –1 and undocks the window. If the window you specify isn't docked anywhere, or you specify a tab-docked or link-docked group that's not docked to the VFP desktop, the command does nothing.

Finally, specify –3 to remove a tab-docked group of windows from a link-docked group. The following commands create the configuration shown in **Figure 4**.

```
DOCK WINDOW Command WINDOW View
DOCK WINDOW Command WINDOW Properties POSITION 0
DOCK WINDOW Document WINDOW Command POSITION 0
```

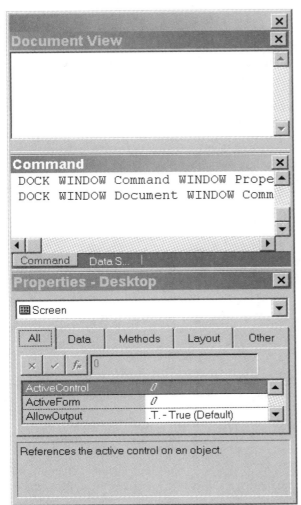

Figure 4. *Complex docking. You can mix tab and link-docking to create unusual arrangements of windows.*

To remove the tab-docked group from the configuration in Figure 4, use either of these commands:

```
DOCK WINDOW Command POSITION -3
DOCK WINDOW View POSITION -3
```

If you specify POSITION –3 for a window that's not part of a tab-docked group link-docked to other windows, you get the same behavior as when you specify POSITION –2 for that window.

Determining what's docked

With the ability to dock windows programmatically, you need a way to determine their current state. That's the job of the new ADOCKSTATE() function. Like the other "A" functions, ADOCKSTATE() fills an array with its results, creating or resizing the array as needed. ADOCKSTATE() accepts two parameters. The first is required; it's the array in which to put the results. The second parameter is optional; passing 1 restricts results to IDE windows only, while passing 2 limits the output to toolbars. Omitting the second parameters includes both IDE windows and toolbars. In all cases, the function returns the number of rows in the resulting array.

The array created by ADOCKSTATE() has four columns, shown in **Table 1**. All visible toolbars are included in the list, whether system or user-defined. Any visible IDE windows that support docking are included. User-defined forms are not included.

Table 1. Determining what's docked. The ADOCKSTATE() function creates a four-column array filled with information about IDE windows and toolbars.

Column	Meaning
1	Name of window or toolbar.
2	Docking state: 1 for docked; 0 for undocked.
3	The position where the window or toolbar is currently docked. Uses the same values as the DOCK WINDOW command.
4	The window to which this window is currently tab-docked or link-docked. Not used for toolbars.

The results of ADOCKSTATE() are a little confusing when windows are tab-docked or link-docked. All windows in the group have 1 (docked) in the second column, but the third and fourth column contents vary.

For tab-docked windows, the window with the left-most tab indicates the docking state of the group as a whole; if it's undocked, this window shows –1 (undocked) in column 3, and the empty string in column 4. All the other windows in the tab-docked group have 4 (tab-docked) in column 3 and the name of the window whose tab is immediately to the left of this window's tab in column 4. For example, **Figure 5** shows the Document View, Properties, and Data Session windows tab-docked. If the only other windows open are the Command Window and the Standard toolbar, executing ADOCKSTATE() at this point gives the results shown in **Table 2**.

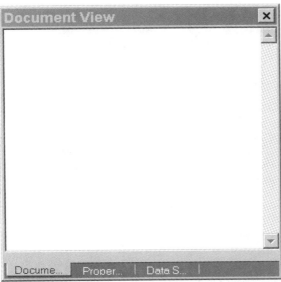

Figure 5. *Tab-docked group. Running ADOCKSTATE() on this group produces the results shown in Table 2.*

Table 2. *Checking on tab-docked groups. With the tab-docked group shown in Figure 5 open, along with the Command Window and the Standard toolbar, the array passed to ADOCKSTATE() gets these contents.*

Row	Window	Dock state	Dock position	Docked window
1	"DOCUMENT VIEW"	1	-1	""
2	"PROPERTIES"	1	4	"DOCUMENT VIEW"
3	"VIEW"	1	4	"PROPERTIES"
4	"Standard"	1	0	"Microsoft Visual FoxPro" (or whatever the VFP caption is)
5	"COMMAND"	0	-1	""

> *Don't count on the order of the items in the array created by ADOCKSTATE(). While windows that are tab-docked or link-docked always seem to be listed in sequence, the overall order of the windows varies.*

The results are similar for link-docked windows. The window at the top or left (or top left in more complex arrangements) contains information indicating how the group as a whole is docked. Each window in the group shows as docked to the window above it, if there is one; if not, it shows as docked to the window to its left. **Figure 6** shows a complex arrangement of link-docked windows. **Table 3** shows the contents of the array created by ADOCKSTATE(), assuming the only other window open is the Standard toolbar.

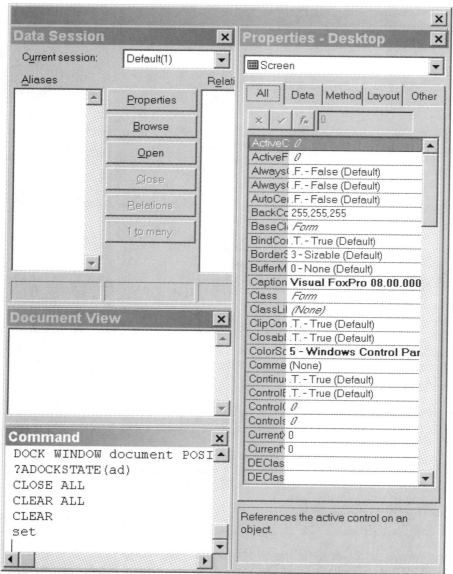

Figure 6. *Complex arrangement. Given this link-docked group of windows, ADOCKSTATE() produces the array in Table 3.*

Table 3. Checking on link-docked windows. Running ADOCKSTATE() on the window arrangement shown in Figure 6 gives these results.

Row	Window	Dock state	Dock position	Docked window
1	"VIEW"	1	-1	""
2	"Document View"	1	3	"VIEW"
3	"COMMAND"	1	3	"Document View"
4	"PROPERTIES"	1	2	"VIEW"
5	"Standard"	1	0	"Microsoft Visual FoxPro" (or whatever the VFP caption is)

Open Debugger windows (including the Debugger toolbar) are also included in the listing, whether the Debugger is set to the FoxPro frame or to the Debug frame.

Better keyboard support

Over the last few years, Microsoft has become more attuned to accessibility issues. VFP 8 reflects this concern with improved keyboard support for developers. You still can't develop a VFP application without either a mouse or software that simulates a mouse, but there are more places in this version where you can keep your hands on the keyboard. In addition, in several places, keystrokes now have their usual Windows meanings rather than legacy meanings from pre-Windows versions of FoxPro.

The most significant change is that Ctrl-Home and Ctrl-End now navigate to the first and last records, respectively, of grids and Browses, making them compatible with other Windows applications. In previous versions, Ctrl-Home opened a selected Memo field in grids and Browses, while Ctrl-End closed a Browse and was ignored in grids.

The behavior of Ctrl-Tab has also changed. In VFP 8, Ctrl-Tab in the development environment most often changes focus from one window to another, mimicking the behavior of Ctrl-F6. Ctrl-Shift-Tab does the same thing, but moves backward through the list of windows. Projects are included in the list of windows here, unless they're "rolled up," but torn-off tabs of projects are included regardless. Many of the IDE windows (such as the Property Sheet and Data Session windows) do not participate.

When focus is on a pageframe or a control within a pageframe, Ctrl-Tab moves to the next page. However, when a grid or a control within a grid has focus, Ctrl-Tab retains its older behavior of moving focus to the next control after the grid.

Several really useful new behaviors take place in the Property Sheet. First, when the Property Sheet has focus, you can now get to the Objects dropdown with Tab. In VFP 7 and earlier, tabbing in the Property Sheet moves you between the currently highlighted property, the page tabs, and when available, the action buttons and textbox for the current property, but not the Objects drop-down. In VFP 8, the list of objects is part of that cycle, so you can change from one object to another without the mouse. (Actually, you've always been able to change to the same property of the next object or the previous object with Ctrl-PgDn and Ctrl-PgUp. This behavior remains in VFP 8.) To make things even easier, once the object list has focus, the arrow keys move between the objects without any need to open the drop-down.

The other keyboard change in the Property Sheet is the behavior of the context menu key (either a dedicated key or the Shift-F10 combination). In VFP 7 and earlier, no matter where focus is on the Property Sheet, the context menu key brings up the context menu for the currently highlighted property. In VFP 8, when focus is on the drop-down list or one of the page tabs, the context menu key brings up the context menu for the Property Sheet as a whole.

IntelliSense enhancements

IntelliSense was a major new feature in VFP 7. VFP 8 includes some minor IntelliSense improvements. First of all, IntelliSense has been enabled for the textbox portion of the Watch window. Both keyword completion and List Members are available. For example, typing "mess()" into the textbox puts "MESSAGE()" into the Watch list. Typing the name of an object followed by a period into the textbox brings up a list of PEMs for that object, so you can choose the property you'd like to watch.

In addition, a number of scripts have been added to the FoxCode table that drives IntelliSense. The ZLOC script brings up a list of all local and public variables and parameters declared in the current method or procedure and lets you pick one from the list. The ZDEF script brings up a list of all #DEFINES available from #DEFINE or #INCLUDE statements in the routine. (Unfortunately, it does not include those from the default Include File specified for the form.) Based on the type ("S") used for them, we suspect these new scripts are designed for use in other scripts, but don't see any scripts that use them.

There are also new scripts for each of VFP's control structures. The new scripts are listed in **Table 4**.

Table 4. *New IntelliSense scripts. The FoxCode table supplied with VFP 8 includes scripts for the VFP control structures.*

Abbreviation	Represents
DOCASE	DO CASE structure with one CASE
DOWHILE	DO WHILE structure
FOREACH	FOR EACH structure
FOREND	FOR loop structure
IFELSE	IF structure with ELSE
IFEND	IF structure without ELSE
SCANEND	SCAN loop
TEXTEND	TEXT command with TEXTMERGE
TRYEND	TRY structure including one CATCH branch
WITHEND	WITH structure
WS	Web service instantiation code wrapped in TRY ...CATCH logic

We're delighted to see these scripts provided, but overall we think they're a little too basic. For example, the FOREND script generates this code:

```
FOR
ENDFOR
```

We're more inclined to include additional structure, to have a result like this (with "VAR" highlighted and ready for replacement):

```
FOR VAR = ~START~ TO ~FINISH~

ENDFOR
```

To do so, open the IntelliSense Manager, switch to the Custom page, and find the listing for FOREND. Click the Script button and modify the script code to look like this:

```
FOR ~Var~ = ~Start~ TO ~Finish~

<<lcSpace>>ENDFOR
```

Of course, we would really love it if marking multiple items in the script made it possible to tab among them and replace them with the right values. An alternate approach is to prompt for the necessary items before performing the replacement. For ideas on doing this and other custom scripts, check out **http://fox.wikis.com/wc.dll?Wiki~IntelliSenseCustomScripts~VFP**.

VFP 8 provides new IntelliSense behavior for some keywords. For the IMPLEMENTS keyword (part of a DEFINE CLASS structure), it provides an option to select the interface from a dialog box. IntelliSense for the DragIcon, MouseIcon, and OLEDragPicture properties can now display the same Open Picture dialog it does for the Icon and Picture properties.

There's one further change in IntelliSense, the addition of two new properties you can set to customize behavior. The first is lDebugScript, which allows you to debug IntelliSense scripts; it's true by default. The second new property is lEnableMultiWordCmdExpansion. It's true by default, but you can set it to false to prevent IntelliSense from adding the second word to a multi-word command. For example, when this property is true, ALTER is expanded to ALTER TABLE. When you set the property to false, the word "TABLE" is not added. (This property doesn't affect OPEN DATABASE, presumably because that command also needs to deal with an MRU list.)

We can't imagine why anyone would set this property to false. Multi-word commands are expanded only when they're unique, that is, when no other command begins with the same word. While learning not to type the second word automatically takes some time, the overall time savings are great and worth the effort of relearning.

Summary

VFP 8 doesn't include revolutionary changes in the editing environment, just some solid enhancements that make everyday life with VFP easier. But the real productivity changes are in the tools arena, with improvements to existing tools and several brand new tools. The next four chapters address tools.

Updates and corrections to this chapter can be found on Hentzenwerke's web site, **www.hentzenwerke.com**. Click on "Catalog" and navigate to the page for this book.

Chapter 2
The Toolbox

It seems every new version of Visual FoxPro introduces some new tools. VFP 8 brings three of them, all written in VFP itself. This chapter looks at the Toolbox, which provides a new way to access controls and much more.

The availability of tools is one of the things that distinguishes a productive development environment from a less productive one. VFP has always included a variety of tools (going back to the FoxBase days), and it seems each new version of the product brings more tools to help us work faster and smarter.

The Toolbox (shown in **Figure 1**) is the new preferred tool for adding controls to forms and classes. It combines the simplicity of the Form Controls toolbar with the flexibility of the Component Gallery to provide a tool better than either.

Figure 1. The Toolbox. The Toolbox offers a marriage of the Form Controls toolbar and the Component Gallery.

The Toolbox is divided into categories, each represented by a bar in the Toolbox. Each category contains a list of items. There are several types of categories and several types of items (described later in the chapter). By default, there are seven categories: Favorites, Text Scraps, VFP Base Classes, VFP Foundation Classes, My Base Classes, My XML Web Services, and My ActiveX Controls.

Also by default, the VFP Base Classes category contains all the base classes, while My Base Classes contains the first-level subclasses from the _Base library in the FoxPro Foundation Classes. (You can change the contents of My Base Classes, but not VFP Base Classes. See "Adding items to the Toolbox" later in this chapter.) VFP Foundation Classes contains a number of the more useful classes (like the About dialog and the Registry class) from the FoxPro Foundation Classes. The initial contents of the other categories are described later in the chapter.

Opening the Toolbox

The easiest way to start the Toolbox is to click on the icon for it (a crossed hammer and wrench) on the Standard toolbar. You can also open the Toolbox by choosing it from the Tools menu or by issuing the command:

```
DO (_TOOLBOX)
```

The _TOOLBOX system variable points to the Toolbox application, by default, ToolBox.APP in the home directory.

Unlike the Form Controls toolbar, the Toolbox doesn't open automatically when you open the Form Designer or Class Designer. (In fact, in VFP 8, the Form Controls toolbar doesn't open automatically any more unless you set it up to do so; see Chapter 5, "Better Tools.") You might want to write a little program that opens the toolbox, and then opens a specified form or class. A very simple version of such a program might look like this:

```
LPARAMETERS cForm

DO (_TOOLBOX)
IF EMPTY(cForm)
   MODIFY FORM ? nowait
ELSE
   MODIFY FORM (cForm) NOWAIT
ENDIF
```

Once the Toolbox is open, it can be resized both horizontally and vertically. The size and position of the Toolbox are stored in the resource file.

By default, the Toolbox is set to be always on top. You can change that setting from the context menu. Another context menu item lets you turn off the Help text pane at the bottom of the Toolbox, providing more room for the contents.

Working with the Toolbox

You can do a variety of things with the Toolbox, but its principal function is to put controls onto forms or classes. To open a category so you can access the items within it, click on the name of the category. If the items in the category don't fit in the Toolbox's area along with the category bars, up arrow and/or down arrow bars are added at the top and bottom to allow you to scroll within the category. (In Figure 1, there's a down arrow bar for the VFP Base Classes category.) Click on one of the arrow bars to scroll up or down one item. Better, holding the mouse over one of these bars scrolls continuously in the specified direction. (You can set the scroll rate—see "Configuring the Toolbox" later in this chapter.)

When the Form Designer or Class Designer is open, double-clicking on a control in the Toolbox (whether one of the built-in controls, a subclass, or an ActiveX control) drops an instance of that control onto the active form or class. If a container class is selected in the Designer, the new control is added to that container. If not, the new control is placed in the upper left corner of the form or class.

You can also drag a control from the Toolbox and drop it onto a form or class. If you drop onto a container control, the new control is added to the container; otherwise, it's placed directly on the form or class at the point you dropped it. (Dropping onto a container doesn't require the container to be selected.)

If you attempt to add a control to something that can't hold the control, you get an error message "Object class is invalid for this container." For example, the error appears if you attempt to drop anything other than an option button onto an option group. Some classes, such as Exception and Session, are really meant only for programmatic use. Attempting to add one of these to a form or class results in the message "This class has no visual representation and therefore cannot be dropped onto this container."

Some of the controls have additional smarts. If you attempt to add a page class onto a form or class, a pageframe is automatically added to hold it. Similarly, adding a grid column class onto an appropriate container other than a grid creates a one-column grid in the container. Adding a single option button creates an option group.

We expected we'd be able to drag classes and other files from the Toolbox into a project to have them added to the project, but dragging onto a project gives the "no drop" symbol. Since the Component Gallery supports this functionality, we're a little disappointed. Of course, once you use a class in a member of a project, the class library will be added to the project automatically.

The Toolbox is also handy when working with code. Drag an object out of the Toolbox into a code editing window and a line of code instantiating the class is added. For example, if you drag the Splash Screen class from the VFP Foundation Classes category into a code window, this line of code is generated:

```
_splash = NEWOBJECT("_splash", "_DIALOGS.VCX")
```

In fact, this is simply default behavior. You can specify two distinct behaviors for dragging into code windows—see "Determining the behavior of class items" later in this chapter. (One change you may want to make is to include the path for the class library in the generated code. The default code doesn't include it, which isn't a problem if you're building an application, but might be for utility code.)

Working with categories

The Toolbox supports five kinds of categories, as shown in **Table 1**. **Table 2** shows the types for the built-in categories.

Table 1. Toolbox category types. Each type of category has some unique characteristics.

Category type	Purpose
General category	Contains classes and other files.
Dynamic folder category	Contains all or a specified subset of the files in a specified folder.
Registered ActiveX controls	Contains ActiveX controls.
Text scraps	Contains fragments of text, which may contain strings to be expanded using text merge.
XML web services	Contains registered XML web services.

Table 2. Built-in category types. The categories that come with the Toolbox demonstrate most of the types.

Category	Type
Favorites	Favorites (special type not available for new categories)
Text Scraps	Text scraps
VFP Base Classes	General
VFP Foundation Classes	General
My Base Classes	General
My XML Web Services	XML Web Services
My ActiveX Controls	Registered ActiveX controls

Although each category has a type, you're actually not restricted to putting items of the specified type in the category. Some of the category types provide special behaviors not included in the General category. For example, a Dynamic folder category always includes all the items from the specified folder. However, you can also add other items to the category if you wish. (See "Adding items to the Toolbox" later in this chapter.) You see this behavior at work in the built-in My XML Web Services category. This category (like all XML web services type categories) includes all registered web services. However, it also includes a number of other items, such as Register and Generic Handler.

To add a new category, open the context menu and choose Add Category. The dialog shown in **Figure 2** appears. Specify the name of the new category and choose its type. When you click OK, the new category is added to the Toolbox, but has no contents.

Add Category
Category name:
Category type:
General category
General purpose category.
OK
Cancel

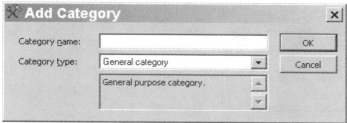

Figure 2. *Adding a new category. When you choose to add a category, this dialog appears. Specify the name and type of the new category.*

To change the settings for a category, right click on the category name in the Toolbox and choose Properties from the context menu. (If the category is expanded, you need to click on the category name before right clicking.) The dialog that appears varies with the category type. **Figure 3** shows the Category Properties dialog for a general category. **Figure 4** shows the dialog for a dynamic folder category. **Table 3** shows the various items that appear in the Category Properties dialog and indicates to which category types they apply.

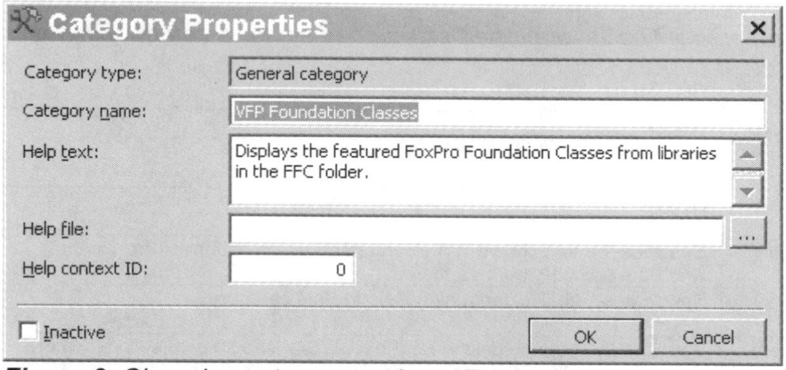

Category Properties
Category type:
General category
Category name:
VFP Foundation Classes
Help text:
Displays the featured FoxPro Foundation Classes from libraries in the FFC folder.
Help file:
Help context ID:
0
Inactive
OK
Cancel

Figure 3. *Changing category settings. For a general category, you can set only a few items.*

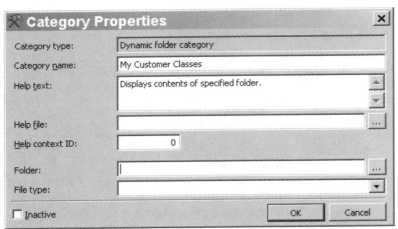

Figure 4. Setting dynamic folder category properties. When a category is the dynamic folder type, you can also specify the folder and the type(s) of files listed.

Table 3. Category properties. The list of properties you can set for a category varies with the category type.

Property	Applies to	Notes
Category type	All category types	Read-only, set when the category is created.
Category name	All category types	Specifies the name displayed for the category in the Toolbox.
Help text	All category types	Specifies the text shown in the Help pane at the bottom of the Toolbox when the category bar has focus.
Help file	All category types	Specifies a Help file containing Help for this category.
Help context ID	All category types	Specifies the help context id for the topic that should be displayed when Help opens. If this is specified and Help file is empty, it refers to the VFP Help file.
Inactive	All category types	Indicates whether the category is displayed in the toolbox at this time.
Folder	Dynamic folder type	Specifies the folder whose files are displayed for this category.
File type	Dynamic folder type	Specifies a set of file extensions. Only files in the specified folder having those extensions are included in the category. One reason to limit the extensions is so you see only the "main" file of items stored across multiple files, like tables (DBF/FPT/CDX) or class libraries (VCX/VCT). The various lists of extensions available include the primary files, but not the supporting files.
Template	XML web services type	Specifies a text merge template used for inserting the necessary code to instantiate and use a web service. If empty, a default text merge template is used.
Class library	XML web services type	Specifies the class and class library used when a web service from this category is dropped on a form or class.

Table 3. Continued

Property	Applies to	Notes
Base class	XML web services type	Indicates the base class of the class specified for the Class library item. Read-only when a class and class library are specified. When no class and class library are specified, this item is a drop-down list of base classes, but as far as we can tell, changing it doesn't affect the behavior of items in the category.
Object name	XML web services type	The name used for web services dropped on forms or classes.
Properties	XML web services type	Property settings to use when web services are dropped on forms or classes. (See "Setting instance properties" later in this chapter.)

Categories of the XML web services type have some properties that belong to individual items in other types of categories. That's because the XML web services type of category is dynamic, and there's no opportunity to specify these characteristics for the individual web services.

Working with items

While categories are helpful for organizing the Toolbox, it's really the items within them that make the tool useful. There are several ways to add items to the Toolbox, and quite a few things you can do to customize their behavior once you've added them.

The Toolbox supports five types of items, listed in **Table 4**. Although most have a connection with a particular category type, you can put any type of item into any category.

Table 4. Item types. The Toolbox allows you to add a variety of item types.

Item type	Notes
ActiveX control	All registered ActiveX controls are eligible.
Class	Class libraries are added as a whole.
File	Behaves in accordance with Registry settings.
Script	Executes specified code and inserts return value.
Text scrap	Inserts text where dropped. May use text merge.

Adding items to the Toolbox

Class items are added to the Toolbox a class library at a time. You can remove individual classes within a library once you've added the whole library and you can hide some classes from a library (see "Customizing the Toolbox" later), but there's no way to add a single class from a class library to the Toolbox.

The most obvious way to add class items is to choose Add Class Library from the context menu. When you do so, the dialog shown in **Figure 5** appears. The category defaults to the one currently expanded, but you can choose any active category. When you specify the class library to add and choose OK, all the classes in the specified library are added to the specified category.

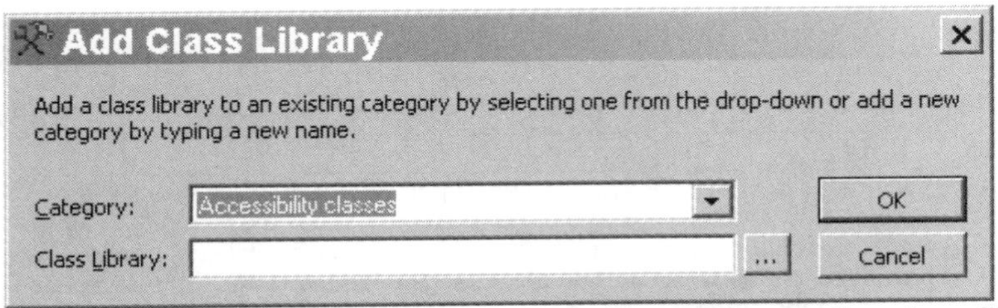

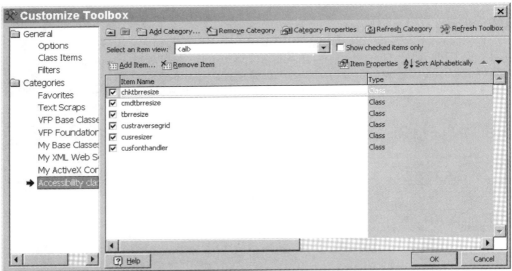

Figure 5. Adding items to the Toolbox. You add an entire class library at once.

You can also add classes by dragging the class library from Windows Explorer and dropping it onto the desired category. In this case, the dialog in Figure 5 never appears.

Both techniques for adding class items allow you to add both VCX-based and PRG-based classes.

All types of items can also be added using the Customize Toolbox dialog (shown in **Figure 6**), accessed through the context menu. (The General items in this dialog are discussed later in the section, "Configuring the Toolbox".)

Figure 6. Adding items to categories. All types of items can be added through the Customize Toolbox dialog.

To add an item in the dialog, choose the correct category from the left pane, and then click the Add Item button. The Add Item dialog shown in **Figure 7** appears, with the default item type for the category highlighted.

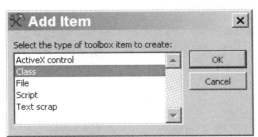

Figure 7. Adding an item. The first step is to indicate the type of item.

Once you choose an item type, you specify the item. The exact sequence of steps varies with the Item type. For Class and File, the Open dialog appears to let you specify the class library (VCX or PRG) or file (any type at all).

If you choose ActiveX control, the main body of the right pane changes to display a list of registered ActiveX controls (as shown in **Figure 8**). You can choose one or more to add to the category by checking them. Note also, in this case, the Select an item view drop-down list changes to "ActiveX controls." To return to a display of the categories contents, you need to change it back to "<all>." (For more on this drop-down list, see "Managing categories" later in this chapter.)

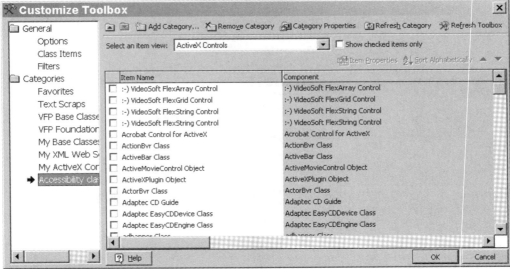

Figure 8. Adding ActiveX controls. All registered controls are listed. Check the ones you want to add to the category.

Specifying Script or Text Scrap for the item type opens the Item Properties dialog, which is described in the next section, "Setting item properties."

When a category has the Dynamic folders type, you don't need to add items to it explicitly. All files in the specified folder with the specified extensions are added to the category automatically. If you change the contents of the folder, you need to explicitly refresh the category. You do so by choosing Refresh Category from the context menu or the Customize Toolbox dialog. (However, dynamic folder categories are all refreshed when the Toolbox is closed and reopened.) Be aware that all items are added to this type of category as File items, even if they contain classes.

Setting item properties

The context menu for items (other than those added automatically to Dynamic folder type categories) includes Properties; choosing it opens the Item Properties dialog. The contents of the dialog vary based on the item type. **Figure 9** shows the dialog for a Class type item, **Figure 10** shows it for a File type item, and **Figure 11** shows it for a text scrap. (The dialogs for the other item types aren't shown here.)

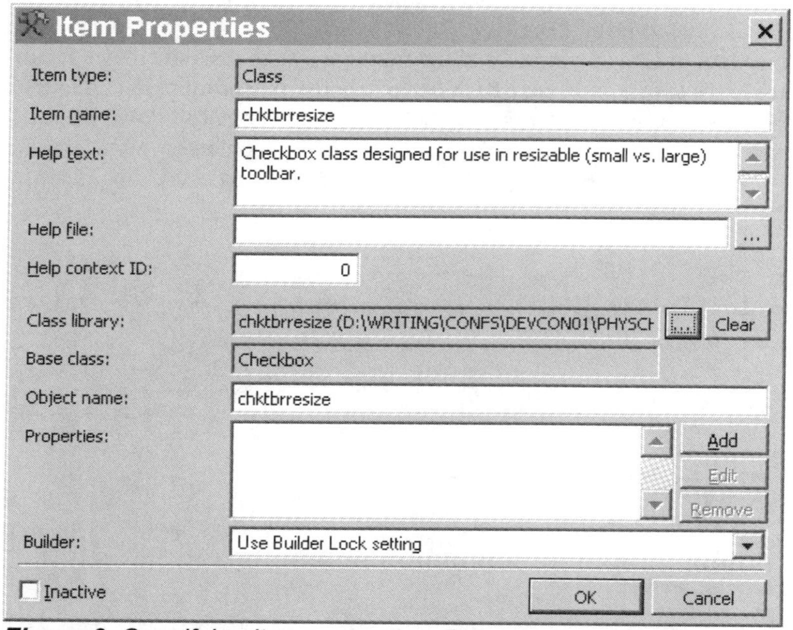

Figure 9. *Specifying item properties. This version of the Item Properties dialog is used for Class type items.*

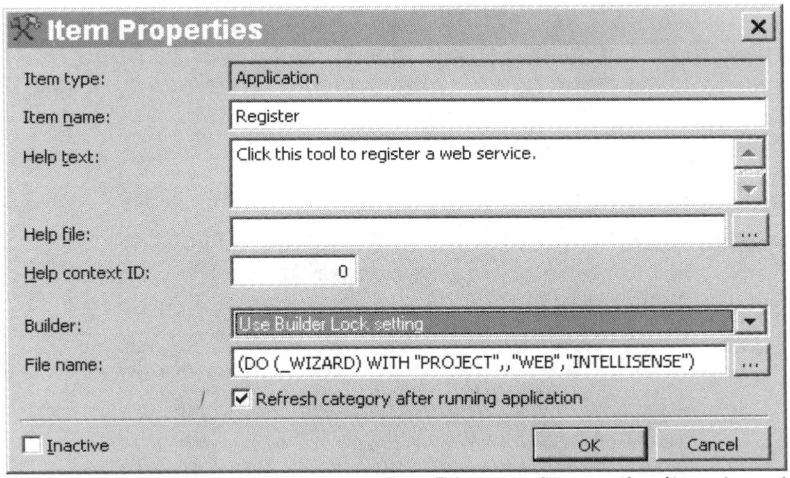

Figure 10. File item properties. For File type items, the Item type text box shows the type of the underlying file, not just "File."

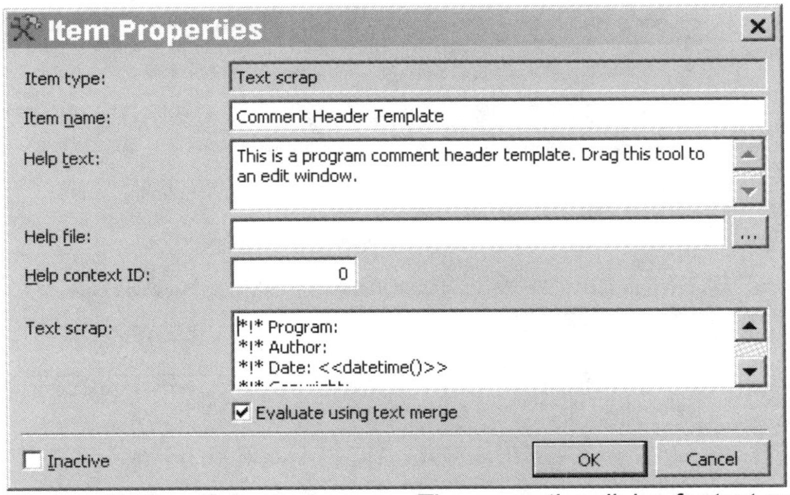

Figure 11. Specifying text scraps. The properties dialog for text scraps and scripts let you specify the item itself.

As with categories, many of the properties you can specify are the same for all types, while others apply to only specific types. **Table 5** lists the properties you can specify in the Item Properties dialog.

Table 5. *Item Properties. The list of things you can specify varies with the item's type. Most intriguing is the ability to set property values for instances of classes created from the toolbox.*

Property	Applies to	Notes
Item type	All item types	Read-only; determined by the item type, and for File type items, by the file's type.
Item name	All item types	Specifies the name that appears for the item in the Toolbox.
Help text	All item types	Specifies the text shown in the Help pane at the bottom of the Toolbox when the item has focus.
Help file	All item types	Specifies a Help file containing Help for this item.
Help context ID	All item types	Specifies the help context id for the topic that should be displayed when Help opens. If this is specified and the Help file property is empty, it refers to the VFP Help file.
Inactive	All item types	Indicates whether the item should be displayed in the Toolbox.
Class library	Class, ActiveX control	Specifies the class library that contains the class or the OCX file that contains the ActiveX control. Read-only; for Class items, an ellipsis button allows you to choose the class and class library.
Base Class	Class	Specifies the class of the item. Read-only; an ellipsis button allows you to choose the class and class library.
Class Name	ActiveX control	The ProgID of the ActiveX control. Read-only.
Object name	Class, ActiveX control	Specifies the name of the control to create when this item is added to a form or class or the name of the object variable when the item is added to a code editor. For a Class item, normally the class name. For an ActiveX item, by default, OLEControl.
Properties	Class, ActiveX control	Specifies property settings to be performed on the fly as the item is added to a form or class. See "Setting instance properties" later in this chapter.
Builder	Class, ActiveX control, File	Determines whether the builder for the item, if one is specified, runs when the item is opened. There are three choices: Use Builder Lock setting, Always invoke Builder, or Never invoke Builder.
File name	File	The name of the associated file. This setting can actually be a call to a program. (See the Register item in the My XML Web Services category for an example.)
Text scrap	Text scraps	Specifies the text to be inserted when the item is used. May include items to be evaluated via text merge.
Evaluate using text merge	Text scraps	Indicates whether the text merge should be performed on the text scrap before inserting it.
Script	Script	Specifies the code to be executed when the item is used. The return value of this code is inserted where the item is dropped.
Complete drag script	Script	Specifies code to be run after dropping the item. The return value isn't used, but you can perform interface or clean-up tasks.

Using items

In "Working with the Toolbox" earlier in this chapter, we described the most common things you do with Toolbox items, double-click or drag and drop them to add controls to forms and classes. However, the Toolbox actually supports far more than this.

The context menu for each item varies depending on the item type. For classes other than the VFP base classes, it includes Modify, which opens the Class Designer. For classes that can be subclassed visually, the menu includes Create Subclass, which opens the New Class dialog. For ActiveX controls, the context menu has Open in Object Browser. For form classes, the context menu includes Create Form, which opens the Form Designer with a new form of the specified class. When any forms or container classes are open in the Form Designer or Class Designer, an Add to item is added to the context menu for many items. It points to a submenu showing each available container and form. Choosing one of those items drops an instance of the class on the chosen container or form.

The context menu for Text Scraps includes Copy to Clipboard. For File type items, the choices vary with the file type, but most common are Modify and Run. When you choose Modify, it opens the file in its native editor (even if it's a different application).

File items are displayed using hyperlinks. Clicking on a File item is equivalent to choosing Modify for that item and opens it in its native editor.

Most items have Rename and Delete options on the context menu that do as their name suggests. (Of course, deleting an item from the Toolbox doesn't actually remove it from the class library. Similarly, Rename affects the name you see in the Toolbox, not the actual name of the class.) In addition, the context menu for all items includes Add to Favorites. Choosing it adds the item to the Favorites category without removing it from the category it's already in. This is an easy way to have overall organization, but put the items you use all the time together.

Setting instance properties

The Item Properties dialog for Class items (shown in Figure 9) and for ActiveX items includes a Properties section. This section lets you specify properties to be set in the Property Sheet when the item is added to a form or class. When you click the Add button, the Set Object Property dialog (shown in **Figure 12**) appears. (For ActiveX controls, the left-hand control is a text box rather than a drop-down list.)

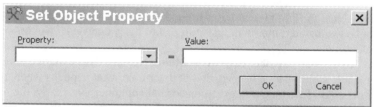

Figure 12. Setting properties on the fly. The settings you perform in this dialog are applied when you add the item to a form or class.

To set a property, choose it from the drop-down list or type in the name, and then specify the value you want in the Value text box. Note there's no IntelliSense or other help for adding values here. You need to know what the appropriate values are. After you click OK, the property setting displays in the Properties area of the Item Properties dialog (as shown in **Figure 13**). Once property settings are added there, you can use the Edit and Remove buttons to modify or delete the settings. Double-clicking on a setting in the list opens the Set Object Property dialog with that setting entered.

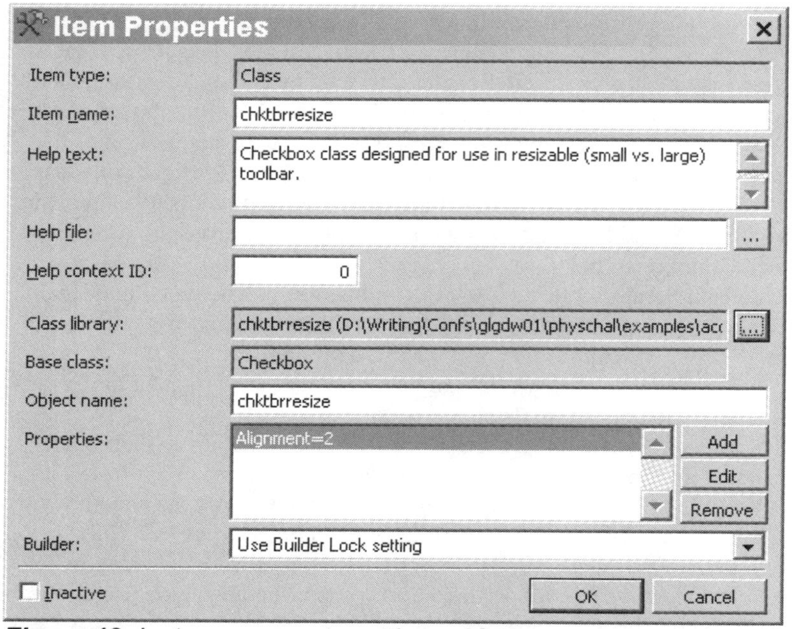

Figure 13. *Instance property settings. After you add property settings, they're displayed in the Properties edit box, where they can be edited or removed.*

It's important to understand that setting properties in this way does not create new subclasses. It's more like a builder in that it sets properties for a particular instance. Don't use this capability when a subclass is appropriate.

However, there are two fairly cool things you can do by setting item properties. First, the value you specify can actually be code. For example, you might set Caption to a value of "(INPUTBOX('Specify caption'))"; when you add the control to a form or class, you'll be prompted to enter the caption. Note the extra parentheses around the function call; they're needed to force the value to be evaluated rather than just assigned to the property. However, don't include the outer quotation marks.

In addition, the property listings for member controls (Column Header, Grid Column, Option Button, and Page) include some special properties that determine what happens when you drop one of these controls onto something other than its normal container. Normally, the appropriate container is added based on the VFP base classes, and then an object of the specified class is added to it. The ContainerClass, ContainerClassLib, and MemberCount properties let you determine what class the container is based on, and how many objects of the chosen class are added. These properties do not appear anywhere except in this dialog.

Customizing the Toolbox

Given everything we've already described, you may be wondering what else we can possibly do to customize the Toolbox. In fact, there are some more global changes you can make.

First, the context menu contains several toggles that affect the Toolbox as a whole. Builder Lock determines whether builders appear for items set to follow the Builder Lock setting. Items in the Toolbox ignore the global Builder Lock setting from the Options dialog on the Tools menu. The setting for the Toolbox is independent of the Options dialog setting.

Display Help Text determines whether the Help pane appears at the bottom of the Toolbox. Always on Top determines whether the toolbox stays on top or drops behind other forms.

Most configuration of the Toolbox, though, is performed in the Customize Toolbox dialog (shown in Figure 6 and Figure 8). In "Adding items to the Toolbox" earlier, we discussed one use for this dialog, but it's far more capable than just editing the list of items in a category. The top section of the left pane provides access to items that affect the Toolbox as a whole.

Configuring the Toolbox

Figure 14 shows the General Options view of the dialog. This section contains a variety of settings for Toolbox behavior, including the three that can be set from the context menu. Run associated builders is the same as the Builder Lock context menu item. Display Toolbox help text section corresponds to the Display Help Text item, and Always on top is a mirror of the Always on Top context menu item.

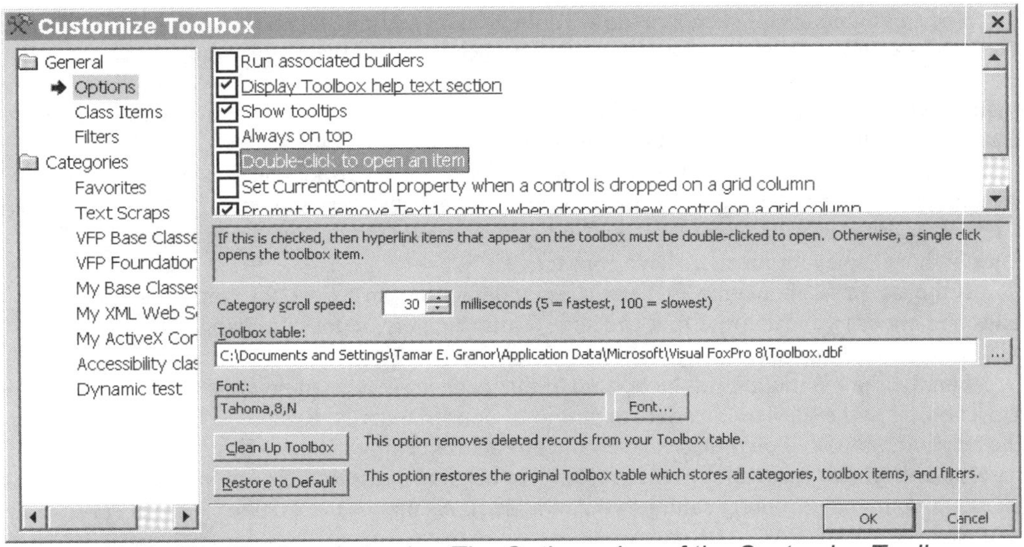

Figure 14. Setting Toolbox behavior. The Options view of the Customize Toolbox dialog contains settings that affect the Toolbox as a whole.

Show tooltips determines whether tooltips are displayed when the mouse hovers over an item. The tooltips use the Help text specified for the items. If space is at a premium for you, turn off the Help text section and leave tooltips on.

Double-click to open an item applies to File items. By default, a single click on a File item opens it in its native editor. When this item is checked, it takes a double-click. If you find you often open items by accident, consider changing this setting.

The next two items, Set CurrentControl property when a control is dropped on a grid column and Prompt to remove Text1 control when dropping a new control on a grid column, combine to determine what happens when you drop controls on grids. When the Prompt item is checked, dropping a control on a grid column that contains a default text box named Text1 brings up the dialog shown in **Figure 15**. If you answer Yes, not only is the control you're dropping added to the column, but the text box is deleted. When the Set CurrentControl option is checked, the newly added control becomes the current control for the column. When this option is not checked, CurrentControl isn't set to the new control, even if you delete the default text box.

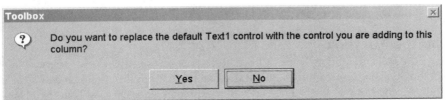

Figure 15. Replacing grid controls. When you drop a control onto a grid column, this dialog lets you get rid of the default text box.

The final item in this section, Allow Toolbox to be minimized, adds a minimize button to the Toolbox and enables the control box, putting Minimize on that list as well.

As noted in the section "Working with the Toolbox" earlier in this chapter, holding the mouse over the arrows at the top and bottom of a category scrolls within that category. The Category scroll speed spinner lets you determine how fast the items scroll.

As you'd expect, the Toolbox table item points to the table that contains the Toolbox data. Among other things, the ability to change this setting means you can maintain several toolbox data sets (perhaps for different projects) and switch among them. (See "Filtering the Toolbox" later in this chapter for an alternative approach.)

If the 8-point Tahoma the Toolbox uses by default doesn't work for you, use the Font button to choose your favorite font and size. (Unfortunately, it doesn't change the font in any of the associated dialogs.)

Finally, the two buttons at the bottom of this page let you clean up after yourself. Clean Up Toolbox packs the Toolbox data to get rid of deleted records. Restore to Default restores the original toolbox, though it gives you the option of keeping categories and items you have added. In that case, all it does is restore the original items to their original settings (for example, removing property settings you've added). A copy of the Toolbox table is saved as a backup.

Determining the behavior of class items

The Class Items view of the dialog (**Figure 16**) lets you determine how Class items are named when added to the Toolbox and what happens when you drag Class items to code editing windows.

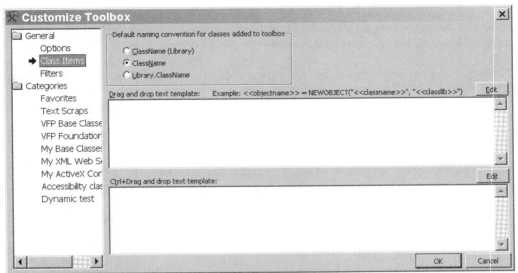

Figure 16. Class item behavior. This page of the Customize Toolbox dialog determines default naming of Class items and their behavior when dropped into code windows.

When you add a class library to the Toolbox, each item is given a name. The Default naming convention option buttons determine the format of that name. (Keep in mind you can change the name in the Item Properties dialog or on the appropriate category's page in the Customize Toolbox dialog.) For a class called cmdMyButton in a class library named MyClasses, the three options are:

- cmdMyButton (MyClasses)

- cmdMyButton

- MyClasses.cmdMyButton

The two edit boxes on this page control what happens when you drag a Class item onto a code editing window. The Drag and drop text template is used for a normal drag, while the Ctrl+Drag and drop text template is used for a drag with the Ctrl button held down. Whatever text you put into the edit box is evaluated using text merge, and then dropped into the code editing window.

By default, dragging a VFP base class generates code like:

```
Text = CREATEOBJECT("Textbox")
```

Dragging any other Class item results in code using NewObject(), like this:

```
_checkbox = NEWOBJECT("_checkbox", "_BASE.VCX")
```

In both cases, the name used for the new object is the object name specified in the Item Properties dialog. If this code isn't what you want, write your own template in the dialog. **Table 6** shows the data related to the item you can use in your template.

Table 6. *Creating text templates. These pieces of data about the item you're dropping are available for text merge in templates.*

Name	Contains
BaseClass	The base class of the item.
ClassLib	The class library of the item, with complete path.
ClassName	The name of the item's class.
ObjectName	The name specified for the object in the Item Properties dialog.

For example, to create documentation for a class, you might put this template in the Ctrl-Drop template:

```
Base Class: <<BaseClass>>
Class Library: <<ClassLib>>
Class Name: <<ClassName>>
Object Name: <<ObjectName>>
```

Filtering the Toolbox

The third page of the General section of the Toolbox (shown in **Figure 17**) lets you define and manage filters that limit the categories displayed in the Toolbox at any time. When any filters are defined, the context menu adds a Filters item that opens a submenu listing all defined filters. Choose a filter from that list and the Toolbox displays only the categories specified for the filter. We can see using filters to manage the different class libraries needed for different clients or different projects.

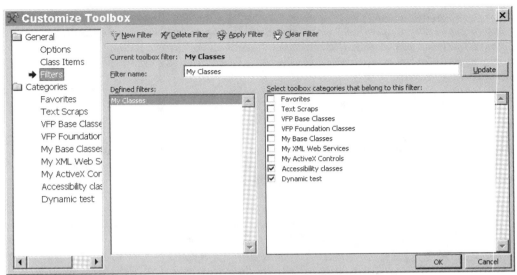

Figure 17. Managing filters. A filter contains one or more categories.

To define a filter, click the New Filter button. The new filter is added in the dialog and focus is set to the Filter name textbox. Type the name for your filter, and then check the categories that should be displayed for the filter. The Update button updates the name of the filter in the Defined filters list.

You can edit any filter by clicking on it in the Defined filters list and changing the chosen categories. As you'd expect, Delete Filter removes a filter from the list.

Apply Filter and Clear Filter let you set and remove a filter, but you can do that right from the context menu as well.

Managing categories

The Categories pages in the Customize Toolbox dialog let you manage the list of categories and their contents. Techniques for adding items to categories are discussed in "Adding items to the Toolbox" earlier in this chapter.

When Categories or any specific category is chosen, a button bar at the top of the dialog (shown in **Figure 18**; see Figure 6 and Figure 8 for the whole dialog) lets you rearrange the list of categories, add, remove and edit categories, and refresh an individual category or the whole Toolbox.

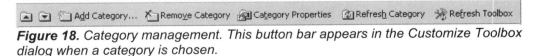

Figure 18. Category management. This button bar appears in the Customize Toolbox dialog when a category is chosen.

The Select an item view drop-down list controls what appears in the main pane of the dialog. The choices in the drop-down list are "<all>," "Visual FoxPro Class Libraries" and "ActiveX Controls." The button bar beneath the drop-down list changes based on the choice in the drop-down list. When "<all>" is chosen, it contains buttons (**Figure 19**) for adding, removing, and editing individual items, as well as sorting and rearranging items. When "Visual FoxPro Class Libraries" is chosen in the drop-down list, the button bar (**Figure 20**) contains items for managing entire class libraries. When "ActiveX controls" is chosen, no buttons are available.

Figure 19. Managing items in the Customize Toolbox dialog. When the item view is set to "<all>," the button bar lets you work with individual items. The up and down arrows let you rearrange items in the category.

Figure 20. Working with libraries. When the item view is set to "Visual FoxPro Class Libraries," the buttons manage entire libraries.

In any view, check or uncheck items to show or hide them in the Toolbox. The Show checked items only check box in the dialog determines whether you see the hidden items while in the Customize Toolbox dialog. Also, no matter what view you're in, the Item Name column is editable—changing it determines what appears for the item in the Toolbox.

Working with the source code

As with other tools written in VFP, the source code for the Toolbox comes with the product. Source for all of the "Xbase tools" is in a file called XSource.ZIP in the HOME() + "Tools\XSource" directory. When you unzip it (make sure to select the Use folder names option), a new directory called VFPSource is created. Each tool has a subdirectory within that directory. The Toolbox project is in a Toolbox directory.

You can modify or subclass any of the code used for the Toolbox and rebuild the application. By default, the Toolbox is Toolbox.APP in the HOME() directory. You can change that by setting the _TOOLBOX system variable.

By default, Toolbox data is stored in a table called Toolbox.DBF in the application data directory (the one indicated by HOME(7)). As noted in "Configuring the Toolbox" earlier in this chapter, you can change the location and file name.

The Toolbox table contains one record for each category and one for each item in the Toolbox. **Table 7** shows the fields in the Toolbox table.

Table 7. Toolbox data. The Toolbox table contains one record for each category and one for each item in the Toolbox.

Field	Type	Purpose
UniqueID	Character	A unique identifier for the record. Recommended format is "vendor.ID". For records added through the Toolbox interface, "user" is filled in for the vendor portion and SYS(2015) is used to provide the ID portion.
ShowType	Character	Indicates the type of item. For example, "C" for category and "T" for (tool) item. See Toolbox.H in the Toolbox project for the complete list.
ToolTypeID	Character	The type of item. For categories, in the form "Category.CategoryType". For items, just "ItemType".
ToolType	Memo	The type of item in readable format. This is the type that appears in the Properties dialog.
ParentID	Character	For items, the UniqueID of the containing category.
ToolName	Character	The descriptive name of the category or item, as it appears in the Toolbox.
ImageFile	Memo	The icon to use for the item. Not used for categories.
ClassType	Character	Indicates the type of item. "CATEGORY" for categories, "CLASS" for class items, and so forth. For file items, the file type, such as "APP."
SetID	Memo	For class items, the containing class library. (Important because class libraries are added and, sometimes, removed as a whole.)
ClassName	Memo	The name of the class used to process this item. For example, by default, "_classtool" for class items and "_activetool" for ActiveX items.
ClassLib	Memo	The class library containing the class named in ClassName. If empty, _toolbox.vcx is used.
ToolTip	Memo	The help text for the category or item. This appears in the Display Help pane and as a tooltip.
HelpFile	Memo	The Help file (including path) containing Help for this item.
HelpID	Numeric	The help context ID for this item in the Help file specified by HelpFile (or in the VFP Help file, if HelpFile is empty).
ToolData	Memo	Data for this category or item. For items, includes the class name, class library, base class, and object name information, as well as the list of properties to set in this instance. For file items, includes the file name. For text scraps, includes the text to insert. For scripts, includes the script. For ActiveX controls, includes the OCX file name, the class name and the object name.
DisplayOrd	Numeric	The display order of this item. For categories, the position in which the category appears. For items, the position of the item in the category.
LockAdd	Logical	For categories, indicates whether items can be added. (True indicates no additions are permitted.) Ignored for items.
LockDelete	Logical	Indicates whether the item or category can be deleted. When this is set to True, Delete does not appear on the context menu and the Remove Item button is disabled in the Customize Toolbox dialog.
LockRename	Logical	Indicates whether the item or category can be renamed. When this is set to True, the Rename item does not appear on the context menu.
Inactive	Logical	Indicates whether the item or category is currently displayed in the Toolbox. (True means the item or category is not displayed.)
User	Memo	Available for user-specified information.
Modified	DateTime	Time stamp of last change to item or category.

Finally, when the Toolbox is running, the variable _oToolbox contains an object reference to it. The oToolboxEngine property points to the object responsible for much of the Toolbox's behavior.

Summary

The Toolbox is an amazingly capable new tool. It offers the power of the Component Gallery without its complexity. We plan to use the Toolbox exclusively and never open the Form Controls toolbar again.

Incredibly, the Toolbox is just one of the new tools in VFP 8. The next two chapters will explore the other two, Code References and the Task Pane Manager. Chapter 5, "Better Tools," looks at changes to existing tools.

Updates and corrections to this chapter can be found on Hentzenwerke's web site, **www.hentzenwerke.com**. Click on "Catalog" and navigate to the page for this book.

Chapter 3
Code References

**Among the cool new tools introduced in VFP 8 is Code References, which lets you
search the files in a project or folder, provides replace capability, and much more.**

FoxPro has had some kind of search capability for many versions. The Filer tool, first
introduced in FoxPro 2.0, provides the ability to search a directory tree. However, there's
never been an easy way to search within a project. In addition, while Filer can find strings,
even in forms, class libraries, and other metadata stores, it can only open files as text.

Enter the Code References tool. It allows you to search a project or a directory tree, opens
the found references in their native format, and provides replace capability. It also maintains a
history of your search results and a log of replacements. In addition, the Code References
engine is used to provide the ability to find the definition of any item in code.

Running the Code References tool

You can start Code References in a number of ways. What you see depends both on how you
start it and what you've done before.

The most obvious way to run the tool is to choose it from the Tools menu. The first time
you do that, the Look Up Reference window (shown in **Figure 1**) appears. You can specify a
string (or a regular expression) to search for and a folder in which to search.

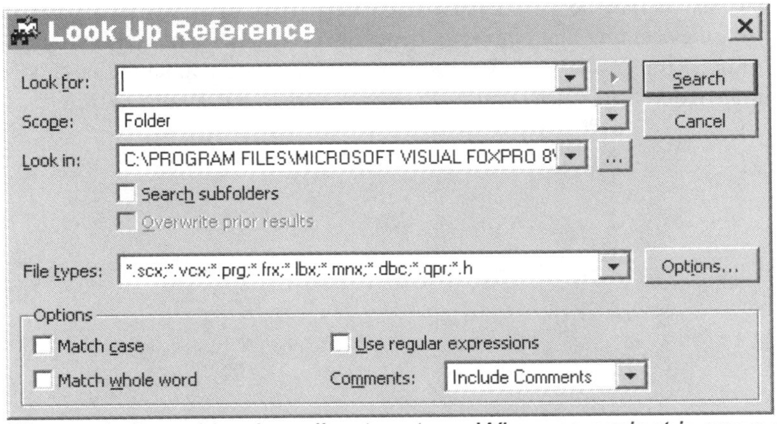

*Figure 1. Searching in a directory tree. When no project is open and you haven't
previously searched, choosing Code References brings up this dialog.*

If a project is open when you choose Tools | Code References, your options change and
you can search within the project (**Figure 2**). (The Scope drop-down list also lets you switch
to searching in a Folder, as in Figure 1.)

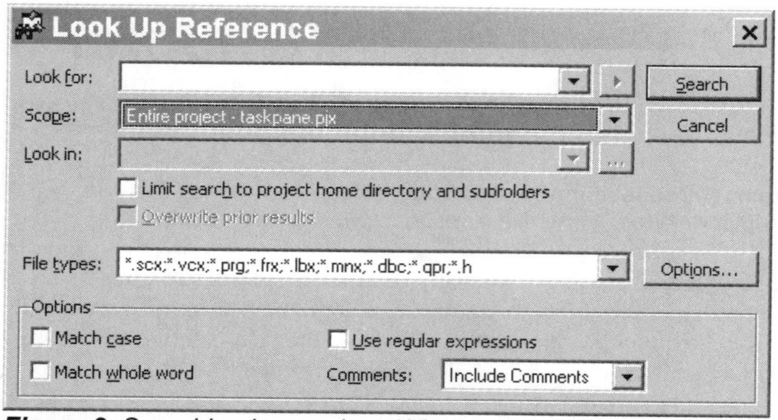

Figure 2. *Searching in a project. When a project is open, the Look Up References dialog assumes you want to search within the project.*

You don't have to start Code References from the menu, though. The context menu for code editing windows now includes a Look Up Reference item. When you choose that item, the Look Up Reference window opens. If any text was highlighted in the code window, it's automatically placed in the Look for text box.

If you've previously done a search, choosing Code References from the menu with no project open behaves differently. In that case, the Code References window (see **Figure 3**) opens, showing the results of previous folder-based searches. (Figure 3 shows the result of searching for "M_PROPERTIES_LOC" in the VFP home directory. As with all the searches shown in this chapter, your results may be different.)

When a project is open, the window that comes up depends on whether you've previously searched in that project. If not, you get the Look Up Reference window. If you have searched within the project before, the Code References window appears, showing previous search results for that project.

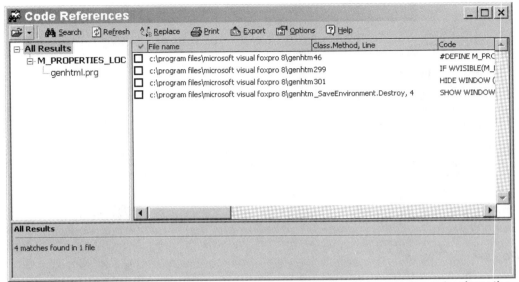

Figure 3. *Code References window. After a search, this window appears to show the results. Once you've performed a search, when you open Code References from the menu without a project open, this window appears as well.*

Searching for strings

The Look Up Reference window (shown in Figure 1 and Figure 2) lets you specify the string to search for, the project or folder to search in, and a variety of options.

If a string is highlighted when you open the tool, it's already specified as the string to search for. The Look for drop-down combo contains a list of strings you've previously searched for. (The list is stored in your resource table in one of several records with an ID of "FOXREF.")

You can modify the search in quite a few ways. Check Match case for a case-sensitive search. Check Match whole word if you only want to search for your string as a word, not within words.

Check Use regular expressions to allow you to specify a regular expression as the search string. Regular expressions use a special notation that provides wildcards and other structure. See the Help topic "Regular Expressions and Operators" for details on how to construct regular expressions. When you check this check box, the arrow key next to the Look for drop-down combo is enabled. Click on it to see a menu of regular expression operators (**Figure 4**). Click on an item in this menu to insert the operator into the Look for expression.

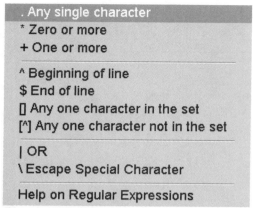

Figure 4. Building regular expressions. This menu is displayed by clicking the arrow button next to the Look for drop-down combo when Use regular expressions is checked. You can combine choices from this menu with characters you type to build a regular expression.

You can determine how comments are treated in the search using the Comments drop-down list. Your choices are to include them, to ignore them, or to search only in comments.

The File types drop-down list determines which files within the folder or project are searched. The drop-down list contains quite a few sets of file types, but if you frequently need to search another set, you can add your own sets to the list. See "Customizing Code References" later in this chapter.

The Scope drop-down list determines whether the search takes place in a project or in a folder. When no projects are open, Folder is the only choice. When any projects are open, the drop-down lists each one, as well as "Folder."

When Scope is set to Folder, the Look in drop-down combo and the ellipsis button next to it let you choose the folder in which to search. The drop-down lists recently searched folders.

As shown in Figures 1 and 2, the caption for the check box beneath the Look in drop-down combo varies depending on the choice of scope. When Folder is chosen, the check box determines whether subfolders should also be searched. When a project is chosen, the check box determines whether all files in the project are searched or only those in the project's home directory and its subdirectories. By checking this item, you can omit common code (such as framework code) that's stored somewhere other than the project folder.

The Overwrite prior results check box is enabled only when previous searches have occurred and haven't yet been cleared. When checked, it indicates the results of this search should replace all search results currently contained in the Code References window. The Options button opens the Code References Options dialog. It's discussed in "Code References Options" later in this chapter.

Once you have the search set up as you want, the Search button begins the search. While the search proceeds, the dialog shown in **Figure 5** is displayed. It indicates progress and shows the name of the file currently being searched.

Figure 5. *Search in progress. While the Code References tool is searching, this progress dialog is displayed.*

Once the search is complete, the Code References window is displayed. (If you cancel the search, partial results are included.)

Examining search results

The Code References window (Figure 3) shows the results of searches. At any given time, it shows the results for a single project or for searches in folders. The Open button lets you open a project and display its results or choose which list of results is displayed. **Figure 6** shows the list of choices; it includes Folder and all open projects. To access the list, click the drop-down arrow portion of the button.

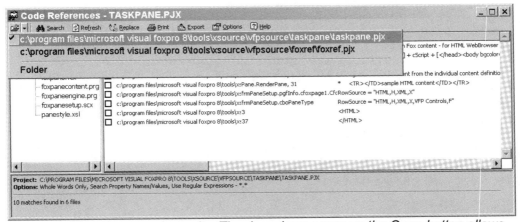

Figure 6. *Choosing search results. The drop-down arrow on the Open button allows you to determine which list of search results display. The list includes every open project and the word "Folder" to choose search results based on folders.*

The Code References window has four panes. The top pane is a button bar. In the middle are two panes side by side. The left pane lists the searches performed while the right pane shows the individual matches for the item selected in the left pane. The bottom pane provides a description of the currently selected items in the left and right panes.

The list of searches

The left pane uses a treeview control to show the list of searches performed in the currently selected project or against folders. The search string is shown as a major item and each file containing a match is a leaf node. You can search for the same string using different options; when you do so, that search string appears multiple times in the treeview. If you repeat a search for a particular string, using exactly the same options, the new results replace the old ones.

When a search string is selected in this pane, the right pane shows all the matches for that string. When an individual file is selected (as in **Figure 7**, created by searching the project TaskPane.PJX first for "collection," and then for "html"), the right pane shows only the matches for that string in the file.

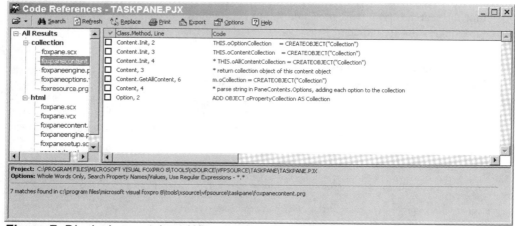

Figure 7. Displaying matches. When a search string is highlighted in the left pane, the right pane shows all matches for that string. When an individual file is highlighted, only matches in that file are displayed in the right pane.

The context menu for the left pane (**Figure 8**) gives you a number of options, most of them for managing the list of searches. The Open item appears only when a file name is highlighted; it opens the specified file. The first match for that file is highlighted. You can also open a file by double-clicking it.

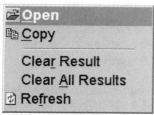

Figure 8. Context menu for Code References window's left pane. Use this menu to manage the list of searches.

The Copy item copies the list of matches to the clipboard in a comma-separated format that includes the search string and all the information about where it was found. With a little work, you could use this information to add items to the Task List for the matches. When a search is selected, all matches for that search are copied. When a file is selected, all matches for that file are copied. When All Results is selected, information about all matches is put on the clipboard.

The Clear Result and Clear All Results items let you remove searches from the list. As you'd expect, Clear Result removes the currently selected item, whether a file or an entire search. Clear All Results does what its name says: it clears all the searches.

The Refresh item updates the results by re-running the search or searches. If a file is highlighted, only that file is searched. If a search is highlighted, the entire search is performed again. (That includes all files in the folder or project, not just the ones where matches were previously found.) If All Results is highlighted when Refresh is chosen, all displayed searches are run again. Be careful with this item, as running a lot of searches again can take a long time.

The list of matches

The right pane uses a grid to show matches found. The list of matches shown depends on what's selected in the left pane. In fact, the set of columns displayed depends on what's selected in the list of searches. When a file is selected (as in Figure 7), the grid has three columns: a selection check box (discussed in "Replacing matches" later in this chapter); the class, method, and line number of the match; and the actual code matched. When a search or All Results is selected (as in Figure 3 and Figure 6), a File Name column appears to the right of the check box. The columns can all be resized (or auto-fitted), except for the check box column.

The context menu for this pane (**Figure 9**) contains some of the same items as the left pane's context menu, but has a number of other options as well. As in the list of searches, Open opens the highlighted item. However, in this case, the selected item is highlighted in the editing window, rather than the first match for the file. As in the list of searches, double-clicking on an item here also opens the file. Copy copies the selected item to the clipboard.

Figure 9. Context menu for list of matches. This menu lets you work with the matches found, as well as start a new search.

The remaining items on this menu refer to the entire list, not to individual members of the list. For example, Refresh performs the search again, searching all items, not just the selected file.

If any items are checked, the Replace item brings up the Replace dialog, discussed in "Replacing matches" later.

The Print and Export items are identical to the Print and Export buttons on the button bar, and are discussed in "Generating output" later in this chapter.

Some options work with the checked items, so there are several context menu items for controlling which items are checked. Select All checks all items in the list of matches in the right pane and Clear All Selections unchecks all of them. Be aware that item selections for a file are retained even when you navigate away from it. That is, if you choose a file in the left pane and check some items, choose another file in the left pane, and then move back to the first file, the items you previously checked are still checked. To clear all selections for all files in a search, choose the search string in the left pane, then choose Clear All Selections in the right pane. In addition, all selections are cleared when you switch to a different project or to folders.

Sort by lets you sort the list of matches in a variety of orders, including file name, the class and method name, selection state, the type of file, and the file location. You can also sort the list by clicking on the headers for the Selected, File name and Class, method, line columns.

Options opens the Options dialog, discussed in "Code References Options" later in this chapter.

The description pane

The bottom pane of the Code References window shows a description of whatever is currently highlighted. To save space, you can turn off this pane using the button bar's context menu.

The description is divided into two sections, separated by a horizontal line. The upper section describes the search, listing the project or folder searched and the search options chosen.

The bottom section changes depending on the type of item currently highlighted. When a search string is highlighted, it shows the number of matches found and the number of files represented by those matches. When a file is highlighted, the bottom section shows the number of matches found and the file name. When a match is highlighted, this section shows the match information: the file name, the class, method and line number, and the line of code. While this may seem redundant, it often provides more complete information, because some of the information may not fit in the grid columns. **Figure 10** shows an example.

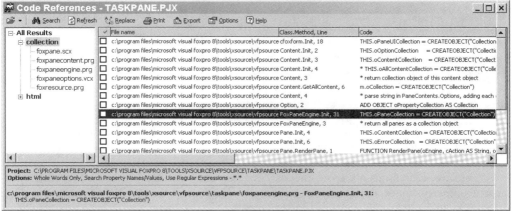

Figure 10. *Using the description pane. The detailed information at the bottom of the description pane is useful when file names and code lines are long.*

Replacing matches

One big feature that distinguishes Code References from Filer is the ability to replace the matched strings.

To replace a string, you have to check the occurrences you want to replace in the list of matches. Then, choose Replace from the button bar or the context menu. The dialog shown in **Figure 11** appears.

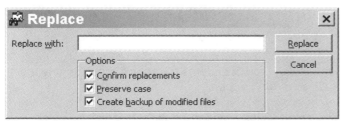

Figure 11. *Replacing matched strings. When you select one or more items, and choose Replace, this dialog appears.*

Only the search string can be replaced. If you've checked matches for more than one search string, in each case, the search string corresponding to the match is replaced.

Enter the replacement string, check the options you want, and then click Replace to perform the replacement. If Confirm replacements is checked, the dialog shown in **Figure 12** appears for each checked match.

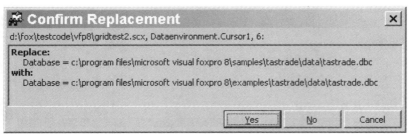

Figure 12. *Confirming replacement. When Confirm replacements is checked, this dialog appears for each replacement.*

There are some limits on replacement ability, however. While the tool can find strings such as property values, it can't make changes to those items. When the list of checked matches includes items that can't be replaced or where replacement could cause problems, the dialog in **Figure 13** appears before the Replace dialog (Figure 11).

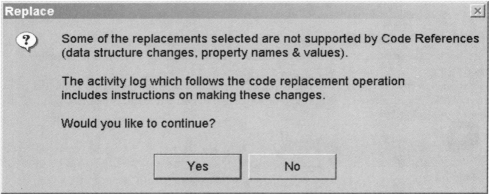

Figure 13. *Replacement warning. When the list of items to replace includes any that can't be replaced automatically, this warning appears.*

After replacement is completed, a replacement log is added to the treeview in the left pane. (Due to a bug, the log doesn't appear immediately if you skip all the replacements.) **Figure 14** shows a replacement log. Each item that was checked appears. If the line was changed, the original and new lines of code are included. If confirmation was on and you chose not to replace that line, it shows as "SKIPPED." If the item couldn't be changed automatically, the log shows the change that needs to be made manually.

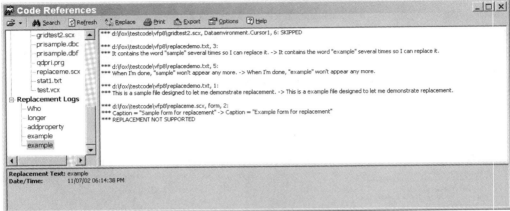

Figure 14. Replacement log. Each replacement you perform creates a log showing exactly what changes were made.

Replacement logs can be removed individually or along with all search results, but there's no way to clear just the replacement logs. Replacement logs aren't included in the text placed in the clipboard by Copy.

Generating output

The Print and Export items on the button bar and the corresponding items on the right pane's context menu let you send search results elsewhere. Print creates a report you can either print or preview, while Export offers six different output formats. Both options let you choose all searches, a particular search, or only selected (checked) items.

Choosing Print displays the dialog in **Figure 15**. The Search set drop-down list and the Scope option buttons determine which items are included in the output. If you specify Selected items only, the report includes the checked items from the chosen search (or all selected items if no search set is specified). **Figure 16** shows a generated report preview.

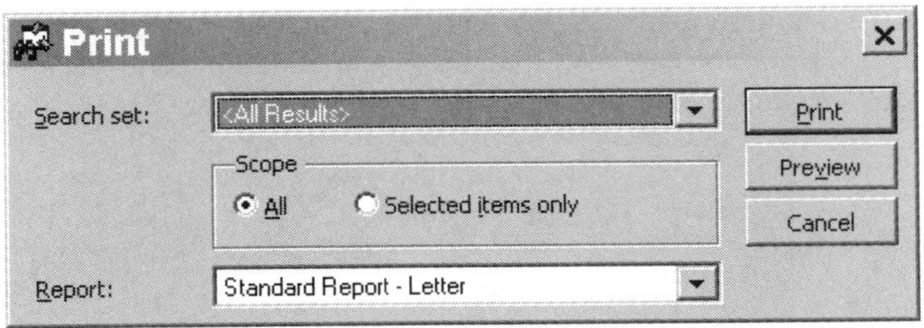

Figure 15. Reporting on search results. The dialog lets you choose all searches (for the current project or for folders), a particular search, or checked items.

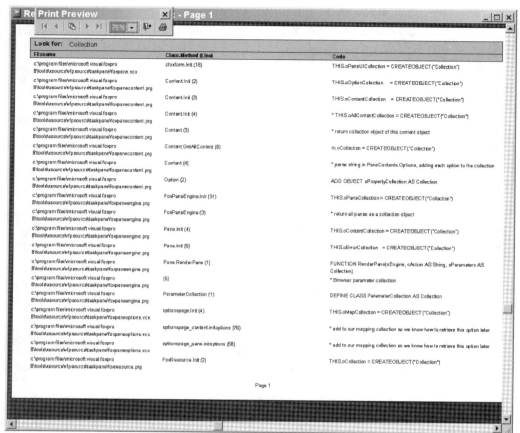

Figure 16. *Code references report. The report shows the details of each match, including the line of code.*

The Export button displays the dialog shown in **Figure 17**. The Type drop-down list lets you choose the type of file created. The options are a VFP table, a comma-delimited text file, XML, HTML, an Excel workbook, or the clipboard.

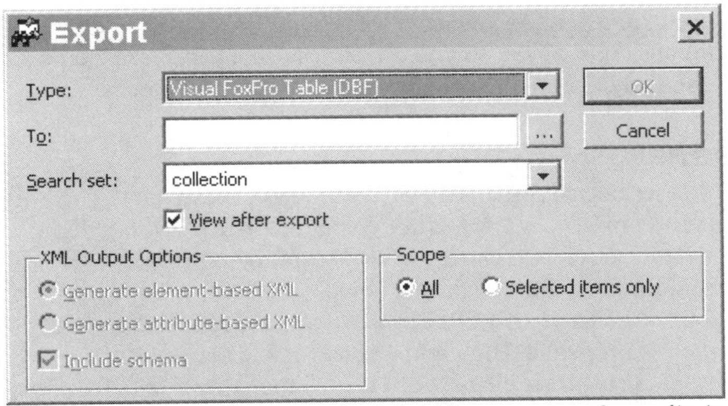

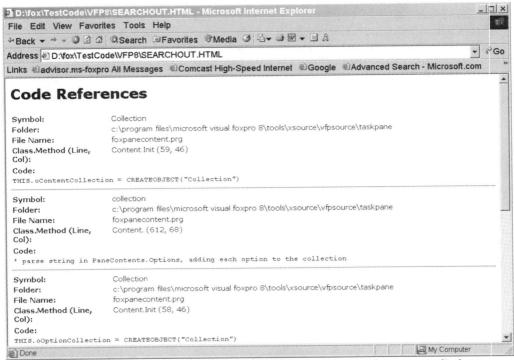

Figure 17. Exporting search data. You can send results to a table, a text file, a spreadsheet, or even the clipboard.

You specify the result file in the To text box or using the ellipsis button. Search set and Scope work together to choose the items to export, as in the Print dialog.

If View after export is checked (the default), the newly created file is opened in the appropriate application. **Figure 18** shows HTML output displayed in Internet Explorer.

Figure 18. Exporting to HTML. Choosing HTML as the export format results in an attractive report.

When you choose XML as the export format, you have some additional options. The controls labeled XML Output Options are enabled, so you can choose whether to use element-centric or attribute-centric XML and whether the output file should include the schema.

Looking for definitions

In addition to the full-blown tool described above, Code References has another face. The context menu in code editing windows offers a View Definition option. When you highlight some code (generally the name of something) and choose View Definition, the Code References engine is used to search for the definition of that item.

For example, when you highlight the name of a PRG-based class, and choose View Definition, the definition for that class is opened. Highlight a constant and choose View Definition, and the #DEFINE for that constant is displayed. This functionality works for pretty much anything that can be defined before it's used, including code-based classes, constants, procedures, functions, methods, properties, and variables.

You can prepare for this kind of searching by allowing Code References to store definition information when you search within a project or folder. (See "Code References Options.") Doing so can speed up View Definition searches at the cost of searching more slowly through the Code References tool.

Code References Options

The Options dialog for the tool (shown in **Figure 19**) is accessed from the Code References window's button bar or the context menu in the list of matches. This dialog lets you modify the behavior of the tool, as well as set the display font and indicate where the data for the tool is stored. Choosing Options in the Look Up Reference window brings up an abbreviated version of the dialog that includes only the check boxes.

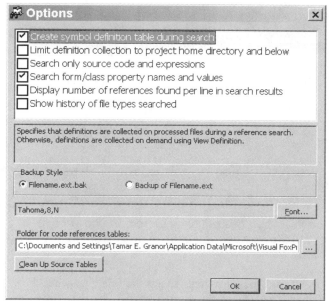

Figure 19. *Code References Options. This dialog lets you specify a variety of settings for the Code References tool. The default settings are shown here.*

Create symbol definition table during search determines whether information about each defined item in a file is stored when that file is searched. This information is used by the View Definition context menu item discussed in "Looking for definitions" earlier in this chapter. Leaving this option checked can slow down the search considerably. However, having the definition information stored speeds up View Definition. (See "Code References data" later in this chapter for more information on the tables involved.)

The next item, Limit definition collection to project home directory and below, offers a compromise position. In this case, definitions are stored only for files in the project's directory tree rather than all files referenced in the project.

The next two items allow you to limit the scope of searches. When Search only source code and expressions is checked, items such as labels in reports, field names, and other textual items are omitted from the search. Search form/class property names and values controls searching in the properties of SCX and VCX files.

Display number of references found per line in search results determines whether a column is added to the list of matches showing how many times the search string was found on the line. When it's checked, the column appears to the right of the checkbox; it's empty for lines with a single reference. **Figure 20** shows an example.

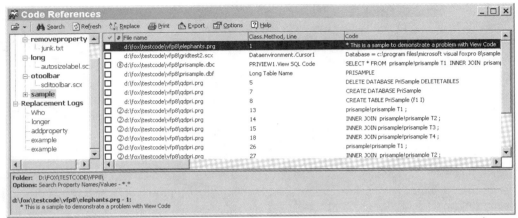

Figure 20. *Including reference counts. When this option is turned on, the second column in the list of matches contains the number of times the search string appears in the specified line, if it's greater than one.*

The final check box, Show history of file types searched, affects the File types checkbox in the Look Up Reference window. When it's checked, the drop-down list first lists those sets of file types previously used for a search, as shown in **Figure 21**.

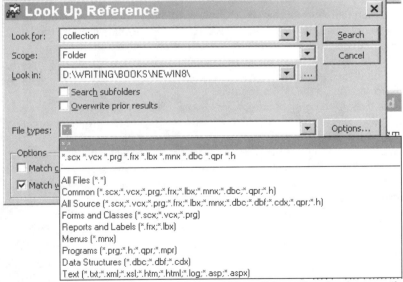

Figure 21. *Showing file type history. When this option is chosen, the File types drop-down list shows sets of file types you've used above the line before providing the complete list below.*

By default, when you perform replacements, the files that are changed are backed up. (You can turn that option off in the Replace dialog, if you wish.) The Backup style option group lets you specify how those backup files are named.

The font you choose in this dialog affects both the list of searches and the list of matches in the Code References window, but has no impact on the Look Up Reference window.

The Code References tool maintains several tables (described in "Code References data"). The Folder for code references tables text box and accompanying ellipsis button lets you specify where those tables are stored. If you change this setting, the existing tables don't disappear, but the tool no longer has access to them. Until you close and reopen the tool, the searches you've already performed are still listed in the treeview, but without their files.

The Clean Up Source Tables button lets you remove outdated information from these tables, then packs them to get rid of deleted records. See the Help topic "Look Up Reference Dialog Box, Options Dialog Box" for the exact list of actions performed. Be aware that this operation can take a little time, since the files involved can be quite large.

Code References data

Code References uses several tables to store data about definitions, searches, and replacements. By default, it's stored in your application data directory (the exact path varies with the Windows version, but it's generally something like C:\Documents and Settings\UserName\Application Data\Visual FoxPro 8—you can find the exact value with HOME(7)), but as noted in the "Code References Options" section, you can change this.

Two tables cooperate to store the list of files and definitions. RefFile.DBF contains one record for each file the tool has looked at, assigning it a unique id. RefDef.DBF contains a record for each definition found, linking it to the file and indicating the type of object defined.

Another set of tables stores information about searches and replacements. Global_Ref.DBF in the application data directory contains this information for folder searches. In addition, a table is created for each project opened in Code References and is stored with the project file itself. The table is named in the form ProjectName_Ref.DBF. So, for example, for a project called AwesomeApp.PJX, the search and replacement data would be stored in AwesomeApp_REF.DBF in the project's home directory.

A table called RefAddin.DBF in the application data directory contains meta-data for the Code References tool itself. You can change or add records in this table to change the behavior of the tool. See "The RefAddin table" later in this chapter.

In addition to the various tables, some information about the state of the tool is stored in the resource file (by default, FoxUser.DBF in the application data directory). Look for records with "FOXREF" in the ID column. While you probably won't want to manipulate this data manually, if you want to restore the tool to its original state, you can delete these records.

Customizing Code References

There are several ways you can modify the behavior of the Code References tool other than through the various options in the user interface.

The RefAddin table

The RefAddin table provides several opportunities for customization. The table includes seven types of records, listed in **Table 1**.

Table 1. *Customizing the Code References tool. The RefAddIn table contains records of different types that determine the behavior of the tool.*

Type field	Purpose
"FINDFILE"	Specifies the class used to search in a particular file type.
"IGNOREFILE"	Indicates a particular file type is ignored by the tool.
"FINDWINDOW"	Specifies the class used to search within an open window.
"REPORT"	Specifies a report for use by the Print option.
"MATCH"	Specifies the search engine class used to perform searches not involving wildcards.
"WILDMATCH"	Specifies the search engine class used for searches involving wildcards.
"FILETYPE"	Specifies a set of file types to include in the File type drop-down list in the Look Up Reference window.

You're most likely to change or add records of type "FILETYPE" in order to modify or add sets of file types to the list in the File type drop-down list. To add a FileType entry, you need to specify only four columns: UniqueId (SYS(2015) works well for this), Type ("FILETYPE"), TimeStamp (use DATETIME()), and Data (put the name and list of extensions you want to use in the form: Name (*.ext, *.ext)). For example, you could add an entry for Office documents, as follows:

```
INSERT INTO RefAddIn (UniqueID, Type, Data, TimeStamp) ;
   VALUES (SYS(2015), "FILETYPE", "Office (*.DOC, *.XLS, *.PPT)", DATETIME())
```

You might also want to design custom reports of search data. For a report record, you need the four fields above, as well as the FileName field. In this case, the Data field contains a descriptive name for the report. For example, to add a report named CodeRefReport.FRX and call it "My Code References Report", use code like this (including the path for the report):

```
INSERT INTO RefAddIn (UniqueID, Type, Data, FileName, TimeStamp) ;
   VALUES (SYS(2015), "REPORT", "My Code References Report", ;
          "CodeRefReport.FRX", DATETIME())
```

When you press Print or Preview, a query is performed before generating a report. **Table 2** shows the fields in the query result; they're available for the report in a cursor named Rptcursor, which is selected. As designed, the query supports a variety of sort orders, but at present, the tool doesn't seem to take advantage of them. The results are sorted by folder, file name, and then line number.

Table 2. Creating custom reports. The query performed before processing a report contains fields from the project or folder reference table (RefTable) and the RefFile table.

Source table	Expression from source (Field name in result, if different)	Meaning
RefTable	SetID	Unique id for the search or replace.
RefTable	Symbol	The search string or replacement string.
RefTable	ClassName	The name of the class containing the search string. Empty for replacement records.
RefTable	ProcName	Name of the method or procedure where the string was found. In some cases, such as property values, name of the object involved. Empty for replacement records.
RefTable	ProcLineNo	Line number within the method or procedure where the match was found.
RefTable	LineNo	Line number within the file where the match was found.
RefTable	ColPos	Column position on the line where the match was found.
RefTable	MatchLen	Length of the match.
RefTable	Abstract	The contents of the line where the match was found.
RefTable	TimeStamp	As of the search, date and time when the file containing the match was last modified. For replacements, date and time of the last replacement.
RefFile	Folder	Path to the file containing the match.
RefFile	FileName	First 100 characters of the name of the file containing the match.
RefFile	LEFT(Folder, 240) (SortFolder)	First 240 characters of the path, to be available for sorting.
RefFile	LOWER(PADR(JUSTEXT(FileTable.Filename), 3)) (SortFileType)	File extension.
RefTable	PADR(RefTable.ClassName, 100) (ClassNameSort)	First 100 characters of class name, to be available for sorting.
RefTable	PADR(RefTable.ProcName, 100) (ProcNameSort)	First 100 characters of procedure/method name, to be available for sorting.

You may want to add or remove IGNOREFILE type records to change the list of file types the tool supports. If you remove such a record, you may need to add a FINDFILE record for that type to indicate what code should be used to search in the file. We suspect you're more likely to add IGNOREFILE records so additional types are skipped.

As supplied, all the FINDFILE records point to subclasses of a class called RefSearch. If you don't like the behavior of the search, you can subclass these classes further, create your own subclasses of RefSearch, or write your own search routine. We don't anticipate doing any of those.

The default RefAddIn table has no MATCH or WILDMATCH type records, meaning the built-in default classes are used. They're subclasses of a class called MatchEngine. Again, you can subclass further, write your own subclasses, or start from scratch. Again, we don't anticipate doing so.

Working with the source code

The source code for Code References comes with VFP 8. It's included in a zip file called XSource.ZIP located in the HOME() + "Tools\XSource" directory. The zip file contains the code for all the tools written in VFP. When you unzip the file (using folder names), each tool lands in its own directory tree beneath a VFPSource directory. The directory for Code References is called FoxRef.

You can modify or subclass the code provided and build a new version of the Code References application. If you call it FoxRef.APP and place it in the home directory, your version will be used automatically.

The report used by default when you choose Print is Foxrefresults.FRX; you may want to use it as a template or simply for guidance in designing custom reports.

Replacing the supplied application

You can also replace the Code References application entirely (whether it's a third-party tool, something of your own devising, or a customized version of the tool supplied). Rather than replacing FoxRef.APP, you can specify a different tool be used by changing the _FOXREF system variable.

You can specify a value for _FOXREF in code or using the File Locations page of the Options dialog.

When you invoke Code References, it receives a single object parameter that indicates how the tool was called, and in some cases what was highlighted at the time. (For more information, examine the main program, FoxRefStart.PRG.)

Running Code References directly

As with the other tools to which a system variable is hooked, you can run Code References directly by calling the program the variable points to:

```
DO (_FOXREF)
```

The call is equivalent to choosing Code References from the Tools menu; that is, the exact behavior depends on whether or not a project is open and, if so, whether the active project has been searched before.

The optional parameter offers access to the View Definition lookup and to pre-populating the search string for the Look Up Reference dialog. While you could create and populate the appropriate parameter object to pass (it seems to be based on the Empty base class), we can't see why you'd want to, since the tool as a whole is interactive. If you really want to automate the tool, dig into the oFoxRef property of the _oFoxRef object created when you start the tool. We haven't tested it out, but we suspect you could perform search and replace operations by manipulating the properties and calling methods of this object.

Summary

The Code References tool fills a major hole in the VFP toolkit, providing a way to search and replace in all the files of a project. While we're sure we'll use this tool on our code, it seems particularly useful for exploring other people's code. In fact, we used Code References to explore all three new tools, to help us understand what they do, how they work, and how they're architected.

Updates and corrections to this chapter can be found on Hentzenwerke's web site, **www.hentzenwerke.com**. Click on "Catalog" and navigate to the page for this book.

Chapter 4
The Task Pane Manager

The last of VFP 8's new tools, the Task Pane Manager, provides easy access to a number of common tasks. It also offers one-click connection to a variety of VFP resources.

The Task Pane Manager is a portal. It collects a number of tasks and tools into a single interface. The tool itself is just a container; it contains "task panes." Each task pane offers some kind of information or functionality. The tool is a manager for those panes. It lets you choose which pane to view at any time, and also contains tools for installing third-party panes, creating new panes and editing existing panes.

Running the Task Pane Manager

As with the other new tools, there are several ways to start the Task Pane Manager. Both the Tools menu and the Standard Toolbar contain Task Pane items. In addition, the new _TASKPANE system variable points to the Task Pane Manager application, so you can run it by issuing:

```
DO (_TASKPANE)
```

You can also pass the unique identifier for the pane you want to see. See "Extending the Task Pane Manager" later in this chapter to learn how to find the identifier. For example, to launch the Task Pane Manager with the Solution Samples page open, use:

```
DO (_TASKPANE) WITH "microsoft.solutions"
```

The first time you start the tool, you see the Start pane (**Figure 1**), which contains getting started information, the My Tools section, lists of the projects and databases you've opened most recently, and quick access to the tool's Options window. (You can specify which pane is displayed at start-up; see "Customizing the Task Pane Manager" later in this chapter.)

Figure 1. *The Start Task Pane. This pane offers links to help you get started and to the projects and databases you've used most recently.*

The button bar across the top allows you to switch among the available task panes. As you'd expect, the Options button opens an Options window. Options that affect the Task Pane Manager as a whole are discussed in "Customizing the Task Pane Manager" later in this chapter. The Options window also includes settings for individual task panes; they're discussed along with the panes themselves.

You wouldn't expect an application like this to need a Refresh button. However, the main display of the Task Pane Manager is an Internet Browser control and some task panes use Internet content. So Refresh allows you to see the most up-to-date content. (Be aware that the Refresh option on the context menu and the F5 key simply re-read the source for the current pane, while the Refresh item on the button bar actually recreates the source before drawing it.)

Depending on the size of the Task Pane Manager (it's resizable), you may see a right-pointing chevron in the button bar (as in Figure 1). When present, it indicates more panes are available, but don't fit on the button bar.

At this point, we'll look at the capabilities of each of the task panes provided.

The Start pane

The Start pane (shown in Figure 1) is the home page for the Task Pane Manager. It has five sections: Start, My Tools, Recent Projects, Recent Databases, and Task Pane Manager startup options.

The Start section provides links to useful information and basic tasks. The items in the What's new in Visual FoxPro list are links to the Help file. Customize my development environment switches to the Environment Manager pane described in "The Environment Manager pane" later in this chapter. Create a new application runs the Application Wizard, while Create a new database runs the Database Wizard. Go to the Visual FoxPro web site opens your browser and navigates to the VFP home page on the MSDN web site.

The My Tools section provides quick access to as many developer tools as you'd like. Click Manage to open the My Tools dialog, shown in **Figure 2**. This dialog lets you add, modify, and remove tools from the list.

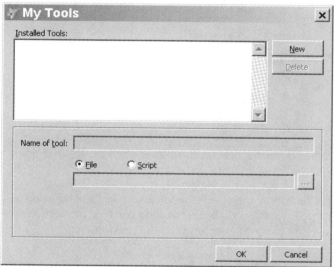

Figure 2. *Adding tools to the Start pane. Use this dialog to put tools just a mouse click away.*

A "tool" in this context is pretty open. It could be a form, a report, a VFP application, or you can write a little code to do what you want.

To add a tool to the list, click the New button. An item is added to the list with the name "New Tool" and the bottom part of the dialog comes alive. In the Name of tool text box, specify the name you want to see in the Start pane. If the tool is file-based, use the text box or the ellipsis button beneath the option buttons to point to the file. **Figure 3** shows the My Tools dialog with an item added for Stonefield Database Toolkit.

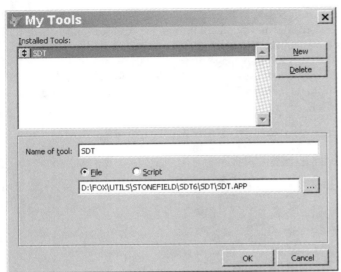

Figure 3. *Adding a file-based tool. To have a file run for a tool, choose File and point to the file.*

When you choose the Script option button, the ellipsis button disappears and the text box changes into an edit box. Type VFP code into the edit box—the code you type forms the tool's script. **Figure 4** shows a script you might create to clean up your VFP environment.

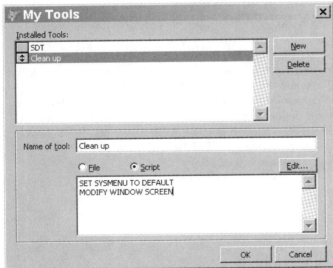

Figure 4. *Adding a script-based tool. Assign a name and create the script in the edit box.*

Once you've added at least one tool, the Start pane changes to allow you to run your tools. **Figure 5** includes a drop-down list of tools and a Run button to execute them.

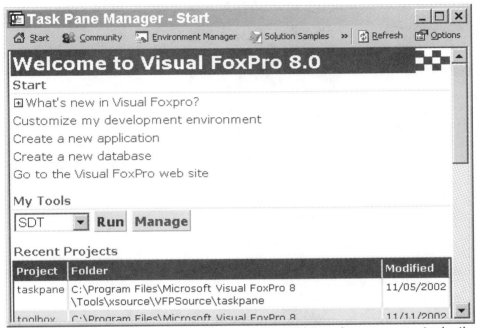

Figure 5. *Making tools available. Once you've registered one or more tools, the My Tools section expands to include a drop-down list of tools and a Run button.*

The Recent Projects and Recent Databases sections of this pane provide a look at what you've recently worked on as well as an easy way to re-open those items. The number of items in each list is based on your setting for Most Recently Used lists. (You can change this setting on the View page of the VFP Options dialog.) The MRU lists themselves are stored in your resource file, so what you see will vary based on whether RESOURCE is on and how it's set.

The Project column of Recent Projects and the Database column of Recent Databases are hyperlinks; click on an item in that column to open it. Beneath each of these sections are two buttons (shown in **Figure 6**), one to open a project or database and one to create a new project or database. Clicking one of these buttons is equivalent to typing the corresponding CREATE or MODIFY command.

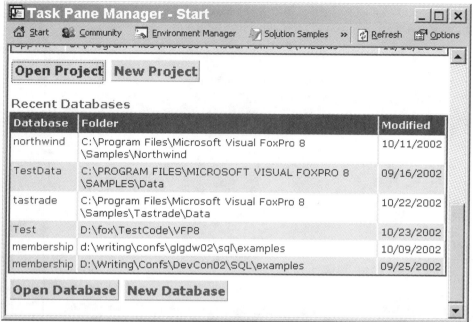

Figure 6. Recent Databases. This section of the Start pane provides quick access to the databases you've used most recently. The buttons are like typing MODIFY DATABASE ? or CREATE DATABASE.

The Recent Projects and Recent Databases lists are not updated dynamically as you work. Use the Refresh button to add projects or databases you've used while the Start pane was displayed.

The Task Pane Manager startup options link opens the Task Pane Options window, with options for the tool as a whole displayed. That window is discussed in "Customizing the Task Pane Manager" later in this chapter.

Start pane options

By default, all five sections described above (Start, My Tools, Recent Projects, Recent Databases, and Task Pane Manager startup options) are included in this pane. However, the Options window for the pane (shown in **Figure 7**) allows you to change that. The Options window shows a General section for each pane; choosing that section is the same as choosing the pane itself.

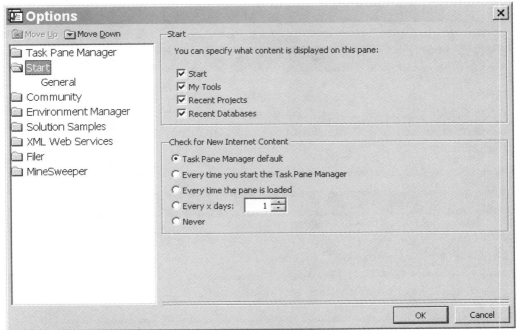

Figure 7. *Start pane options. You can turn off one or more of the sections of the start pane, as well as determine how often the display for this pane is updated.*

A number of the panes can be updated on the fly. This provides the ability for, say, Microsoft, to put new content on its website and have that content appear in the specified pane. For example, when white papers describing new features of VFP 8 become available, they might be added to the Start pane. The Check for New Internet Content option group lets you decide how often any given pane looks for new content. Setting a default for the tool is discussed in "Customizing the Task Pane Manager" below.

The Community pane

The Community pane (shown in **Figure 8**) provides links to support sites for VFP and the latest VFP news. This pane has two sections: Community and News.

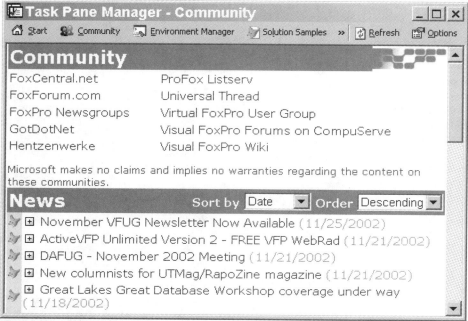

Figure 8. *Links to the VFP community. The Community pane lets you get directly to online VFP help sites, as well as keeping you up-to-date on what's going on.*

The Community section lists a number of websites that provide support for VFP developers. Most of them include peer-to-peer support forums or newsgroups. (This is another area we can imagine Microsoft updating over time.) Each item in this section is a hyperlink; click on one to open your browser and navigate to the specified site.

By default, the News section shows recent news item from the **www.FoxCentral.net** website. The two drop-down lists let you sort the news items as you desire.

The headline for each news item is displayed. You expand an item by clicking on the plus sign to read the full item. In addition, each headline is a hyperlink to the provider for that news item.

Community pane options

The Community pane has several pages of options. Its general page lets you set the frequency of new content checks (as in Figure 7). It also lets you choose sources for the News section. There are three choices: Universal Thread News, FoxCentral News and the FoxPro wiki. You can choose any combination of the three.

Each of the news sources has additional options. For each, you can specify how many days worth of news to include. In addition, for the Universal Thread, you need to provide your username and password (presumably to access the web service that provides the news items). The Universal Thread options page also lets you specify the type of item that's included. **Figure 9** shows the options page for Universal Thread News.

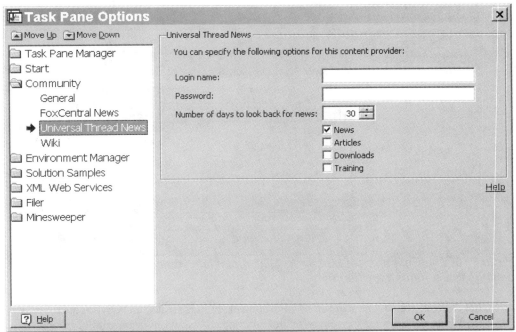

Figure 9. Setting news options. You need a (free) username and password to access Universal Thread news.

There's a heavy overlap between the FoxCentral and Universal Thread news listings, so you'll probably want to choose one or the other, but not both.

The Environment Manager pane

The Environment Manager pane provides a solution to an old problem: how to easily switch between projects and make sure everything's set up the way it should be. VFP developers have tried various solutions to this problem over the years, from using the menu to switch between projects to setting things up via a project hook. The Environment Manager offers another solution.

When you first visit this pane, it includes a single link captioned "Manage Environments." Clicking the link opens the Environment Manager dialog shown in **Figure 10**.

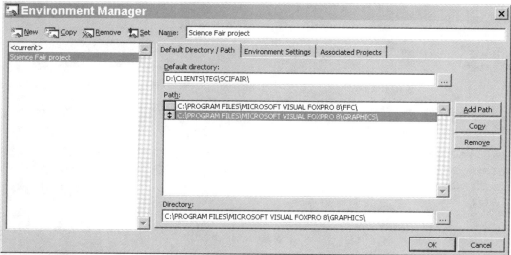

Figure 10. *The Environment Manager. This applet lets you combine a variety of settings into a named environment.*

Click New to create a new group of environment settings (called an "environment set" by the tool). When you do so, a new item (by default, named "New Environment Set *n*," where *n* is the number of sets you've created in this VFP session) is added and the dialog comes alive. You can edit the name in the Name text box.

As its name suggests, the Default Directory / Path page lets you set up a default folder and a path. Both default to the current settings. To add a folder to the path, click the Add Path button. Doing so clears the Directory text box. Use the text box or the associated ellipsis button to specify a folder. Once you've added more than one folder to the list of paths, you can rearrange the list to ensure files are located in the right order.

The Environment Settings page (**Figure 11**) lets you specify values for various SET commands, as well as scripts to run before and after loading the environment. For each setting listed in the grid, you can leave it set to the default value or specify one of the allowed values.

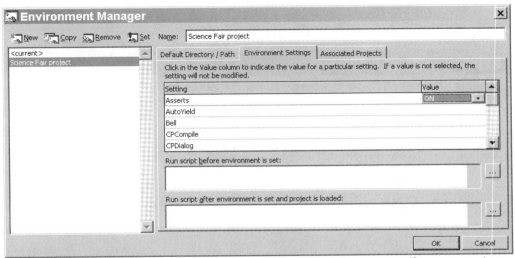

Figure 11. *Specifying environment settings. This page lets you specify some system settings and run any VFP code you'd like.*

The two scripts let you handle items not included elsewhere in the tool. The first runs before any of the settings are changed. The second runs after everything has been done. You can include any VFP code in the scripts.

The Associated Projects page lets you connect one or more projects to an environment set. Once you've done so, the projects are listed along with this environment set. Clicking on a project establishes the settings, and then opens the project. (Note that you have to open the project from the Environment Manager page to have the settings put in place.)

The Copy button lets you copy an environment set, presumably to use as the starting point for a new set. Remove deletes an environment set. The Set button executes that environment set, making its settings current.

When you've added one or more groups of settings, the Environment Manager page expands to list them (as shown in **Figure 12**). The name of a group of settings and any projects listed underneath are hyperlinks. Clicking the name establishes the settings. Clicking a project establishes the settings and opens that project. Clicking the Design icon on the right opens the Environment Manager dialog with this group of settings highlighted.

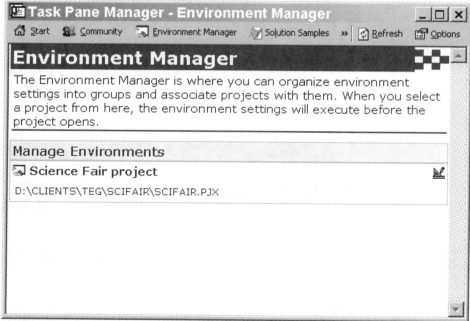

Figure 12. *The Environment Manager pane. Once you've defined some groups of settings, you can set them and open associated projects from this pane.*

The Environment Manager pane has no settable options.

The Solution Samples pane

Since version 5, VFP has shipped with an extensive set of sample forms, programs, and classes, known as the Solution Samples, designed to demonstrate features of the language. In different versions of the product, Microsoft has tried a variety of strategies to make the Solution Samples easy to find. In VFP 8, they've included a task pane for them (shown in **Figure 13**).

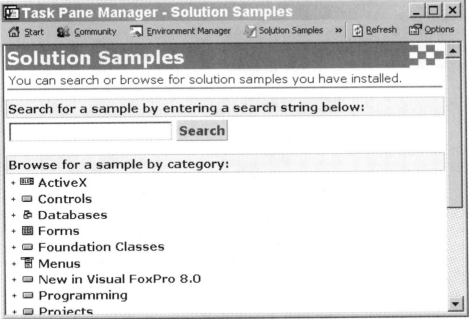

Figure 13. *Solution Samples pane. You can run any sample or explore the code from within this pane.*

When you drill into any category in the list of samples, the name of the sample is a hyperlink that runs the sample. There's also an icon to show the code behind the sample.

The search text box and button let you find samples related to a particular topic. For example, **Figure 14** shows the results of searching for "grid." (To remove the search results from the pane, clear the textbox and click Search again.)

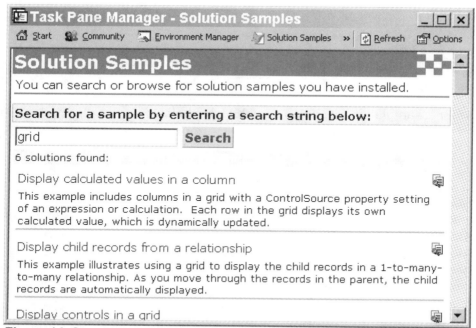

Figure 14. Searching for a sample. Click on the name of the sample to run it, or the icon at the right to see the code.

At the bottom of the page, there are two additional sections. The first, Solution Sample Add-Ins, is for installing new samples. Expect Microsoft (and, perhaps, others) to periodically provide additional samples in the form of an XML file. When you click the Install Sample button, you're prompted to point to the new samples. Navigate to the appropriate manifest.xml file and the new samples are added.

The second section, Links to sites that have Add-Ins available, presumably will list places you can get additional samples. As of this writing, the section is empty.

Solution Samples pane options

This pane has only a few options. As with a number of other panes, you can choose the frequency of content checks. In addition, check boxes allow you to determine whether the Solution Samples and the links to add-ins are displayed. We can't imagine why you'd uncheck the Solution Samples checkbox; there's no point in having this pane without the samples.

The XML Web Services pane

This pane (shown in **Figure 15**) is a one-stop shop for everything you'd want to do with web services, except actually use them in an application. It contains three sections: XML Web Services Tools, Explore an XML Web Service, and XML Web Services Resources.

Figure 15. *Working with web services. This pane lets you register and publish web services, dig into individual web services, and offers access to a variety of resources.*

The XML Web Service Tools section offers access to the three tools listed in it. All three are discussed in Chapter 10, "COM and Web Services Enhancements."

The Explore an XML Web Service section of the XML Web Services pane lets you see what a web service offers without leaving VFP. It's also discussed in Chapter 10.

The XML Web Services Resources section of the pane contains links to various Help topics, articles on the Microsoft web site, and other documentation.

XML Web Services pane options

For this pane, the Options window has two groups. As with other panes, the bottom group controls the frequency with which the tool checks for updates. The upper group lets you decide which sections of the pane are displayed. Check boxes let you control each of the three sections independently.

The Filer pane

This pane (shown in **Figure 16**) provides easy access to the Filer tool that lets you search for files in directory trees. Except for being housed in the Task Pane Manager and having a snazzier appearance, running Filer here is the same as issuing DO FORM HOME() + "Tools\Filer\Filer".

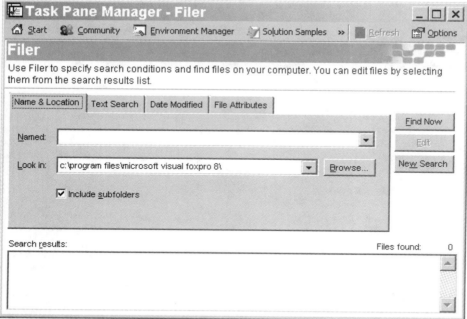

Figure 16. The Filer pane. This pane provides quick access to the Filer form.

The Filer pane has no options to set.

The Minesweeper pane

The final pane provided by Microsoft (**Figure 17**) offers a VFP version of the Minesweeper game. The game was written to demonstrate (and, undoubtedly, test) the new Collection class (discussed in Chapter 9, "OOP Improvements.").

Figure 17. The Minesweeper pane. Something to do when you need a break. Explore the underlying code for an example of the Collection class.

While the game is missing some of the features of the original, it has some nice features of its own, including the ability to determine the size of the grid, which you do on the Options page for this pane.

Errors happen

Occasionally, things may go wrong when working in a task pane. The tool is equipped to deal with that. When it has a problem it can't resolve, an error message appears right in the tool. Click on the message to see exactly what's wrong. Click it again to remove the details.

Figure 18 shows what happens when you attempt to retrieve news for the Universal Thread without providing a username and password. Once the problem is resolved, the error message goes away.

Figure 18. Dealing with errors. When the task pane has a problem, it displays an error message.

Customizing the Task Pane Manager

Along with the options you can set for individual panes (described in the relevant sections earlier), there are a variety of settings for the tool itself, which you can set through the Task Pane Options window (shown in **Figure 19**). The options for the tool itself are divided into two pages, General and Customize.

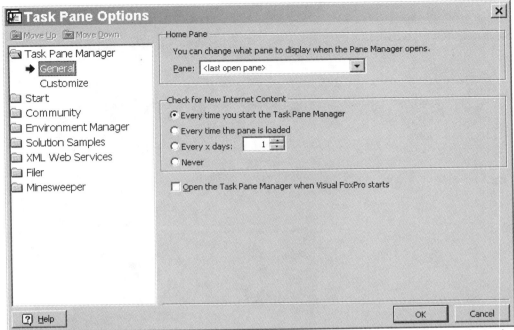

Figure 19. Setting Task Pane Manager options. These settings affect the whole tool.

The General page contains options that determine how the tool works. The Home Pane drop-down list allows you to specify what you see when you open the Task Pane Manager. By default, it reopens to the last pane, but you can choose a particular pane if you prefer.

The next section, Check for New Internet Content, determines the default setting for how often the tool looks for updates. As noted above, those sections that can be updated include individual settings for this option, which allow them to use the default setting or make a different choice.

If you decide to make the Task Pane Manager (especially the Start pane) your portal for development, you'll probably want it open all the time. In that case, check Open the Task Pane Manager when Visual FoxPro starts. (Be aware that CLEAR ALL closes the tool, because it's a VFP app.)

The Customize page (shown in **Figure 20**) lets you determine where Task Pane data is stored, and allows you to manipulate that data, including adding and modifying panes.

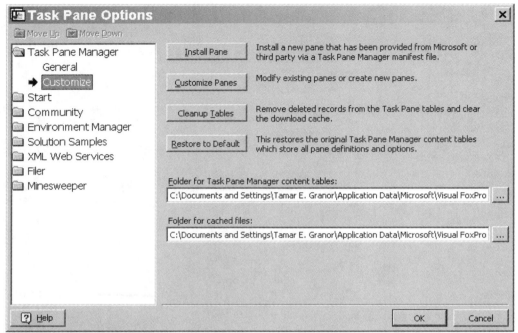

Figure 20. *Customizing Task Pane Manager content. These options let you add panes, modify existing panes, and more.*

Install Pane lets you add panes provided by others to the tool. Customize Panes lets you tweak the panes that are there, as well as create your own. Both are discussed in "Extending the Task Pane Manager" later in this chapter.

The next two items here let you clean up if you've made a mess. Cleanup Tables packs the data. Like the other new tools, the Task Pane Manager application contains clean copies of its own data tables. When you click the Restore to Default button, those tables are copied out to the data directory, overwriting whatever's there.

The last two items determine where the Task Pane Manager stores its data. The content tables specify what panes are available and what they contain. By default, they're stored in a subdirectory called TaskPane of your application data directory (use HOME(7) to find out what it is). The tool creates a variety of files on the fly to hold the actual content of the panes. By default, they're stored in a subdirectory called PaneCache of the directory holding the content tables. (See "Extending the Task Pane Manager" later for more on Task Pane Manager data.)

Working with the source code

As with the other Xbase tools, the source code for the Task Pane Manager is included in the XSource.ZIP file in HOME() + "Tools\XSource." When you unzip the file, the Task Pane Manager project is found in the TaskPane folder of the VFPSource folder.

You can replace or subclass the various components to build your own version of the tool. To use your version, change the _TASKPANE variable or the Task Pane settings in the File Locations page of the Tools | Options dialog to point to your version.

Extending the Task Pane Manager

The Task Pane Manager is designed to allow you to add additional task panes. Our impression is that Microsoft hopes third-party vendors (such as the framework makers) will provide task panes for their tools.

Two tables are used to store Task Pane data. TaskPane.DBF contains a record for each pane, while PaneContent.DBF contains records describing the actual content of each pane. Fortunately, you shouldn't need to dig into the data because the tool itself lets you do what you need to add new panes and edit existing ones.

Adding third-party panes

Not surprisingly, given Microsoft's focus on XML, the mechanism for distributing new task panes is XML. The supplier of a task pane provides you with an XML file that describes the new pane and its functionality.

To install a pane in your Task Pane Manager, click Install Pane on the Task Pane Manager-Customize page of the Task Pane Options window (described in "Customizing the Task Pane Manager" earlier in this chapter). When you do so, you're prompted to point to the appropriate file. The tool reads the file and updates its data accordingly. When control returns, you're looking at the Options page for the new pane in the Task Pane Options window. When you close that window, the new pane appears in the Task Pane Manager.

 *The Developer Downloads available at **www.hentzenwerke.com** include an XML file (Mortgage_Calculator.XML) that allows you to add a simple Mortgage Calculator pane. See "Specifying a VFP Controls pane" later in the chapter to learn how to create this pane.*

Creating and modifying panes

Adding someone else's pane is the easy part. Creating your own is somewhat trickier. To be more accurate, it's not hard to create a simple, fairly static pane, but creating complex panes like those that come with the product is non-trivial.

The Customize Panes button on the Task Pane Manager-Customize page of the Task Pane Options window opens the Pane Customization window (shown in **Figure 21**). Each installed pane is included in the list on the left-hand side. When you choose a pane, the right-hand side of the window shows the data that describes the pane. The Inactive checkbox at the bottom left lets you determine whether a given pane appears in the Task Pane Manager at this time.

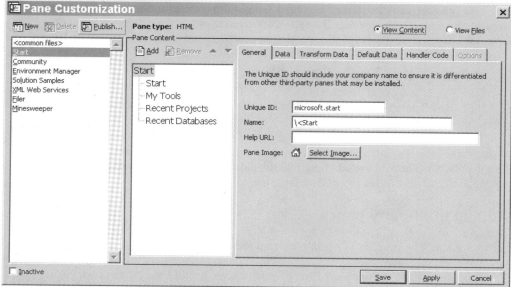

Figure 21. Adding and editing task panes. The Pane Customization window provides tools for changing the behavior of existing panes, creating new panes, and creating the XML file needed to distribute your panes.

To add a new task pane, click the New button in the button bar. The Pane dialog (shown in **Figure 22**) appears. When you fill in the Vendor text box, the Unique ID field is modified to include the vendor name as part of the ID. (The dialog automatically generates a value for ID using SYS(2015), but you can replace it with anything you want.) The name you specify in this dialog is the "friendly" name for the pane—it appears in the Task Pane Manager's button bar, in the Task Pane Manager's title bar when the pane is active, and in the various windows accessed through the Task Pane Options window.

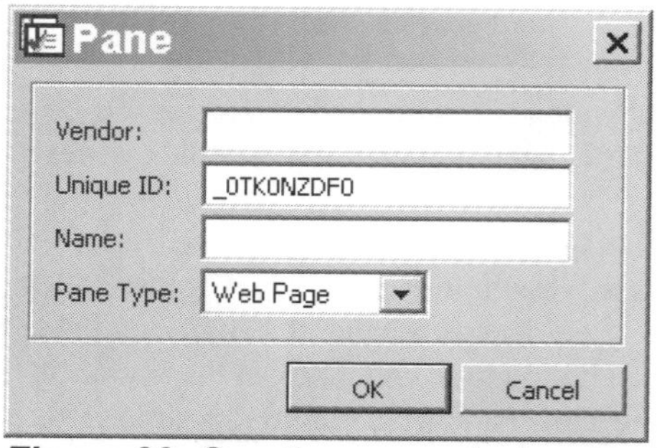

Figure 22. Creating a new task pane. This dialog lets you specify the name and type of the pane.

There are four types of task panes: Web Page, HTML, XML, and VFP Controls. The choice you make in this dialog is permanent; the interface provides no way to change the type of a task pane once it's created. (You can, of course, do so in the underlying data.) The type of pane is shown in the button bar of the Pane Customization window.

Once you click OK in the Pane dialog, the new page is added to the list in the Pane Customization window, and you can specify its contents.

The General tab (shown in Figure 21) describes the pane as a whole, or if you click on a section of the pane (for example, the My Tools section of the Start pane), it describes that section. Help URL is the address for any help file for the pane or subsection. The Select Image button lets you specify the graphic that appears next to the name in the button bar.

The contents and availability of the remaining pages (except for Options) vary depending on the pane type.

Specifying pane options

The Options page of the Pane Customization window lets you determine what appears in the Task Pane Options window for each pane. You can specify one or more items that let the user customize the pane. **Figure 23** shows the Options page for the Minesweeper pane; it indicates the user can specify a value for Size. Items from the Options pane can be used in specifying the pane contents by surrounding them with "##" pairs; for example, to use the Minesweeper Size parameter, you'd write it as "##size##". You can use this approach for passing an option's value to a web service's method, for example. In addition, a method is provided for retrieving the value of an option item for use in VFP code; see "Specifying a VFP Controls pane" later in this chapter for an example.

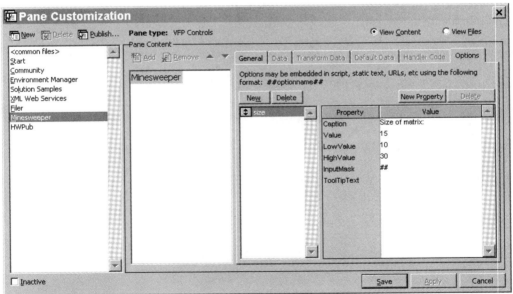

Figure 23. Pane options. The Options page lets you determine what items appears in the Task Pane Options window for a given pane.

To add an option item to a pane, click New on the page and the New Option dialog (**Figure 24**) appears. For each option, you specify a name, the type of control to use for that option (text box, check box, spinner, or password—choosing password provides a text box with a PasswordChar mask), and the caption to appear for the control.

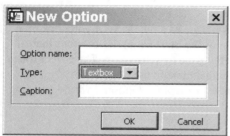

Figure 24. Adding pane options. Use this dialog to add items to the Task Pane Options window for a specific pane.

When you click OK, the new option item appears in the list of items. The grid shows properties you can set for the specified control. A default set of properties appears initially, but the New Property button lets you add other properties of the control to the list, and the Delete button lets you remove properties from the list. You can edit the values for any of the properties to determine the appearance and behavior of the controls on the Options page for that pane.

The list of items has mover bars that let you determine the order in which the items appear on the Options page for the pane. The Delete button immediately above the list removes option items from the list.

Be aware that the values the user enters for these options are saved between VFP sessions, so when you open a task pane, it uses the last values entered by the user.

Specifying a Web Page pane

For a pane whose type is Web Page, things are quite simple. The Data page (shown in **Figure 25**) contains one available text box where you specify the URL. When you choose this pane in the Task Pane Manager, the specified page is displayed.

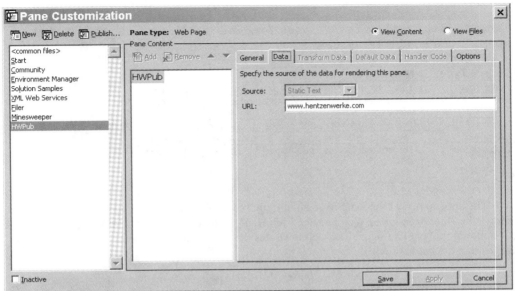

Figure 25. Configuring a Web Page task pane. For a Web Page task pane, the only thing to specify is the URL.

You can set up an option item for this type of pane, but the only thing you could do with it is substitute it into the URL. This seems like a rather complex way of choosing which web page to display.

None of the panes provided are Web Page panes.

Specifying an HTML or XML pane

The HTML and XML choices for pane type are quite similar, so we'll discuss them together. HTML and XML panes offer a wide variety of choices. Unlike Web Page panes, they're not confined to displaying just the data from a particular URL. The pane contents are created at the time the pane is displayed.

HTML and XML panes can be divided into multiple sections, each of which has its own configuration. To add a section to a pane, click the Add button above the Pane Content list. Then, specify the contents for that section. (Be aware that HTML and XML panes can't have options, but sections of these panes can.)

When you specify an HTML or XML pane, the Data page offers five choices for the source of the content. **Table 1** shows the choices and their meanings.

Table 1. *HTML and XML content types. An HTML or XML pane can draw its data from any of a number of sources.*

Source Type	Meaning
Static Text	The content for the pane is specified as HTML or XML text.
URL	The content for this pane is specified as the URL for an XML file or web page.
Script	The content for the pane comes from VFP code that returns XML.
File	The content for this pane comes from a file containing HTML or XML
Web service	The content for this pane comes from a call to a method of a web service.

The appearance of the Data page changes based on the source type you specify. **Figure 26** shows the Data page when Web Service is chosen—in this case, it's for the Wiki section of the Community pane. (The figure also demonstrates the use of an option item—the daysold item appears in the method call.)

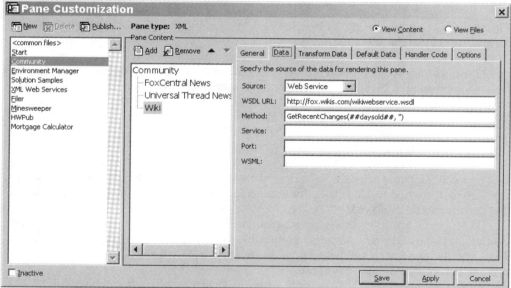

Figure 26. *Getting content from a web service. When you choose Web Service as the Source, the Data page lets you fill in the details.*

The Transform Data page determines how the data is formatted for display. You have three choices: no transformation, application of an XSL style sheet, or application of a script. When you choose XSL or script, you have the same five choices for the source of the XSL style sheet or the script as shown in Table 1 for supplying the data. **Figure 27** shows the Transform Data page for the Recent Projects section of the Start pane, which uses XSL transformation with a static text style sheet.

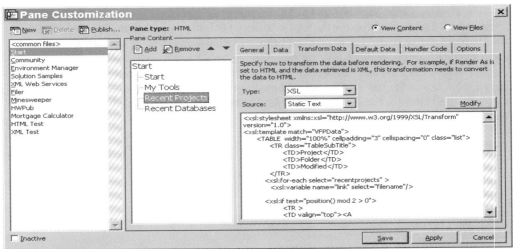

Figure 27. Rendering the data. The Transform Data lets you specify how the data is converted for display.

The Default Data page lets you supply data to be used if, for some reason (such as no Internet connection), the real data can't be loaded. While you can edit this data in place, there's also a Modify button to zoom it out into an editing window. (Other pages also offer a Modify button when appropriate.) **Figure 28** shows the default data for the Start section of the Start pane.

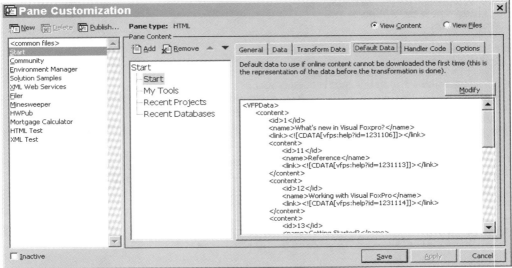

Figure 28. Specifying default data. If the actual data for this section or pane can't be loaded, the data specified on the Default Data page is used.

The Handler Code page lets you put links on a pane that actually run code, not just jump to other text. The convention for the tool is for any URL that begins with "vfps:" (presumably for "Visual FoxPro script") to invoke the handler code for that pane or section. The handler code receives four parameters: a string representing the action specified for the link, an object reference to a parameters collection containing the parameters passed in the link, an object reference to the browser object, and an object reference to the pane content itself. For example, in the Recent Projects section of the Start pane, the name of each project is a link like this:

```
vfps:modifyproject?filename="PATH\Project.PJX"
```

Here's the handler code for the Recent Projects section:

```
LPARAMETERS cAction, oParameters, oBrowser, oContent
LOCAL cFilename
LOCAL oResource
LOCAL nProjectCnt

m.nProjectCnt = _VFP.Projects.Count

DO CASE
CASE m.cAction == "modifyproject"
  m.cFilename = oParameters.GetParam("filename")
  IF EMPTY(m.cFilename)
    MODIFY PROJECT ? NOWAIT
  ELSE
    MODIFY PROJECT (m.cFilename) NOWAIT
  ENDIF

CASE m.cAction == "createproject"
  CREATE PROJECT ? NOWAIT
ENDCASE

IF _VFP.Projects.Count > m.nProjectCnt
  * Update the MRU List
  IF FILE(HOME() + "TaskPane.app")
    m.oResource  = NEWOBJECT("FoxResource", "FoxResource.prg", ;
                            HOME() + "TaskPane.app")
    m.oResource.AddToMRU("MRUL", _VFP.Projects(1).Name)
  ENDIF
ENDIF
```

When you click the Modify button on this page, an editing window opens up displaying the handler code. If there's no handler code already specified, the opening section of the code is created automatically. It looks like this:

```
* Any link clicked on that begins with "vfps:" will
* be passed to this handler.  For example:
*   <a href="vfps:showmsg?text=Sample Text">...</a>
*
```

```
* <cAction>      = action text (ex: "showmsg")
* <oParameters> = collection of parameters
* <oBrowser>     = reference to browser object
* <oContent>     = reference to content object
LPARAMETERS cAction, oParameters, oBrowser, oContent
```

The handler code can include any VFP code. Several of the supplied panes have code that creates an object and calls methods to perform the desired action.

Several handler actions are predefined and can be used in custom panes without writing any code. They're shown in Table 2. The Start pane demonstrates several of these. For example, the link for "Customize my development environment" is:

```
vfps:gotopane?uniqueid=microsoft.environmgr
```

and the link for "Go to the Visual FoxPro web site" is:

```
vfps:linkto?url=http://msdn.microsoft.com/vfoxpro/
```

Table 2. *Built-in handler actions. The Task Pane Manager includes the code to perform several actions, so you don't have to write it.*

Action	Purpose
gotopane	Switches to the specified pane.
help	Displays the specified Help topic.
linkto	Opens a browser to the specified URL.
message	Displays a message box.
options	Displays the Task Pane Options window.
refresh	Reloads the current pane.

The Developer Downloads available at ***www.hentzenwerke.com*** *include a very rudimentary HTML pane that provides easy access to the electronic version of a few Hentzenwerke books. Install Hentzenwerke_Books.XML as a task pane. To make it work, you'll need to modify the handler code-it has the location of the e-books hard-coded.*

The Start, Solutions Samples, and XML Web Services panes are HTML panes; the Community and Environment Manager panes are XML panes.

Specifying a VFP Controls pane

Task panes of the VFP Controls type are much like forms. They're built from FoxPro controls and code. However, you can't use just any VFP form; in fact, you can't use a form at all.

The best way to build a VFP Controls pane is to subclass it from the PaneContainer class in the FoxPane class library that's part of the TaskPane project. PaneContainer is a subclass of Container and includes a number of custom methods the Task Pane Manager expects to find. You need to create your PaneContainer subclass before defining the new task pane.

Depending on the content of your pane, you may not need to do anything with the custom methods of PaneContainer. If your pane is simple, you may be able to just drop the necessary controls on the pane, and write your method code. You can subclass PaneContainer visually or in a PRG file.

Once you've defined the PaneContainer subclass, you can add the pane to the Task Pane Manager. For a VFP Controls pane, the General page of the Pane Customization window expands to let you specify the class and class library for your subclass (as in **Figure 29**).

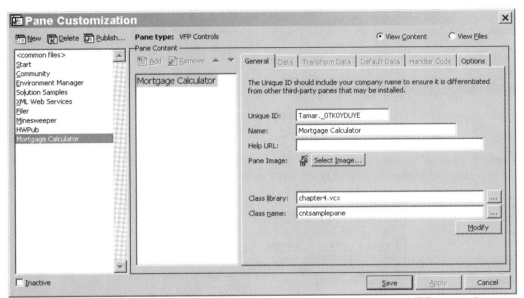

Figure 29. Adding a VFP-based pane. When the pane is based on VFP controls, you specify the class and class library containing the pane.

 *The Developer Downloads available at **www.hentzenwerke.com** include a subclass of PaneContainer that shows a simple mortgage calculator. The code is in Chapter4.VCX.*

You can use option items in this type of pane. To read their values, you need to put code in the custom OnRender method. The method receives two parameters: oPane and oContent. You can retrieve the value of an option item with a line like:

```
cValue = oContent.GetOption(cOptionName, cDefaultValue)
```

The second parameter (cDefaultValue) is optional. Note that all option values are returned as character, so you have to convert the result if you need data of another type.

The Mortgage Calculator pane has one option item, a check box that indicates whether the interest rate is annual or monthly. The OnRender method contains this code:

```
LPARAMETERS oPane, oContent

LOCAL cResult

cResult = oContent.GetOption("isannual")

This.lIsAnnual = IIF(cResult = ".T.", .T., .F.)

IF This.lIsAnnual
   This.lblInterest.Caption = "Interest rate (annual %)"
ELSE
   This.lblInterest.Caption = "Interest rate (monthly %)"
ENDIF
```

Two of the panes that come with VFP 8 are VFP Controls panes: Filer and Minesweeper. It is worth opening their code (using the Modify button) to see how they were fitted to task panes.

Publishing panes
Once you've created a pane, making it available to others is easy. With the pane you want to publish chosen in the left-hand list of the Pane Customization window, click the Publish button. The Publish Pane dialog (shown in **Figure 30**) appears. Choose the appropriate settings for your pane and click OK. You're then prompted to specify a file name—by default, it's the pane name plus an XML extension. Click Save in that dialog and the pane information is saved.

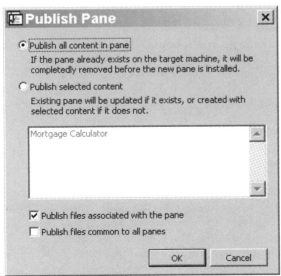

Figure 30. Publishing task panes. This dialog lets you specify what's put in the XML file you create to distribute a task pane.

The option buttons determine what happens when the pane is installed. If Publish all content in pane is chosen, this definition entirely replaces any existing definition for the pane. If Publish selected content is chosen, the pane is updated if it already exists, and installed otherwise.

The files associated with a task pane are stored with Task Pane Manager data. The two checkboxes determine which of those files are actually encoded into the XML file you distribute. The first, Publish files associated with this pane, determines whether files that are part of the pane definition are included in the XML. The second, Publish files common to all panes, determines whether files used across multiple panes (such as the HTML message that tells you data is being loaded from the Internet) are included.

To distribute your pane, just send the XML file. Others can install the pane as described in "Adding third-party panes" earlier in this chapter.

Panes and files

The data for all panes is stored in the two Task Pane tables (TaskPane.DBF and PaneContent.DBF), which are normally located in a TaskPane subdirectory of the user's application data directory (HOME(7)), and in a set of directories beneath that one. When you specify that a particular piece of information comes from a file, that file is copied into the appropriate field of the tables or to the directory. The Task Pane Manager then uses the copy of the file to generate the contents.

This structure has two consequences. First, once you've specified a file to be used in a pane (say, as the data or to perform the transformation), changing the original file doesn't affect the pane unless you return to the Pane Customization window and point to the file again. Clicking Modify where it's available opens the copy of the file, not the original. If you modify the copy, your modifications will be overwritten if you later point to the file, causing it to be copied in again.

Second, the XML files you create to distribute panes can be quite large, because they include the contents of every relevant file.

You can see what files are being stored for a given pane by choosing the View Files button on the button bar of the Pane Customization window. **Figure 31** shows the files view for the Solution Samples pane. This view also lets you add, edit, and remove files.

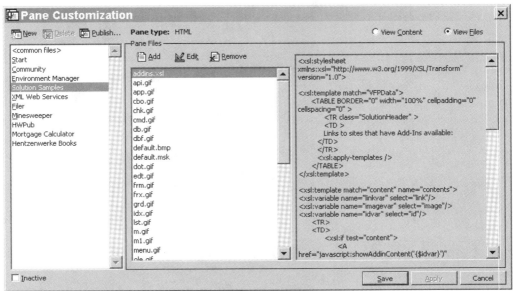

Figure 31. *Looking at pane files. Choosing the View Files option button lets you see what files are stored for a given pane.*

Summary

The Task Pane Manager offers a whole new approach to working in VFP. If third-party vendors choose to present their applications through task panes, we imagine it will become the preferred approach for many developers. The ability to add your own common tasks to the Start pane also makes this portal very attractive, as does the dynamic updating capability.

Updates and corrections to this chapter can be found on Hentzenwerke's web site, **www.hentzenwerke.com**. Click on "Catalog" and navigate to the page for this book.

Chapter 5
Better Tools

Along with a good selection of new tools (described in Chapters 2, 3 and 4), VFP 8 brings significant improvements to a couple of existing tools and small changes to many of the rest.

Two of VFP's tools, the Query/View Designer and the Report Designer, haven't seen any major modifications for quite a few versions. VFP 8 changes that with significant enhancements to both of them. In addition, the Form Designer and Class Designer have quite a few tweaks and there's a new version of InstallShield Express. Several other tools feature small improvements too.

A working Query/View Designer

In VFP 7 and earlier, the Query/View Designer (QD/VD) is of limited use because it's unable to create a wide variety of complex queries. VFP 8 addresses these deficiencies in several ways. There are also a number of other changes in the QD/VD that make it easier to use.

> *While the Query Designer and the View Designer are treated as separate tools both by the VFP IDE and Help, in fact, they're really a single tool with the View Designer offering one extra page to handle update criteria for views.*

The first change to the QD/VD is that it's significantly wider than in earlier versions. This is to accommodate the changes to the Join page. You may find it hard to work with at lower resolutions, depending on your version of Windows and your font settings.

Getting joins right

The most important change is in the way joins are handled. The SQL-SELECT syntax provides two styles for specifying joins in the FROM clause: a nested style in which all the tables are listed first followed by the ON clauses that specify the join conditions and a sequential style in which tables alternate with ON clauses. In VFP 7 and earlier, the QD/VD supports only the nested style. In VFP 8, the tool supports both styles and uses the sequential style by default.

This change is tied into a redesign of the Join page of the QD/VD. The updated Join page is shown in **Figure 1**. In VFP 8, it includes the aliases of the tables involved in each join, as well as two priority columns that let you determine the order of the joins and the order of evaluation for conditions within a specific join.

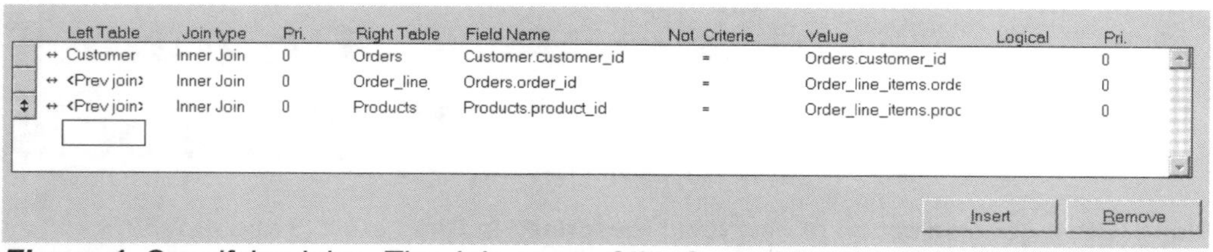

	Left Table	Join type	Pri.	Right Table	Field Name	Not	Criteria	Value	Logical	Pri.
↔	Customer	Inner Join	0	Orders	Customer.customer_id		=	Orders.customer_id		0
↔	<Prev join>	Inner Join	0	Order_line	Orders.order_id		=	Order_line_items.orde		0
↕ ↔	<Prev join>	Inner Join	0	Products	Products.product_id		=	Order_line_items.proc		0

[Insert]   [Remove]

Figure 1. *Specifying joins. The Join page of the Query/View Designer contains a lot more information in VFP 8.*

The Left Table and Right Table columns, together with the first of the two Priority columns, let you determine the logical order of the joins. When the Left Table column for a join specifies "<Prev join>", the sequential style is used. So the joins shown in Figure 1 correspond to this FROM clause:

```
FROM ;
    tastrade!customer ;
  INNER JOIN tastrade!orders ;
  ON  Customer.customer_id = Orders.customer_id ;
  INNER JOIN tastrade!order_line_items ;
  ON  Orders.order_id = Order_line_items.order_id ;
  INNER JOIN tastrade!products ;
  ON  Products.product_id = Order_line_items.product_id
```

> The logical order of joins in a query isn't necessarily the order in which they're performed. The Rushmore engine examines the query and determines the optimal order for joining the tables. The choice of sequential or nested style for a join doesn't affect optimization.

Choosing "<Next join>" in the Right Table column specifies the nested style. **Figure 2** shows a join for the same tables as in Figure 1, but using the nested style. (In the example, you also need to change the left table from "<Prev join>" to the appropriate table.) The resulting FROM clause is:

```
FROM ;
    tastrade!customer ;
  INNER JOIN  tastrade!orders ;
  INNER JOIN  tastrade!order_line_items ;
  INNER JOIN tastrade!products ;
  ON  Products.product_id = Order_line_items.product_id ;
  ON  Orders.order_id = Order_line_items.order_id ;
  ON  Customer.customer_id = Orders.customer_id
```

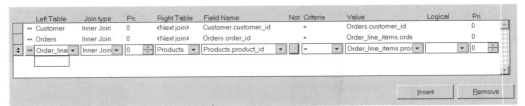

		Left Table	Join type	Pri.	Right Table	Field Name	Not	Criteria	Value		Logical	Pri.	
	↔	Customer	Inner Join	0	<Next join>	Customer.customer_id		=	Orders.customer_id			0	
	↔	Orders	Inner Join	0	<Next join>	Orders.order_id		=	Order_line_items.orde			0	
↕	↔	Order_line ▼	Inner Join ▼	0	Products ▼	Products.product_id ▼		= ▼	Order_line_items.proc ▼		▼	0	↕

Insert   Remove

Figure 2. *Nested joins. Choosing "<Next join>" for the Right Table indicates the nested style of join should be used.*

You can mix and match the nested and sequential styles within a single query. **Figure 3** shows a query using the nested style as in Figure 2, but then adds the Employee table using the sequential style. The resulting FROM clause is:

```
FROM ;
    tastrade!customer ;
  INNER JOIN  tastrade!orders ;
  INNER JOIN  tastrade!order_line_items ;
  INNER JOIN tastrade!products ;
  ON  Products.product_id = Order_line_items.product_id ;
  ON  Orders.order_id = Order_line_items.order_id ;
  ON  Customer.customer_id = Orders.customer_id ;
  INNER JOIN tastrade!employee ;
  ON  Employee.employee_id = Orders.employee_id
```

		Left Table	Join type	Pri.	Right Table	Field Name	Not	Criteria	Value		Logical	Pri.	
	↔	Customer	Inner Join	0	<Next join>	Customer.customer_id		=	Orders.customer_id			0	
	↔	Orders	Inner Join	0	<Next join>	Orders.order_id		=	Order_line_items.orde			0	
	↔	Order_line	Inner Join	0	Products	Products.product_id		=	Order_line_items.proc			0	
↕	↔	<Prev join ▼	Inner Join ▼	0	Employee ▼	Employee.employee_ic ▼		= ▼	Orders.employee_id ▼		▼	0	↕

Insert   Remove

Figure 3. *Mixed joins. You can mix nested and sequential joins in a single query.*

The left-hand Priority column lets you change the order of the joins; in particular, it allows you to put sequential joins inside nested joins. The lower the value in the Priority, the earlier the join is performed. **Figure 4** shows an example; the resulting join clause is:

```
FROM ;
    products ;
  INNER JOIN  order_line_items ;
  INNER JOIN  orders ;
  INNER JOIN customer ;
  ON  Orders.customer_id = Customer.customer_id ;
  INNER JOIN shippers ;
  ON  Orders.shipper_id = Shippers.shipper_id ;
  ON  Orders.order_id = Order_line_items.order_id ;
  ON  Products.product_id = Order_line_items.product_id
```

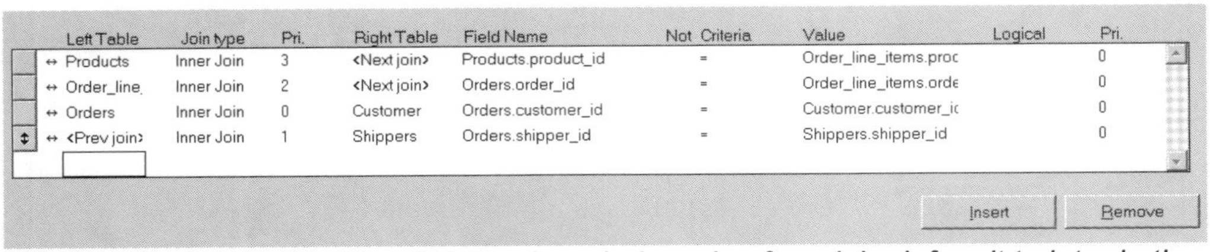

Left Table	Join type	Pri.	Right Table	Field Name	Not	Criteria	Value	Logical	Pri.
↔ Products	Inner Join	3	<Next join>	Products.product_id		=	Order_line_items.proc		0
↔ Order_line	Inner Join	2	<Next join>	Orders.order_id		=	Order_line_items.orde		0
↔ Orders	Inner Join	0	Customer	Orders.customer_id		=	Customer.customer_id		0
↔ <Prev join>	Inner Join	1	Shippers	Orders.shipper_id		=	Shippers.shipper_id		0

Insert   Remove

Figure 4. Using join priority. Raising the priority value for a join defers it to later in the sequence.

The right-hand Priority column lets you determine the order in which logical conditions that are part of a single join condition are evaluated. The Filter page and Having dialog each include an analogous column discussed later in the section "Specifying expressions."

The last join-related change allows you to list tables in the FROM clause, but put the join conditions in the WHERE as in VFP 3 and earlier. The Join type drop-down list contains an item called "Cross Join." When you choose this item, the specified tables are listed in the FROM clause separated by a comma. You can then use the Filter page to specify the join condition or, for those rare occasions when a Cartesian join is appropriate, omit a join condition altogether.

Two-way editing

The other major change to the QD/VD is the addition of two-way editing. The Designer has always had a window to show you the SQL query being designed, but through VFP 7, the contents were read-only. In VFP 8, this window is editable; changes you make there are parsed and reflected in the Designer.

The output of the Query Designer is stored in a text file with a QPR extension. The View Designer stores its results directly in a database, but again it's a textual query that's stored. In VFP 7 and earlier, if you use the QD/VD to open a query or view that it can't parse properly, the query or view may get mangled. In VFP 8, when the QD/VD can't parse the query/view you hand it, it brings up a dialog (see **Figure 5**) that asks what to do. If you choose not to reload the Designer, you can continue to edit your query in the SQL window without damaging it. You'll see this dialog again each time you try to click into the Designer pane.

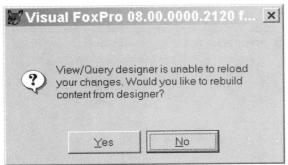

Figure 5. *Query can't be parsed. When the VFP 8 Query/View Designer encounters a query it can't parse, you get a choice of actions. Unless you tell it to, the Designer won't destroy your query.*

When dealing with a query the QD/VD can't parse, saving the query and closing the Designer can be a little tricky. For views, you can use the File | Save menu item or the Save button on the toolbar to save the query. Unfortunately, the same strategy doesn't work for queries.Tthe dialog shown in **Figure 6** appears. Clicking Yes doesn't actually save the query, though. To save a query that can't be parsed, you have to close the designer (as described in the next paragraph) and click "Yes" to the "Do you want to save changes" dialog. Then click "Yes" again when the dialog in Figure 6 appears.

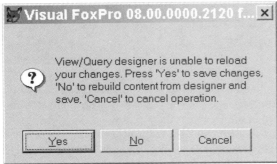

Figure 6. *Saving a query that can't be parsed. This dialog appears when you attempt to save a query that the QD/VD can't parse. Choose Yes to save it anyway.*

To close the QD/VD when you have a query/view that can't be parsed, you have to avoid clicking into the Designer pane. Instead, click the "X" close button on the Designer pane.

Specifying local aliases and field names

In VFP 7 and earlier, the QD/VD doesn't provide a way to specify local aliases for the tables used in a query. If a query uses the same table twice (or two tables with the same name), the second and subsequent instances of the table are assigned aliases based on the table name suffixed with an underscore and a letter of the alphabet. (For example, the second instance of the Customer table is given the alias "Customer_a.")

VFP 8 recognizes the difficulty in working with such results, and provides a way to specify local aliases for tables. The Add Table or View dialog (**Figure 7**) allows you to provide a local alias for each table at the time you add it. You can also add local aliases in the SQL window. Once you specify a local alias for a table, it appears throughout the designer.

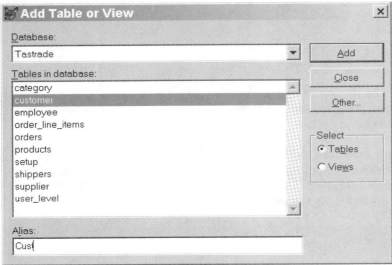

Figure 7. *Adding local aliases. Local aliases specified in the Add Table or View dialog appear in the resulting query, giving you better control.*

Specifying expressions

There are several changes that apply to the three places in the QD/VD where expressions can be entered: the Join page, the Filter page (**Figure 8**), and the Having dialog. The changes make it possible to build a far wider range of queries in the Designer than in previous versions.

First, each includes a new Priority column that lets you add parentheses to the expressions. The priority specification is only relevant when an expression includes both of the logical operators (AND and OR). Without parentheses, compound expressions follow the normal VFP precedence rules, which state that AND is evaluated before OR. Parentheses change that order.

As with join priority (discussed in "Getting joins right" earlier), a higher value in the priority column results in later execution. The priority value applies to the logical operator next to it, not to the expression on that line. So, expressions joined with a logical operator having a lower priority are surrounded by parentheses to force earlier execution.

Figure 8 shows the Filter page for a query that chooses all customers in the UK that have either a phone number or a fax number listed. Here's the corresponding WHERE clause:

```
WHERE  Customer.country = "UK";
   AND  (  NOT (Customer.phone == "");
   OR  NOT (Customer.fax == "") )
```

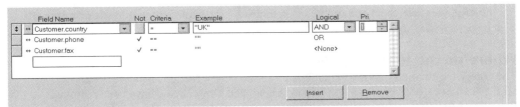

***Figure 8.** Adding parentheses to expressions. The Priority column on the Filter page lets you add parentheses to expressions, changing the order of evaluation.*

On the Join page, the right-hand Priority column is used for this purpose. While it's unusual for a join condition to include a compound expression that uses both AND and OR, one such situation is an outer join where you want to restrict results based on the "some" side of the join. For example, **Figure 9** shows the Join page for a query that returns all customers along with any orders placed in January, 1994 or January, 1995. Because this is an outer join, the filters can't be moved to the WHERE clause; put there, they'd remove any customers without orders and any customers with no orders in the specified months from the result. Here's the FROM clause; note that the Query Designer takes a very liberal attitude toward parentheses, putting them around any expression specified in the Value textbox:

```
FROM ;
      tastrade!customer ;
      LEFT OUTER JOIN tastrade!orders ;
ON  Customer.customer_id = Orders.customer_id;
    AND  ( (  Orders.order_date >= ( {^1994/01/01} );
    AND  Orders.order_date <= ( {^1994/01/31} ) );
    OR  (  Orders.order_date >= ( {^1995/01/01} );
    AND  Orders.order_date <= ( {^1995/01/31} ) ) )
```

Left Table	Join type	Pri.	Right Table	Field Name	Not	Criteria	Value	Logical	Pri.
↔ Customer	Left Outer	0	Orders	Customer.customer_id		=	Orders.customer_id	AND	3
↔		0		Orders.order_date		>=	({^1994/01/01})	AND	1
↔		0		Orders.order_date		<=	({^1994/01/31})	OR	2
↔		0		Orders.order_date		>=	({^1995/01/01})	AND	1
↔		0		Orders.order_date		<=	({^1995/01/31})		0

Insert   Remove

***Figure 9.** Adding parentheses to join conditions. The right-hand priority column allows you to create this complex join condition in the Designer.*

It's often easier to add the parentheses in the SQL window, and let the Designer figure out the priority values.

The second change to these pages is the inclusion of additional items in the Criteria column. All three now include an "Is True" item so you can specify logical items without an extraneous "=.T." or "=.F." In addition, the list of Criteria on the Filter page also includes EXISTS, increasing the number of queries involving subqueries you can handle with the Designer.

Finally, the Case checkbox on the Filter page and the Having dialog has been removed. You have to write the code yourself to force a field to uppercase or lowercase.

Where do the results go?

The Query Destination dialog (available only in the Query Designer) has fewer choices in VFP 8 than in earlier versions. The Report, Label, and Graph items have been removed. Report and Label are relocated to the Miscellaneous page (**Figure 10**), where each has a button. Pressing the button brings up a dialog similar to what was added to Query Destination for each choice in earlier versions. The Graph option is gone entirely.

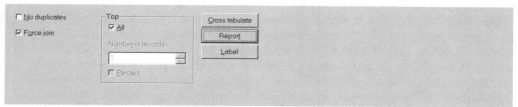

Figure 10. Sending results to reports and labels. The options for sending query results to reports and labels are now on the Miscellaneous page. Pressing one of these buttons brings up a dialog to specify the report or label to use, as well as reporting options.

Odds and ends

There are a number of other, smaller changes to the Query/View Designer.

In VFP 7 and earlier, the list of available fields on the Order By page includes only those fields selected on the Fields page. In VFP 8, all fields from all tables in the query are listed.

When you click on a field in the Available fields list of the Fields page, it now appears in the Functions and expressions textbox. That makes it easy to create simple expressions or add a result field name without opening the Expression Builder.

In addition, the Fields page now lets you control whether the "*" notation for all fields is used. The list of available fields includes items for all fields from all tables and for all fields from each table in the query. (See **Figure 11**.) If you explicitly choose all the named fields from a table, the query is created with the list of fields rather than the "*" notation. In addition, adding a field to the Selected fields list no longer disables it in the Available fields list.

Figure 11. Specifying fields. VFP 8 lets you decide whether to use the "" notation for all fields or list each field separately.*

The Cross tabulate checkbox on the Miscellaneous page of the VFP 7 and earlier QD/VD has been replaced with a button. Pressing the button brings up a confirmation prompt (**Figure 12**)—choosing Yes adds an INTO CURSOR clause and a call to _GENXTAB to the generated query.

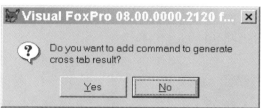

Figure 12. Creating a cross tab. This dialog appears when you press the Cross tabulate button on the Miscellaneous page.

Another change to the Miscellaneous page is the addition of a Force checkbox that allows you to add the FORCE keyword to a query. This clause tells VFP not to attempt to optimize the joins, but to simply perform them in the logical order shown.

In the Properties dialog (**Figure 13**) available from the Fields page of the View Designer, the fields are numbered sequentially, making it easier to keep track when you're going through the list making changes.

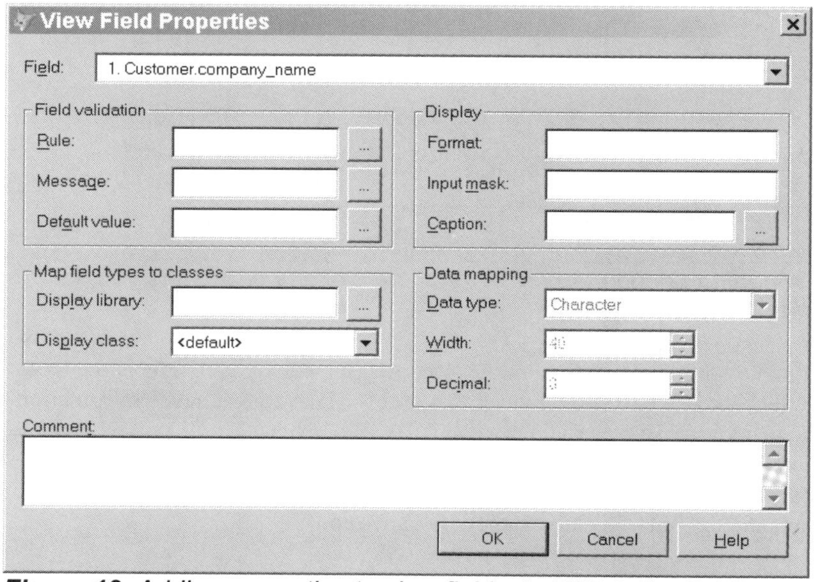

Figure 13. Adding properties to view fields. In VFP 8, the fields are numbered in the drop-down list.

Improved reporting

While VFP 8 still doesn't offer an object-oriented Report Designer, there are a number of changes that make creating and running reports easier.

Setting report options

The first change isn't in the Report Designer itself, but in the Options dialog. There's a new Reports page (**Figure 14**) that lets you specify default behaviors.

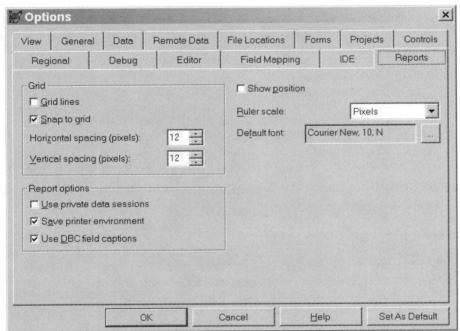

Figure 14. Setting reporting options. A new page in the Options dialog lets you set up standards for creating reports.

The choices you make on this page affect all new reports. Especially welcome is the Save printer environment checkbox—when you uncheck this one, VFP no longer saves information in the report about the printer in use when you created it.

You can also make the choice about the printer environment for individual reports. The Report menu contains a Printer Environment item, which is a toggle. It starts with the value specified in the Options dialog, but you can change it for any report.

More control over header and footer

Two changes make it easier to get your pages to look as you want. First, you can now specify that the contents of the page header and page footer bands appear on the summary page. In older versions, when the summary is placed on a separate page, it doesn't include the page header and page footer. In VFP 8, new options in the Title/Summary dialog (shown in **Figure 15**) make it your decision.

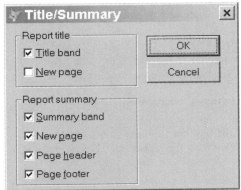

Figure 15. *Have it your way. New options in the Title/Summary dialog let you decide whether to put the page header and page footer on the summary page.*

In addition, the Page Footer and Summary bands support floating and stretching. In earlier versions, the options related to positioning were disabled for fields in those bands. The ability to have stretching fields in those bands means you can't count on the band height. The band may adjust itself to fit the specified text.

Adding captions
In VFP 7 and earlier, when you drag fields from a report's data environment and drop them on the report surface, only the field is dropped. In VFP 8, the field name or caption comes with it as a label. **Figure 16** shows the result of dragging the Company_Name field from the Northwind Customer table into the detail band.

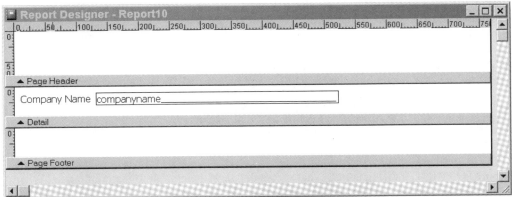

Figure 16. *Drag and drop captions. When you drag a field from the data environment, its caption comes with it. If no field caption is defined, the field name comes along.*

Page x of y

Creating reports that use a "Page x of y" formulation has always been difficult in VFP. Although a system variable, _PAGENO, provides the current page number, prior to VFP 8, there was no easy way to get the total number of pages. The solution was to run the report twice, sending it to a file the first time, and grabbing the page count at that point.

VFP 8 makes the process much simpler. The new _PAGETOTAL system variable provides the total number of pages in the report. To include "Page x of y" in your report, you might put an expression like the following in the Page Header or Page Footer band:

```
"Page " + TRANSFORM(_PAGENO) + " of " + TRANSFORM(_PAGETOTAL)
```

Be aware that because the only way to find out the number of pages in the report is by running the report, when you use _PAGETOTAL, VFP runs the report once before generating your output.

Output issues

Several new features give you more control over what happens when you run reports. Two new keywords combine to let you number pages across multiple reports and continue printing on the same sheet of paper. Another new clause lets you turn off the "Printing" dialog. In addition, there's now a way to distinguish running a preview and printing the report.

Many situations call for a series of reports with pages numbered sequentially rather than starting from 1 in each report. The new NORESET clause of REPORT FORM gives you this ability. When you add it to the second and subsequent reports in a series, the _PAGENO and _PAGETOTAL variables are not reset to 0 when you start processing those reports.

While this ability is really useful for _PAGENO, it's not that helpful with _PAGETOTAL. The problem is the reporting engine doesn't look ahead, so if the first report has two pages, _PAGETOTAL is 2 for that report. Then, if the next report in the sequence has five pages, _PAGETOTAL is set to 7. But if you use a "Page x of y" formulation in the first report, its pages will be labeled as "Page 1 of 2" and "Page 2 of 2." There's also a problem combining NORESET, PREVIEW and _PAGENO in a page footer. If the user uses the mouse to zoom a report after the first, _PAGENO in the footer changes.

When a printer is capable of printing on both sides of the page, it's convenient to begin a report on the back of the page if the previous report ended on the front. Specify NOPAGEEJECT for every report except the last in a series to get this behavior.

You're likely to combine the NORESET and NOPAGEEJECT clauses, along these lines:

```
REPORT FORM FirstReport TO PRINT NOPAGEEJECT
REPORT FORM SecondReport TO PRINT NORESET NOPAGEEJECT
REPORT FORM ThirdReport TO PRINT NORESET
```

The third new clause for REPORT FORM is NODIALOG. Ordinarily, when you send a report TO PRINT, a dialog appears that shows the pages being sent to the print queue. When you add NODIALOG to the command, that dialog is not displayed. Since the dialog can't be customized, many developers prefer not to show it. Note that, even with NODIALOG, you still can't print reports from within a DLL-based VFP COM object.

Finally, a new SYS() function, SYS(2040), lets you determine whether you're currently previewing a report or printing it. The function returns "0" when you're not in a report at all, "1" for a preview, and "2" for printing. You might use it to log the fact that a particular report was printed. Help points out another interesting use: when you include the _PAGETOTAL variable in a report, the reporting engine has to process it twice. You might want to leave out the page total in previews, and include it only in printed reports. You can do so by wrapping that part of the "Page x of y" expression in an IIF() testing SYS(2040).

More data choices
The data environment for reports has additional options in VFP 8. In addition to choosing existing tables and views, you can add CursorAdapters to a report for access to both native and non-VFP data sources. In addition, the data environment's context menu offers access to the DataEnvironment Builder, which lets you specify a data source and gives you access to the CursorAdapter Builder.

For details on CursorAdapters and both new builders, see Chapter 6, "Improved Data Access."

More keyboard support
VFP allows you to use Tab to move from control to control in the Report Designer. In earlier versions, you had to use Ctrl+Tab.

Improved Form Designer and Class Designer
With all the changes to the Query/View Designer and the Report Designer, the Form Designer (FD) and Class Designer (CD) haven't been left out. There are a number of changes to these tools that enhance their usability. In addition, the list of classes you can subclass in the Class Designer has grown.

Support for non-visual classes
Perhaps the biggest change is the ability to use the Class Designer to subclass a number of VFP's base classes that previously could be subclassed only in code. **Table 1** shows the list of classes newly able to be subclassed in the CD. (Several of these classes are new in VFP 8 and are discussed in other chapters.)

Table 1. *Visual subclassing—these classes have been added to the list of those that can be subclassed visually.*

Base class	Notes
Collection	New base class in VFP 8
Cursor	Visual subclassing new in VFP 8
CursorAdapter	New base class in VFP 8
DataEnvironment	Visual subclassing new in VFP 8
Page	Visual subclassing new in VFP 8
Relation	Visual subclassing new in VFP 8
XMLAdapter	New base class in VFP 8
XMLTable	New base class in VFP 8
XMLField	New base class in VFP 8

In addition, the Form Designer's Save As Class dialog now offers the option of saving the data environment as a class.

Most of these additions are related to the new ability to specify the "leaf" class for the various container classes restricted to a particular base class. (For example, you can now specify the Page class used in a PageFrame.) This change is covered in Chapter 9, "OOP Enhancements."

Method editor changes

There are several changes to the method editor, the window that opens when you choose Code from the context menu or the View menu.

One of the most popular third-party tools for VFP has been the SuperClass toolbar, which provides easy access to code from the parent class (and those above it in the class hierarchy) of the class currently being edited. In VFP 6, the toolbar was made available through the Class Browser. VFP 8 goes one better and puts the same functionality and more right into the base product.

The method editor of the FD and CD has a button labeled "View Parent Code." When the method currently displayed has code at a higher level in the class hierarchy or in the container object, the button is enabled. When you click it, it shows you a list of all the parent classes and any container object (see **Figure 17**)—those containing code in this method are enabled, while those without code are disabled. Choose one of the enabled classes and a read-only window opens showing the current method for the chosen class.

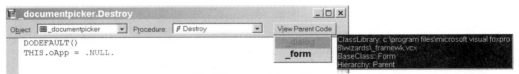

Figure 17. *Access to parent code. The new View Parent Code button shows the inheritance hierarchy for the current class. Choose a class from the hierarchy and the code in that class for the current method is displayed. The tooltip shows the class library and base class for each class in the hierarchy.*

In addition, the drop-down list of events and methods in the editor (labeled "Procedure:" in Figure 17) now includes an icon to show whether an item is a method or an event.

Property sheet improvements
There are a couple of changes in the Property Sheet. First, parent code can also be accessed via the Property Sheet. Right-click on a method with inherited code and the context menu contains a View Inherited Code item. When you choose the item, a read-only window opens showing the code for that method from the first class above it in the hierarchy with code, that is, the one that would display first on the list from the View Parent Code button.

Item tips have been added; hold the mouse over any property whose current value doesn't fit and the value is shown in a tip. **Figure 18** shows an example.

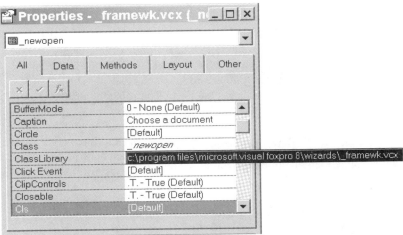

Figure 18. Item tips for the Property Sheet. Hold the mouse over any item whose value isn't fully displayed and an item tip appears.

Another option is available for read-only properties. Before VFP 8, determining the value of read-only properties could be quite tricky. Now, in addition to item tips, the context menu for read-only properties includes a Zoom item. Choosing it opens a window that displays the full value of the property, as shown in **Figure 19**.

Figure 19. *Zoom read-only properties. A new option on the context menu for read-only properties lets you open a window to see their value.*

Odds and ends

One of the first changes you're likely to notice in VFP 8 is that, when you open the Form Designer or Class Designer the Form Controls toolbar no longer opens automatically. Rather than being an annoyance, this is because there's a new, better tool to replace it. The Toolbox provides the functionality of the Form Controls toolbar and much more. It's discussed in Chapter 2, "The Toolbox." However, you can still use the Form Controls toolbar if you prefer, and if it's open when you save a given form or class, it'll reopen the next time you edit that form or class.

VFP provides two ways to set the tab order for a form or class, List and Interactive. When using the Interactive method, it's always been difficult to remember which control you set most recently. In VFP 8, the number displayed on the item last clicked uses different colors than the other items, making it easy to find. **Figure 20** shows an example.

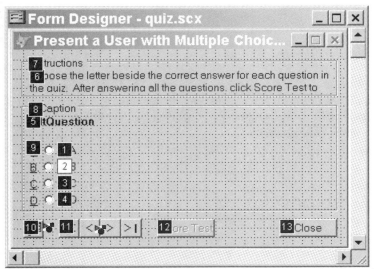

Figure 20. *Setting tab order. The control most recently clicked when setting tab order interactively is numbered in different colors than the other controls.*

The Options dialog allows you to determine the maximum size of newly created forms. In VFP 7 and earlier versions, the default for this setting is 640x480. In VFP 8, the default is "None," meaning that there's no limit on form size.

Finally, the drop-down list for the FontName property shows only font families. In earlier versions, it showed every variation of every font. For more on this change, see Chapter 13, "Language Improvements."

Moving menu items

In earlier versions of VFP, there's no easy way to move a menu item from one place to another, except within the same menu pop-up. If you decide an item should be on the Tools menu rather than the File menu, you have to add it manually to the Tools menu, cut-and-paste any code from the File menu, then delete the item from the File menu.

VFP 8 provides direct support for moving an item. There's a Move Item button in the Menu Designer. When you press it, the dialog in **Figure 21** appears to let you choose the destination.

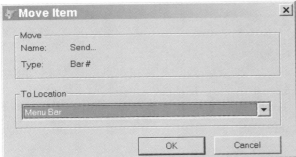

Figure 21. Moving menu items. This dialog appears when you choose the Move Item button in the Menu Designer. Choose the new location from the drop-down list.

The item is placed at the end of the group you specify, and the Menu Designer shows you the item at its new location. If necessary, use the mover bars to reposition the item in its new group.

Working with source code

There are several changes that make managing your code easier. First, Beautify returns to the context menu for editor windows. In addition, Beautify now works on code blocks rather than on everything in the active window. Highlight the code you want to reformat, and then choose Beautify from the context menu or the Tools menu.

In addition, source code now prints in color when sent to a color-capable printer.

Projects and source control

Several changes affect the Project Manager and interaction with Visual SourceSafe.

In earlier versions of VFP, you can only add one file at a time to a project through the Project Manager interface. When you choose the Add button, the Open dialog that appears supports only single selection. In VFP 8, that dialog supports multiple selection, so you can add several files of the same type to a project at once.

Be warned: if you add files of a type other than the one chosen in the Project Manager, they get added to the specified group anyway. VFP doesn't examine the files to see whether you're putting them in the right place. That's different than what happens when you drag files into a project.

In older versions, when you open a project attached to a different Visual SourceSafe (VSS) database than the one currently in use, an error is generated. VFP 8 handles this situation more gracefully by allowing you to browse for the appropriate database.

One other change impacts source control. In order to allow the various VFP components stored in tables (such as forms and classes) to be compared within VSS, the program SCCTEXT.PRG converts them to a textual format. In VFP 7 and earlier, when you edit a form or class in such a way that the order of the methods for an object changes in the memo field where method code is stored, comparing one version of the text file with another is a problem—that's because SCCTEXT puts them in the order they appeared in the source. In VFP 8, the program has changed to list the methods in alphabetical order so they're less sensitive to minor changes.

Distributing applications

VFP 7 introduced the InstallShield Express Visual FoxPro Limited Edition for building installation packages. VFP 8 includes a later version of the product, version 3.54. The major change in the new version is the ability to provide upgrade paths for an application. In the version that came with VFP 7, this capability is disabled. There are several other new capabilities, including support for Windows Installer 2.0. The complete list of changes is included in the Readme.HTM file that comes with VFP 8.

Summary

In addition to the new tools described in previous chapters, VFP 8 includes significant changes to existing tools. The modifications to the Query/View Designer make it a tool every VFP developer will want to explore. Changes to the other tools should make you more productive.

Updates and corrections to this chapter can be found on Hentzenwerke's web site, **www.hentzenwerke.com**. Click on "Catalog" and navigate to the page for this book.

Chapter 6
Improved Data Access

There are several ways you can access non-VFP data (such as SQL Server or Oracle) in VFP applications: remote views, SQL Pass-Through, ADO, and XML. VFP 8 introduces an exciting new technology called CursorAdapter that makes accessing remote data much easier than it was in earlier versions.

More and more VFP developers are storing their data in something other than VFP tables, such as SQL Server or Oracle. There are a lot of reasons for this, including fragility of VFP tables (both perceived and actual), security, database size, and corporate standards. Microsoft has made access to non-VFP data easier with every release, and has even been encouraging it with the inclusion of MSDE (Microsoft Data Engine, a free, stripped-down version of SQL Server) on the VFP CD, starting with version 7.

However, accessing a back-end database has never been quite as easy as using VFP tables. In addition, there are a variety of mechanisms you can use to do this:

- Remote views, which are based on ODBC connections.

- SQL Pass-Through (SPT) functions, such as SQLCONNECT(), SQLEXEC(), and SQLDISCONNECT(), which are also based on ODBC connections.

- ActiveX Data Objects (ADO), which provide an object-oriented front end to OLE DB providers for database engines.

- XML, which is a lightweight, platform-independent, data transport mechanism.

If you've spent any time working with these mechanisms, one of the things you've likely noticed is no two are alike. That means you have a new learning curve with each one, and converting an existing application from one mechanism to another is a non-trivial task.

To help with this problem, Microsoft added a new base class in VFP 8: CursorAdapter. CursorAdapter is one of the biggest new features in VFP 8 because:

- It makes it easier to use ODBC, ADO, or XML, even if you're not very familiar with these technologies.

- It provides a consistent interface to remote data regardless of the access mechanism you choose.

- It makes it easier to switch from one access mechanism to another.

Here's an example of the last point. Suppose you have an application that uses ODBC with CursorAdapters to access SQL Server data, and you want to change to use ADO instead. All you need to do is change the DataSourceType of the CursorAdapters, change the connection to the back-end database, and you're done. The rest of the components in the application neither know nor care about this; they still see the same cursor regardless of the mechanism used to access the data.

One thing to keep in mind is CursorAdapter is well-named; it acts as an adapter between a source of data and a VFP cursor. So, CursorAdapter creates and manages a VFP cursor, but your forms, reports, and code still operate on the cursor to display and update data.

CursorAdapter PEMs

Let's start examining CursorAdapters by looking at their properties, events, and methods (PEMs).

DataSourceType

This property is very important because it determines the overall behavior of the class and what kinds of values to put into some of the other properties. DataSourceType indicates the mechanism you're using to access the data. The valid choices are "Native" (which indicates you're using native FoxPro tables), "ODBC", "ADO", or "XML".

DataSource

This is the means to access the data. VFP ignores this property when DataSourceType is set to "Native" or "XML". For ODBC, set DataSource to a valid ODBC connection handle (note you have to manage the connection yourself). In the case of ADO, DataSource must be an ADO Recordset with its ActiveConnection property set to an open ADO Connection object (again, you have to manage this yourself).

Alias

As with normal Cursor objects, this property contains the alias of the cursor associated with the CursorAdapter.

UseDEDataSource

This property determines whether the CursorAdapter uses the DataEnvironment's DataSourceType and DataSource properties. If it is set to True (the default is False), you can leave the DataSourceType and DataSource properties alone because the CursorAdapter will use the DataEnvironment's properties instead (VFP 8 adds DataSourceType and DataSource to the DataEnvironment class as well). For example, if you want all the CursorAdapters in a DataEnvironment to use the same ODBC connection, you'd set this to True and use the DataSourceType and DataSource properties in the DataEnvironment to specify the ODBC connection.

SelectCmd

This is the command used to retrieve the data. In the case of all DataSourceTypes except XML, this is typically a SQL SELECT command (such as SELECT * FROM CUSTOMERS) or a stored procedure (for example, EXEC GetCustomersByID 'ALFKI'). In the case of XML, this can either be a valid XML string or an expression (such as a function or method) that returns a valid XML string. In either case, VFP uses an internal XMLTOCURSOR() call to convert the XML to a VFP cursor.

CursorSchema

This property holds the structure of the cursor in the same format you'd use in a CREATE CURSOR command (everything between the parentheses in such a command). Here's an example: CUST_ID C(6), COMPANY C(30), CONTACT C(30), CITY C(25). Although it's possible to leave this blank and tell the CursorAdapter to determine the structure when it creates the cursor, it's better to fill in CursorSchema. For one thing, if CursorSchema is blank or incorrect, you'll either get errors when you open the DataEnvironment of a form or you won't be able to drag and drop fields from the CursorAdapter to the form to create controls. Another reason is this allows you to specify exactly what the structure of the cursor should be. For example, if you want a DateTime field from SQL Server to be converted to a Date field in the VFP cursor, specify "D" for the data type for that field in CursorSchema.

Since VFP has a 255-character limit for values entered into the Property Window, you may have to specify the value for this property in code. Fortunately, the CursorAdapter Builder that comes with VFP (see "Builders" below) can automatically do this for you.

AllowDelete, AllowInsert, AllowUpdate, and SendUpdates

These properties, which default to True, determine whether deletes, inserts, and updates can be done and whether changes are sent to the data source.

KeyFieldList, Tables, UpdatableFieldList, and UpdateNameList

These properties serve the same purpose as the identically-named CURSORSETPROP() properties for views. They are required if you want VFP to automatically update the data source with changes made in the cursor. KeyFieldList is a comma-delimited list of fields (without aliases) that make up the primary key for the cursor. Tables is a comma-delimited list of tables the cursor is based on. UpdatableFieldList is a comma-delimited list of fields (without aliases) that can be updated. UpdateNameList is a comma-delimited list that matches field names in the cursor to field names in the table. The format for UpdateNameList is as follows: CURSORFIELDNAME1 TABLE.FIELDNAME1, CURSORFIELDNAME2 TABLE.FIELDNAME2, ... Note that even if UpdatableFieldList doesn't contain the name of the primary key of the table (because you don't want that field updated), the primary key must still be included in UpdateNameList or updates won't work.

*Cmd, *CmdDataSource, *CmdDataSourceType

If you want to specifically control how VFP deletes, inserts, or updates records in the data source, you can assign the appropriate values to these sets of properties (replace the * above with Delete, Insert, or Update). For example, if you want to use a stored procedure to delete records, set DeleteCmd to something like "EXEC DeleteCustomer CustomerID", and set DeleteCmdDataSource and DeleteCmdDataSourceType to the proper values for the connection.

ConversionFunc

This property specifies conversion functions to be applied to fields when automatic updating is performed. The format for ConversionFunc is as follows: CURSORFIELDNAME1 FUNCTION, CURSORFIELDNAME2 FUNCTION, ... (Do not include parentheses at the end of the function name.) Each function must accept the field name as its only parameter. The function can be a built-in VFP function or a user-defined function (UDF).

For example, if you use the SQL Server VarChar data type, which doesn't have trailing spaces, for customer name and city fields, you'll want to trim the fields in the VFP cursor before sending them to SQL Server. To do that, specify "COMPANY TRIM, CITY TRIM" for ConversionFunc.

Other properties

CursorAdapter has several properties identical to the equivalent CURSORSETPROP() properties: AllowSimultaneousFetch, BatchUpdateCount, CompareMemo, FetchAsNeeded, FetchMemo, FetchSize, MaxRecords, Prepared, UpdateType, UseMemoSize, and WhereType. There are a few other properties as well:

- BufferModeOverride determines how the cursor is buffered (row or table).

- UpdateGram contains the changes made in the cursor in updategram format when the *DataSourceType properties are set to "XML". This property isn't filled in as changes are made, but rather when an update is about to be performed (such as when TABLEUPDATE() has been executed).

- The Flags property contains settings to use when VFP creates the updategram; it has the same values as the Flags parameter in the XMLUPDATEGRAM() function.

- UpdateGramSchemaLocation contains the name and location of a mapping schema if you want to use one; as with Flags, this property works like the equivalent parameter in XMLUPDATEGRAM().

- BreakOnError determines what VFP does when an error occurs in VFP code in any of the CursorAdapter events. If this property is True (the default is False), VFP displays an error message immediately when an error occurs; otherwise, the normal error handling mechanism in place is used.

CursorFill(lUseCursorSchema, lNoData, nOptions, oSource)

This method creates the cursor and fills it with data from the data source (although you can pass True for the lNoData parameter to create an empty cursor). Pass True for the first parameter to use the schema defined in CursorSchema or False to have VFP create an appropriate structure from the data source. We'll discuss the use of the other two parameters later in this chapter.

MULTILOCKS must be set on or this method will fail. If CursorFill fails for any reason, it returns False rather than raising an error; use AERROR() to determine what went wrong (although be prepared for some digging, since the error messages you get often aren't specific enough to tell you exactly what the problem is).

CursorRefresh()

This method is similar to the REQUERY() function: it refreshes the cursor's contents.

CursorAttach(cAlias, llnheritCursorProperties) and CursorDetach()

These methods allow you to attach an existing cursor to a CursorAdapter object or to free the cursor attached to a CursorAdapter. Attaching a cursor means it will be under the control of the CursorAdapter—updates are handled by the CursorAdapter, the cursor is closed when the CursorAdapter is destroyed, and so forth. If you want a cursor to exist after its CursorAdapter is destroyed or no longer want it to be under the control of the CursorAdapter, use CursorDetach.

Before*() and After*()

CursorAdapter has many before and after "hook" events that allow you to customize the behavior of the CursorAdapter. In the case of the Before events, you can return False to prevent the action that triggered it from occurring (this is similar to database events). **Table 1** shows a list of these events.

Table 1. CursorAdapter has several Before and After events that allow you to hook in additional behaviors when various operations are done to the cursor.

Event	When Fired
BeforeCursorAttach, AfterCursorAttach	Before and after the CursorAttach method, respectively.
BeforeCursorClose, AfterCursorClose	Before and after the cursor is closed, respectively.
BeforeCursorDetach, AfterCursorDetach	Before and after the CursorDetach method, respectively.
BeforeCursorFill, AfterCursorFill	Before and after the CursorFill method, respectively.
BeforeCursorRefresh, AfterCursorRefresh	Before and after the CursorRefresh method, respectively.
BeforeCursorUpdate, AfterCursorUpdate	Before and after TABLEUPDATE(), respectively; these methods do not fire if the back end is updated implicitly, such as by moving the record pointer when row buffering is used. These events are wrapped around the appropriate Before/AfterDelete, Insert, or Update events, depending on what is happening to the data. For example, for an update operation performed with TABLEUPDATE(), the order of events is BeforeCursorUpdate, BeforeUpdate and AfterUpdate for each record being updated, and finally AfterCursorUpdate.
BeforeDelete, AfterDelete	Before and after a delete operation is sent to the database (even when the delete is done implicitly), respectively. Fires once per record; doesn't fire if BatchUpdateCount is greater than 1.
BeforeInsert, AfterInsert	Before and after an insert operation is sent to the database (even when the insert is done implicitly), respectively. Fires once per record; doesn't fire if BatchUpdateCount is greater than 1.
BeforeUpdate, AfterUpdate	Before and after an update operation is sent to the database (even when the update is done implicitly), respectively. Fires once per record; doesn't fire if BatchUpdateCount is greater than 1.

Some of these events are very interesting and useful. For example, in AfterCursorFill, you can create indexes for the cursor so they're available for SEEK statements or creating relationships between cursors. The before and after events for delete, insert, and update operations (for example, BeforeInsert) receive parameters describing what is happening to the data, including field and record state (the same value you'd get from GETFLDSTATE(-1)), whether changes are being forced or not, the SQL UPDATE or INSERT command being sent to the database engine (very useful when trying to debug problems), and, if updates are done by deleting the old records and inserting new ones (UpdateType = 2), the SQL DELETE command sent to the database. You can change the commands sent to the database in the Before events if necessary, giving you complete control over how updates are done.

Putting CursorAdapter to work

Here's an example that gets certain fields for Brazilian customers from the Customers table in the Northwind database that comes with SQL Server. The cursor is updateable, so if you make changes in the cursor, close it, and then run the program again, you'll see your changes were saved to the back end.

```
local loCursor as CursorAdapter, ;
  laErrors[1]
set multilocks on
loCursor = createobject('CursorAdapter')
with loCursor
  .Alias             = 'Customers'
  .DataSourceType    = 'ODBC'
  .DataSource        = sqlstringconnect('driver=SQL Server;' + ;
    'server=(local);database=Northwind;uid=sa;pwd=;trusted_connection=no')
  .SelectCmd         = "select CUSTOMERID, COMPANYNAME, CONTACTNAME " + ;
    "from CUSTOMERS where COUNTRY = 'Brazil'"
  .KeyFieldList      = 'CUSTOMERID'
  .Tables            = 'CUSTOMERS'
  .UpdatableFieldList = 'CUSTOMERID, COMPANYNAME, CONTACTNAME'
  .UpdateNameList    = 'CUSTOMERID CUSTOMERS.CUSTOMERID, ' + ;
    'COMPANYNAME CUSTOMERS.COMPANYNAME, CONTACTNAME CUSTOMERS.CONTACTNAME'
  if .CursorFill()
    browse
  else
    aerror(laErrors)
    messagebox(laErrors[2])
  endif
endwith
```

 The Developer Download files for this chapter, available at **www.hentzenwerke.com**, *include this code in CursorAdapterExample.PRG. You may have to change the setting for the DataSource property to use the appropriate connection information, such as user name and password.*

DataEnvironment, Form, and other changes

To support the new CursorAdapter class, several changes have been made to the DataEnvironment and Form classes and their designers.

First, as mentioned earlier, the DataEnvironment class now has DataSource and DataSourceType properties. It doesn't use these properties itself but they're used by any CursorAdapter member with UseDEDataSource set to True. Second, you can now create

DataEnvironment subclasses visually using the Class Designer. You can even save the DataEnvironment of a form as a class by choosing Save As Class from the File menu when you're in the Form Designer and selecting the DataEnvironment option.

As for forms, you can now specify a DataEnvironment subclass to use by setting the new DEClass and DEClassLibrary properties. If you do this, anything you've done with the existing DataEnvironment (cursors, code, etc.) will be lost, but at least you're warned first.

CURSORGETPROP('SourceType') returns a new range of values: if the cursor was created with CursorFill, the value is 100 + the old value (for example, 102 for remote data). If an existing cursor was attached to the CursorAdapter with CursorAttach, the value is 200 + the old value. If the data source is an ADO Recordset, the value is 104 (CursorFill) or 204 (CursorAttach). You can get a reference to the ADO Recordset object associated with a cursor using CURSORGETPROP('ADORecordset').

Builders

VFP 8 includes new DataEnvironment and CursorAdapter builders that make it easier to work with these classes.

The DataEnvironment Builder is brought up in the usual way; by right-clicking on the DataEnvironment of a form or on a DataEnvironment subclass in the Class Designer and choosing Builder. The "Data Source" page of the DataEnvironment Builder (see **Figure 1**) is where you set data source information. Choose the desired data source type and where the data source comes from. If you choose "Use existing connection handle" (ODBC) or "Use existing ADO Recordset" (ADO), specify an expression containing the data source (such as "goConnectionMgr.nHandle"). You can also choose to use one of the DSNs on your system or a connection string. The Build button, which is only enabled if you choose "Use connection string" for ADO, displays the Data Link Properties dialog, which you can use to build the connection string visually. If you select either "Use DSN" or "Use connection string", the builder generates code in the BeforeOpenTables method of the DataEnvironment to create the desired connection. If you choose "Native", you can select a VFP database container as a data source; in that case, the generated code ensures the database is open (you can also use free tables as the data source).

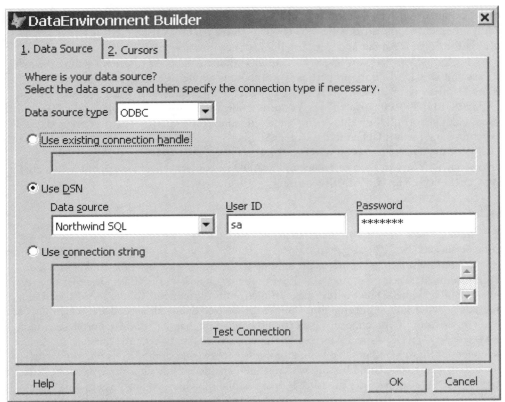

Figure 1. *The Data Source page of the DataEnvironment Builder allows you to specify what type of data source to use and how to connect to it.*

The "Cursors" page, shown in **Figure 2**, allows you to maintain the CursorAdapter members of the DataEnvironment. (Cursor objects don't show up in the builder, nor can they be added.) The Add button allows you to add a CursorAdapter subclass to the DataEnvironment, while New creates a new base class CursorAdapter; in either case, the CursorAdapter Builder is automatically launched so you can work on the new object. Remove deletes the selected CursorAdapter and Builder invokes the CursorAdapter Builder for the selected CursorAdapter. You can change the name of the CursorAdapter object, but you'll need the CursorAdapter Builder to set any other properties.

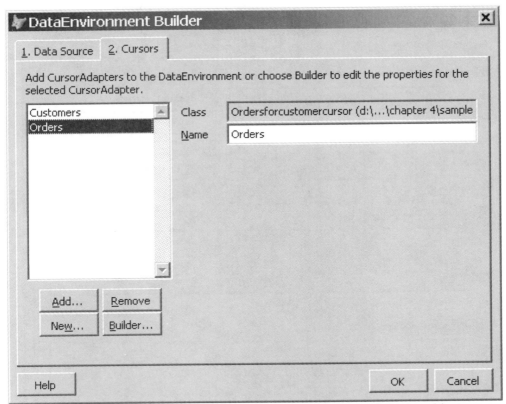

Figure 2. In the Cursors page, you can add or remove CursorAdapter objects or launch the CursorAdapter Builder for the selected one.

The CursorAdapter Builder can be invoked by choosing Builder from the shortcut menu for a CursorAdapter or from the DataEnvironment Builder. The "Properties" page (see **Figure 3**) shows the class and name of the object (Name can only be changed if the builder is brought up from a DataEnvironment, since it's read-only for a CursorAdapter subclass), the alias of the cursor it'll create, whether the DataEnvironment's data source should be used or not, and if not, the connection information to use. As with the DataEnvironment Builder, the CursorAdapter Builder generates code to create the desired connection (in the CursorFill method in this case) if you select either "Use DSN" or "Use connection string". You can also specify a connection for the builder to use temporarily; in that case, the builder doesn't generate code for the connection.

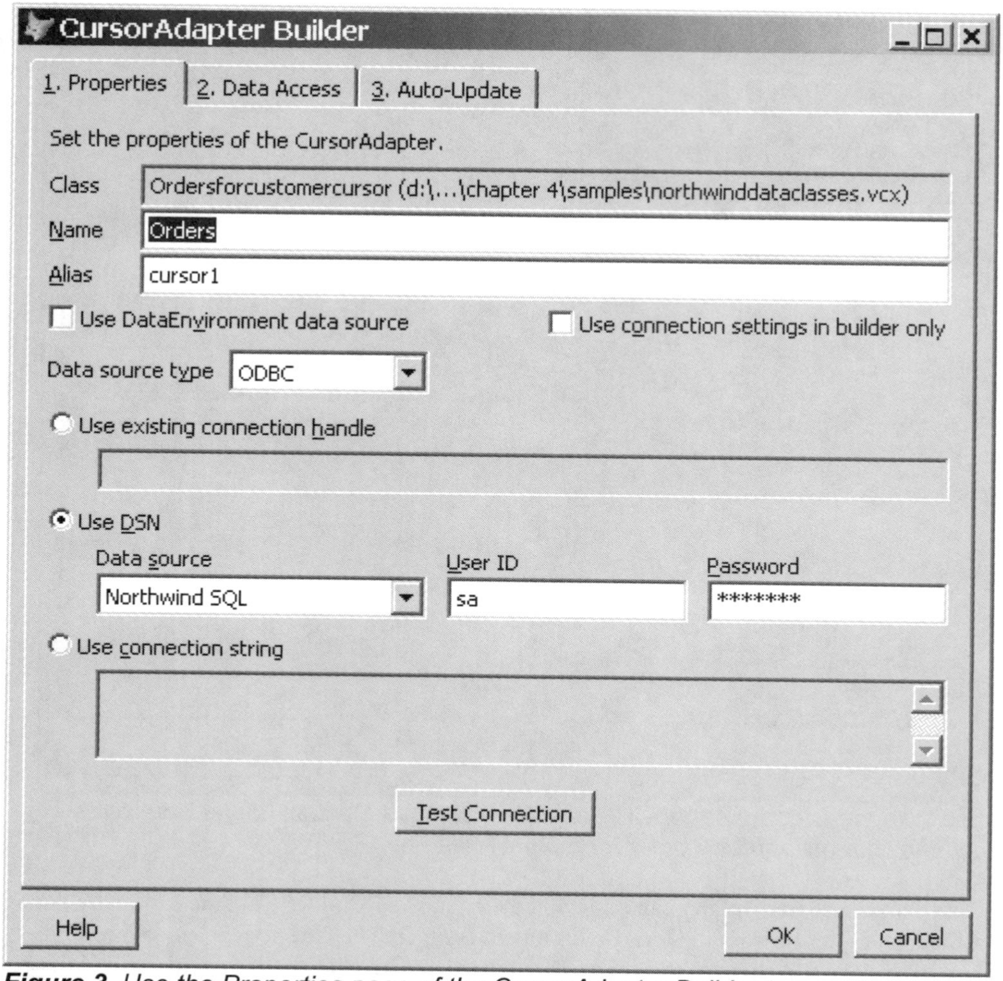

Figure 3. Use the Properties page of the CursorAdapter Builder to specify several settings for a CursorAdapter, including how it's connected to the database.

The "Data Access" page, shown in **Figure 4**, allows you to specify the SelectCmd, CursorSchema, and other properties. If you specified connection information, you can click on the Build button for SelectCmd to display the Select Command Builder, which makes it easy to create the SelectCmd. The schema must be less than 255 characters or you'll get a warning message when you click on the OK button.

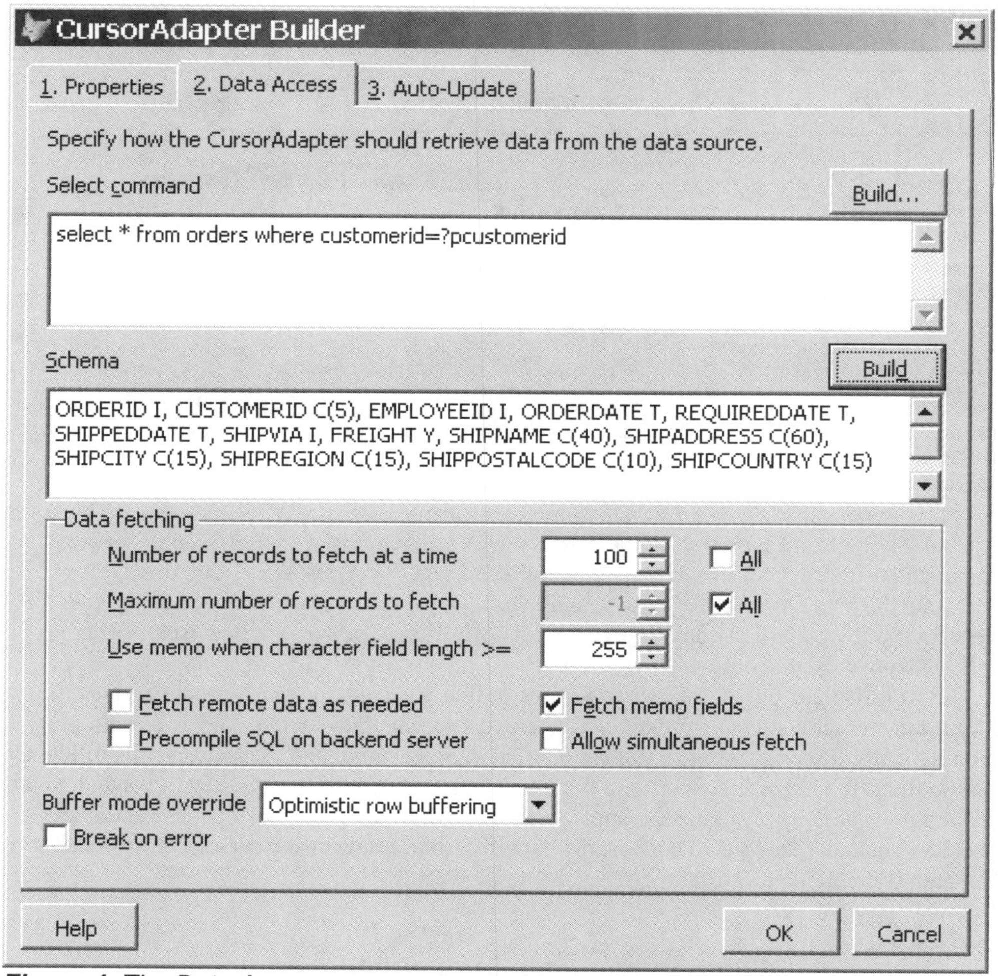

Figure 4. The Data Access page makes it easy to fill in the SelectCmd and CursorSchema properties, as well as specifying how data access should work.

The Select Command Builder, illustrated in **Figure 5**, makes short work of building a simple SELECT statement. Choose the desired table from the table drop-down list, and then move the appropriate fields to the selected side. In the case of a native data source, you can add tables to the Table combo box (for example, if you want to use free tables). When you choose OK, the SelectCmd is filled with the appropriate SQL SELECT statement.

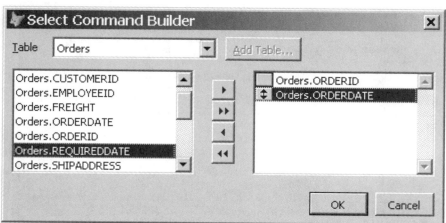

Figure 5. *The Select Command Builder provides a visual tool for creating a SQL SELECT statement.*

Click on the Build button for the CursorSchema to have this property filled in for you automatically. In order for this to work, the builder actually creates a new CursorAdapter object, sets the properties appropriately, and calls CursorFill to create the cursor. If you don't have a live connection to the data source, or CursorFill fails for some reason (such as an invalid SelectCmd), this obviously won't work.

The Auto-Update page is shown in **Figure 6**. Use this page to set the properties necessary for VFP to automatically generate update statements for the data source. The Tables property is automatically filled in from the tables specified in SelectCmd, and the fields grid is filled in from the fields in CursorSchema. As in the View Designer, you select the key fields and which fields are updatable by checking the appropriate column in the grid. You can also set other properties, such as functions to convert the data in certain fields of the cursor before sending it to the data source.

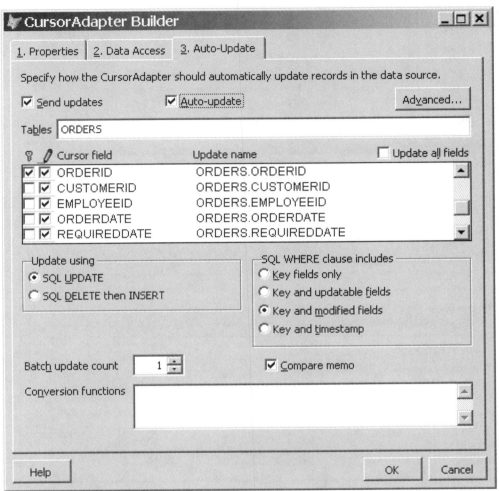

Figure 6*. Use the settings in the Auto-Update page to specify how VFP should generate update statements for the cursor.*

If you want more control over how updates are done, click on the Advanced button to bring up the Advanced Update Properties dialog, shown in **Figure 7**. The Update, Insert, and Delete pages have a nearly identical appearance. They allow you to specify values for the sets of Update, Delete, and Insert properties. This is especially important for XML, because VFP can't automatically generate update statements.

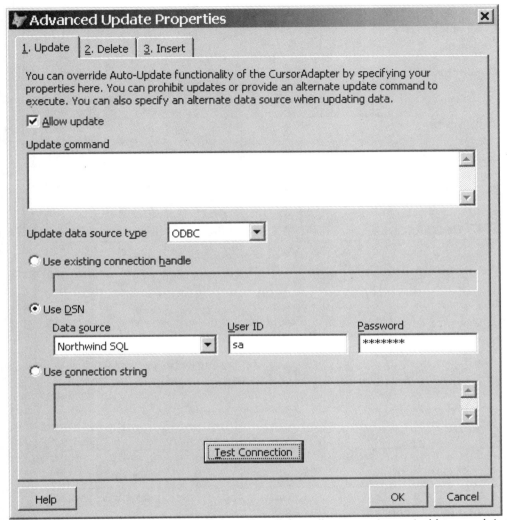

***Figure 7.** The Advanced Update Properties dialog allows you to control how updates are sent to the database.*

Data source specifics

The DataSourceType property indicates what mechanism the CursorAdapter uses to talk to the database engine: native (for VFP data), ODBC, ADO, or XML. Each of these types has its own set of rules about how it works, so let's look at the specific details for each one.

Using native data

Even though it's clear CursorAdapter was intended to standardize and simplify access to non-VFP data, you can use it as a substitute for Cursor by setting DataSourceType to "Native". Why would you do this? Mostly as a look toward the future when your application might be upsized; by simply changing the DataSourceType to one of the other choices (and likely changing a few other properties such as setting connection information), you can easily switch to another DBMS such as SQL Server.

When DataSourceType is set to "Native", VFP ignores DataSource. SelectCmd must be a SQL SELECT statement, not a USE command or expression, which means you're always working with the equivalent of a local view rather than with the table directly. You're responsible for ensuring that VFP can find any tables referenced in the SELECT statement, so if the tables aren't in the current directory, you either need to set a path or open the database the tables belong to. As usual, if you want the cursor to be updateable, be sure to set the update properties (KeyFieldList, Tables, UpdatableFieldList, and UpdateNameList).

The following code creates an updateable cursor from the Customer table in the TestData VFP sample database:

```
local loCursor as CursorAdapter, ;
  laErrors[1]
set multilocks on
open database (_samples + 'data\testdata')
loCursor = createobject('CursorAdapter')
with loCursor
  .Alias              = 'customercursor'
  .DataSourceType     = 'Native'
  .SelectCmd          = "select CUST_ID, COMPANY, CONTACT from CUSTOMER " + ;
    "where COUNTRY = 'Brazil'"
  .KeyFieldList       = 'CUST_ID'
  .Tables             = 'CUSTOMER'
  .UpdatableFieldList = 'CUST_ID, COMPANY, CONTACT'
  .UpdateNameList     = 'CUST_ID CUSTOMER.CUST_ID, ' + ;
    'COMPANY CUSTOMER.COMPANY, CONTACT CUSTOMER.CONTACT'
  if .CursorFill()
    browse
    tableupdate(1)
  else
    aerror(laErrors)
    messagebox(laErrors[2])
  endif
endwith
close databases all
```

*The Developer Download files at **www.hentzenwerke.com** include this code in NativeExample.PRG.*

Using ODBC

ODBC is actually the most straightforward of the four settings of DataSourceType. You set DataSource to an open ODBC connection handle, set the usual properties, and call CursorFill to retrieve the data. If you fill in KeyFieldList, Tables, UpdatableFieldList, and UpdateNameList, VFP will automatically generate the appropriate UPDATE, INSERT, and

DELETE statements to update the back end with any changes. If you want to use a stored procedure instead, set the *Cmd, *CmdDataSource, and *CmdDataSourceType properties appropriately.

Here's an example that calls the CustOrderHist stored procedure in the Northwind database to get total units sold by product for a specific customer:

```
local loCursor as CursorAdapter, ;
  laErrors[1]
set multilocks on
loCursor = createobject('CursorAdapter')
with loCursor
  .Alias         = 'CustomerHistory'
  .DataSourceType = 'ODBC'
  .DataSource    = sqlstringconnect('driver=SQL Server;server=(local);' + ;
    'database=Northwind;uid=sa;pwd=;trusted_connection=no')
  .SelectCmd     = "exec CustOrderHist 'ALFKI'"
  if .CursorFill()
    browse
  else
    aerror(laErrors)
    messagebox(laErrors[2])
  endif
endwith
```

 *The Developer Download files at **www.hentzenwerke.com** include this code in ODBCExample.PRG.*

Using ADO

Using ADO as the data access mechanism with CursorAdapter has a few more issues than using ODBC:

- DataSource must be set to an ADO Recordset with its ActiveConnection property set to an open ADO Connection object.

- If you already have an open ADO Recordset (such as one returned by a middle tier object in an n-tier application), pass it as the fourth parameter to CursorFill. If you do this, the DataSource property is ignored. Also, CursorRefresh works a little differently in this case; you're responsible for refreshing the parameter values before calling CursorRefresh. See the Help topic for CursorRefresh for details.

- For updates to work, the ADO Recordset object must support the Bookmark property. That's only available with client-side cursors, so you should set the CursorLocation property of the Recordset to 3.

- If you want to use a parameterized query (which is usually a better choice than retrieving all records), you have to pass an ADO Command object with its ActiveConnection property set to an open ADO Connection object as the fourth parameter to CursorFill. VFP will take care of filling the Parameters collection of the Command object for you (it parses SelectCmd to find the parameters), but of course the variables containing the values of the parameters must be in scope.

- If you'd rather specify your own delete, insert, or update commands rather than using automatic update, set the appropriate *CmdDataSourceType property to "ADO", *CmdDataSource to an ADO Command object with its ActiveConnection property set to an open ADO Connection object, and *Cmd to the command to execute.

- Using one CursorAdapter with ADO in a DataEnvironment is straightforward; you can set UseDEDataSource to True if you wish, and then set the DataEnvironment's DataSource and DataSourceType properties as you would with the CursorAdapter. However, this doesn't work if there's more than one CursorAdapter in the DataEnvironment. The reason is the ADO Recordset referenced by DataEnvironment.DataSource can only contain a single CursorAdapter's data; when you call CursorFill for the second CursorAdapter, you get a "Recordset is already open" error. So, if your DataEnvironment has more than one CursorAdapter, you must set UseDEDataSource to False and manage the DataSource and DataSourceType properties of each CursorAdapter yourself (or perhaps use a DataEnvironment subclass that manages it for you).

The sample code below shows how to retrieve data using a parameterized query with the help of an ADO Command object. This example also shows the use of the new structured error handling features in VFP 8, discussed in more detail in Chapter 12, "Error Handling". The call to the ADO Connection Open method is wrapped in a TRY structure to trap the COM error the method will throw if it fails. Finally, it shows the use of CursorRefresh to refresh the cursor when the parameter query changes.

```
local loConn as ADODB.Connection, ;
  loCommand as ADODB.Command, ;
  loException as Exception, ;
  loCursor as CursorAdapter, ;
  lcCountry, ;
  laErrors[1]
set multilocks on
loConn = createobject('ADODB.Connection')
with loConn
  .ConnectionString = 'provider=SQLOLEDB.1;data source=(local);' + ;
    'initial catalog=Northwind;uid=sa;pwd=;trusted_connection=no'
  try
    .Open()
  catch to loException
    messagebox(loException.Message)
    cancel
  endtry
endwith
loCommand = createobject('ADODB.Command')
loCursor  = createobject('CursorAdapter')
with loCursor
  .Alias          = 'Customers'
  .DataSourceType = 'ADO'
  .DataSource     = createobject('ADODB.Recordset')
  .SelectCmd      = 'select * from customers where country=?lcCountry'
  lcCountry       = 'Brazil'
  .DataSource.ActiveConnection = loConn
  loCommand.ActiveConnection   = loConn
  if .CursorFill(.F., .F., 0, loCommand)
```

```
   browse
   lcCountry = 'Canada'
   .CursorRefresh()
   browse
  else
    aerror(laErrors)
    messagebox(laErrors[2])
  endif
endwith
```

 *The Developer Download files at **www.hentzenwerke.com** include this code in ADOExample.PRG.*

Using XML

There are some issues to be aware of when using XML with CursorAdapters. They are:

- The DataSource property is ignored.

- The SelectCmd property must be set to a source of XML. For example, you can use an expression that returns the XML for the cursor, such as a UDF or object method name. You can also specify the name of an XML document; in that case, pass 512 as the third parameter to CursorFill (which tells it the XML is coming from a file rather than a string).

- Changes made to the cursor are converted to an updategram, which is XML that contains before and after values for changed fields and records, and placed in the UpdateGram property when the update is required.

- In order to write changes back to the data source, UpdateCmdDataSourceType must be set to "XML" and UpdateCmd must be set to an expression (again, likely a UDF or object method) that handles the update. You'll probably want to pass "This.UpdateGram" to the UDF so it can send the changes to the data source. If BufferModeOverride is set to 5-optimistic table buffering, the function specified in UpdateCmd will be called once for each modified record and UpdateGram will only contain changes for record currently being updated.

The XML source for the cursor could come from a variety of places. For example, you could call a UDF that converts a VFP cursor into XML using CURSORTOXML() and returns the results:

```
use CUSTOMERS
cursortoxml('customers', 'lcXML', 1, 8, 0, '1')
return lcXML
```

The UDF could call a Web Service that returns a result set as XML. Here's an example IntelliSense generated from a Web Service. (The details aren't important; it just shows an example of a Web Service. See Chapter 10, "COM and Web Services Enhancements", for a discussion of Web Services.)

```
local loWS as dataserver web service
loWS = NEWOBJECT("Wsclient",HOME()+"ffc\_webservices.vcx")
loWS.cWSName = "dataserver web service"
loWS = loWS.SetupClient("http://localhost/SQDataServer/dataserver.WSDL", ;
  "dataserver", "dataserverSoapPort")
lcXML = loWS.GetCustomers()
return lcXML
```

It could use SQLXML to execute a SQL Server query stored in a template file on a Web Server (for more information on SQLXML, go to **http://msdn.microsoft.com** and search for SQLXML). The following code uses an MSXML2.XMLHTTP object to get all records from the Northwind Customers table via HTTP; this is explained in more detail later.

```
local loXML as MSXML2.XMLHTTP
loXML = createobject('MSXML2.XMLHTTP')
loXML.open('POST', 'http://localhost/northwind/template/' + ;
  'getallcustomers.xml', .F.)
loXML.setRequestHeader('Content-type', 'text/xml')
loXML.send()
return loXML.responseText
```

Handling updates is more complicated. The data source must either be capable of accepting and consuming an updategram (as is the case with SQL Server 2000) or you have to figure out the changes yourself and issue a series of SQL statements (UPDATE, INSERT, and DELETE) to perform the updates.

Here's an example that uses a CursorAdapter with an XML data source. Notice both SelectCmd and UpdateCmd call UDFs. In the case of SelectCmd, the name of a SQL Server XML template and the customer ID to retrieve is passed to a UDF called GetNWXML, which we'll look at in a moment. For UpdateCmd, VFP passes the UpdateGram property to SendNWXML, which we'll also look at later.

*The Developer Download files at **www.hentzenwerke.com** include all the code necessary for this example: XMLExample.PRG, GetNWXML.PRG, SendNWXML.PRG, and CustomersByID.XML.*

```
local loCustomers as CursorAdapter, ;
  laErrors[1]
set multilocks on
loCustomers = createobject('CursorAdapter')
with loCustomers
  .Alias                = 'Customers'
  .CursorSchema         = 'CUSTOMERID C(5), COMPANYNAME C(40), ' + ;
    'CONTACTNAME C(30), CONTACTTITLE C(30), ADDRESS C(60), ' + ;
    'CITY C(15), REGION C(15), POSTALCODE C(10), COUNTRY C(15), ' + ;
    'PHONE C(24), FAX C(24)'
  .DataSourceType       = 'XML'
  .KeyFieldList         = 'CUSTOMERID'
  .SelectCmd            = 'GetNWXML([customersbyid.xml?customerid=ALFKI])'
  .Tables               = 'CUSTOMERS'
  .UpdatableFieldList   = 'CUSTOMERID, COMPANYNAME, CONTACTNAME, ' + ;
```

```
        'CONTACTTITLE, ADDRESS, CITY, REGION, POSTALCODE, COUNTRY, PHONE, FAX'
      .UpdateCmdDataSourceType = 'XML'
      .UpdateCmd               = 'SendNWXML(This.UpdateGram)'
      .UpdateNameList          = 'CUSTOMERID CUSTOMERS.CUSTOMERID, ' + ;
        'COMPANYNAME CUSTOMERS.COMPANYNAME, ' + ;
        'CONTACTNAME CUSTOMERS.CONTACTNAME, ' + ;
        'CONTACTTITLE CUSTOMERS.CONTACTTITLE, ' + ;
        'ADDRESS CUSTOMERS.ADDRESS, ' + ;
        'CITY CUSTOMERS.CITY, ' + ;
        'REGION CUSTOMERS.REGION, ' + ;
        'POSTALCODE CUSTOMERS.POSTALCODE, ' + ;
        'COUNTRY CUSTOMERS.COUNTRY, ' + ;
        'PHONE CUSTOMERS.PHONE, ' + ;
        'FAX CUSTOMERS.FAX'
   if .CursorFill(.T.)
      browse
      tableupdate(.T.)
   else
      aerror(laErrors)
      messagebox(laErrors[2])
   endif
endwith
close tables
```

The XML template this code references, CustomersByID.XML, looks like the following:

```
<root xmlns:sql="urn:schemas-microsoft-com:xml-sql">
  <sql:header>
    <sql:param name="customerid">
    </sql:param>
  </sql:header>
  <sql:query client-side-xml="0">
    SELECT *
    FROM    Customers
    WHERE CustomerID = @customerid
    FOR XML AUTO
  </sql:query>
</root>
```

Place this file in an IIS virtual directory for the Northwind database (see Appendix 1, "Setting Up SQL Server 2000 XML Access", for details on configuring IIS to work with SQL Server).

Here's the code for GetNWXML. It uses an MSXML2.XMLHTTP object to transfer XML via HTTP. The Open method opens a connection to a URL, which in this case specifies a SQL Server XML template on a Web server. The SetRequestHeader method tells the XMLHTTP object what type of data is being transferred. The Send method sends the request to the server and puts the results into the ResponseText property. The name of the template (and optionally any query parameters) is passed as a parameter to this code.

```
lparameters tcURL
local loXML as MSXML2.XMLHTTP
loXML = createobject('MSXML2.XMLHTTP')
loXML.open('POST', 'http://localhost/northwind/template/' + tcURL, .F.)
loXML.setRequestHeader('Content-type', 'text/xml')
loXML.send()
return loXML.responseText
```

SendNWXML looks similar, except it expects to be passed an updategram, loads the updategram into an MSXML2.DOMDocument object, and passes that object to the Web server, which will in turn pass it via SQLXML to SQL Server for processing.

```
lparameters tcUpdateGram
local loDOM as MSXML2.DOMDocument, ;
  loXML as MSXML2.XMLHTTP
loDOM = createobject('MSXML2.DOMDocument')
loDOM.async = .F.
loDOM.loadXML(tcUpdateGram)
loXML = createobject('MSXML2.XMLHTTP')
loXML.open('POST', 'http://localhost/northwind/', .F.)
loXML.setRequestHeader('Content-type', 'text/xml')
loXML.send(loDOM)
```

To see how this works, run XMLExample.prg. You should see a single record (the ALFKI customer) in a browse window. Change the value in some field, close the window, and run the PRG again. You should see your change was written to the back end.

Update issue

You have a lot of flexibility when updating the original data source from changes in the cursor created by CursorAdapter. The easiest thing to do is let VFP handle the updates by setting the KeyFieldList, Tables, UpdatableFieldList, and UpdateNameList properties. For more control, set the *Cmd, *DataSource, and *DataSourceType properties (where "*" is "Delete", "Insert", or "Update"). However, there's an issue you should be aware of; update conflicts don't work the same way they do with VFP data.

With UpdateType set to 1 (the default) and automatic updates, VFP sends a SQL UPDATE command to the data source. The UPDATE command is usually something like the following (in this case, CUSTOMERID is the key field and the value of the COMPANYNAME field was changed):

```
UPDATE CUSTOMERS SET COMPANYNAME=?customer.companyname
  WHERE CUSTOMERID=?OLDVAL('customerid','customer') AND
  COMPANYNAME=?OLDVAL('companyname','customer')
```

What happens if another user also changed the company name? In that case, the WHERE clause will fail because no record with the former name of the company can be found. However, this doesn't cause an error. As a result, it appears the update succeeded—TABLEUPDATE() returns True.

This situation may be better or worse if UpdateType is set to 2. In that case, VFP generates SQL DELETE and INSERT commands similar to the following:

```
DELETE FROM CUSTOMERS WHERE CUSTOMERID=?OLDVAL('customerid','customer') AND
   COMPANYNAME=?OLDVAL('companyname','customer')
INSERT INTO CUSTOMERS (CUSTOMERID, COMPANYNAME, CONTACTNAME, CONTACTTITLE,
   ADDRESS, CITY, REGION, POSTALCODE, COUNTRY, PHONE, FAX) VALUES
   (?customer.customerid, ?customer.companyname, ?customer.contactname,
   ?customer.contacttitle, ?customer.address, ?customer.city, ?customer.region,
   ?customer.postalcode, ?customer.country, ?customer.phone, ?customer.fax)
```

In the case of a conflict, the DELETE command will fail, but not cause an error. The INSERT command will fail with a duplicate primary key error if the table has a primary key (which is good, since TABLEUPDATE() will return False) or will succeed and create a duplicate record if the table doesn't have a primary key (which is bad).

One way to handle this is to change the SQL UPDATE and DELETE commands so they cause an error if they fail. In the case of SQL Server, you can use code like the following in the BeforeUpdate method of the CursorAdapter to modify the UPDATE and DELETE commands to raise an error if the process failed:

```
lcErrorCode      = " if @@ROWCOUNT=0 RAISERROR('Update conflict!', 16, 1)"
cUpdateInsertCmd = cUpdateInsertCmd + lcErrorCode
cDeleteCmd       = iif(empty(cDeleteCmd), '', cDeleteCmd + lcErrorCode)
```

Reusable data classes

One thing VFP developers have asked Microsoft to add to VFP for a long time is reusable data environments. For example, you may have a form and a report with exactly the same data setup, but you have to manually fill in the DataEnvironment for each one because DataEnvironments aren't reusable. Some developers (and almost all frameworks vendors) made it easier to create reusable DataEnvironments by creating DataEnvironments in code (they couldn't be subclassed visually) and using a "loader" object on the form to instantiate the DataEnvironment subclass. However, this was kind of a kludge and didn't help with reports.

Now, in VFP 8, we have the ability to create both reusable data classes, which can provide cursors from any data source to anything that needs them, and reusable DataEnvironments, which can host the data classes. Unfortunately, you can't use a DataEnvironment subclass in a report, but you can add CursorAdapters or CursorAdapter subclasses to the report's DataEnvironment to take advantage of reusability there.

Here's an example. If you want a CursorAdapter that works with the Northwind Customers table, it makes more sense to create a subclass to do that rather than create separate instances and fill in the properties every time you need one. **Table 2** shows the properties for a subclass of CursorAdapter called CustomersCursor.

Table 2. The properties of the CustomersCursor class provide a CursorAdapter that knows how to access and update the Northwind Customers table.

Property	Value
Alias	Customers
CursorSchema	CUSTOMERID C(5), COMPANYNAME C(40), CONTACTNAME C(30), CONTACTTITLE C(30), ADDRESS C(60), CITY C(15), REGION C(15), POSTALCODE C(10), COUNTRY C(15), PHONE C(24), FAX C(24)
KeyFieldList	CUSTOMERID
SelectCmd	select * from customers
Tables	CUSTOMERS
UpdatableFieldList	CUSTOMERID, COMPANYNAME, CONTACTNAME, CONTACTTITLE, ADDRESS, CITY, REGION, POSTALCODE, COUNTRY, PHONE, FAX
UpdateNameList	CUSTOMERID CUSTOMERS.CUSTOMERID, COMPANYNAME CUSTOMERS.COMPANYNAME, CONTACTNAME CUSTOMERS.CONTACTNAME, CONTACTTITLE CUSTOMERS.CONTACTTITLE, ADDRESS CUSTOMERS.ADDRESS, CITY CUSTOMERS.CITY, REGION CUSTOMERS.REGION, POSTALCODE CUSTOMERS.POSTALCODE, COUNTRY CUSTOMERS.COUNTRY, PHONE CUSTOMERS.PHONE, FAX CUSTOMERS.FAX

You can use the CursorAdapter Builder to do most of the work, especially setting the CursorSchema and update properties. The trick is to turn on the "use connection settings in builder only" option, fill in the connection information so you have a live connection, fill in the SelectCmd, and use the builder to build the rest of the properties for you.

Now, anytime you need records from the Northwind Customers table, you simply use the CustomersCursor class. Of course, we haven't defined any connection information, but that's actually a good thing, because this class shouldn't have to worry about things like how to get the data (ODBC, ADO, or XML) or even what database engine to use (there are Northwind databases for SQL Server, Access, and, new in version 8, VFP). Here's an example that uses the CustomersCursor class; notice it just needs to set the connection information in order to have a fully updateable cursor of Northwind Customers.

```
loCursor = newobject('CustomersCursor', 'NorthwindDataClasses')
with loCursor
  .DataSourceType = 'ODBC'
  .DataSource     = sqlstringconnect('driver=SQL Server;' + ;
    'server=(local);database=Northwind;uid=sa;pwd=;' + ;
    'trusted_connection=no')
  if .CursorFill()
    browse
  else
    aerror(laErrors)
    messagebox(laErrors[2])
  endif
endwith
```

*The Developer Download files at **www.hentzenwerke.com** include this code as TestCustomersCursor.PRG, plus NorthwindDataClasses.VCX, which has the CustomersCursor class definition. Additional sample code not described here is also provided, including subclasses of CursorAdapter and DataEnvironment called SFCursorAdapter and SFDataEnvironment that provide additional functionality and can serve as the parent classes for specialized subclasses.*

One thing to be aware of when you subclass CursorAdapter is the unique order in which events fire at instantiation. For a CursorAdapter instantiated in code, the Init event fires before all others, as you'd expect. However, for a CursorAdapter in the DataEnvironment of a form, here's the event order:

```
DataEnvironment.OpenTables
DataEnvironment.BeforeOpenTables
CursorAdapter.AutoOpen
CursorAdapter.BeforeCursorFill
CursorAdapter.CursorFill
CursorAdapter.AfterCursorFill
CursorAdapter.Init
DataEnvironment.Init
```

Since Init fires after CursorFill, you can't put code that initializes properties such as DataSource and DataSourceType into Init—that code would execute too late. Instead, put this code into BeforeCursorFill or CursorFill.

You can add base class CursorAdapters to the DataEnvironment of a report but you can't add CursorAdapter subclasses, at least not visually. The reason is VFP stores only the class name, not the class library, in the FRX, so when you reopen or run the report, VFP doesn't know where the CursorAdapter subclasses are defined. If you want to use CursorAdapter subclasses, add them programmatically using AddObject or NewObject in the Init of the DataEnvironment.

Summary

CursorAdapter is one of the biggest and most exciting enhancements in VFP 8 because it provides a consistent and easy-to-use interface to remote data, makes it easy to switch from one access mechanism to another, and allows you to create truly reusable data classes.

VFP 8 has a lot of other data-related changes as well. We'll examine these in detail in the next two chapters.

Updates and corrections to this chapter can be found on Hentzenwerke's web site, **www.hentzenwerke.com**. Click on "Catalog" and navigate to the page for this book.

Chapter 7
XML Classes

VFP 8 greatly improves upon the XML features added in VFP 7 by providing new base classes that can work with more types of XML and provide more control over XML input and output. The existing XML functions also have a few improvements.

Several years ago, Microsoft discovered the usefulness of XML and has been adding support for it to every product since then. VFP is no exception. In version 7, they added three XML-related functions that allow you to convert between XML and a VFP cursor (the CURSORTOXML() and XMLTOCURSOR() functions) and create XML containing changes made to a cursor (XMLUPDATEGRAM()). However, there are several shortcomings with these functions:

- XMLTOCURSOR() is picky about the format of the XML. It can't, for example, create a cursor from the XML representation of an ADO.NET DataSet.

- XMLTOCURSOR() can't handle hierarchical XML, where data from more than one table is intertwined (we'll see an example of hierarchical XML shortly).

- You don't have any control over the choices VFP makes when converting the various XML data types specified in the schema to VFP data types.

- Although XMLUPDATEGRAM() can create an updategram another application, such as SQL Server, can use, VFP 7 lacks a function that does the opposite: accept an updategram and apply the changes described in it to local tables. Visual FoxPro MVP Alex Feldstein wrote a routine to do this (available from the FoxForum Wiki at **http://fox.wikis.com/wc.dll?Wiki~XMLUpdateGramParse**), but a native means would be better.

Fortunately, VFP 8 overcomes all of these issues and adds even more capabilities. Rather than enhancing the existing XML functions or adding new ones, the Fox team at Microsoft decided to take a better approach—they added three new XML-related base classes.

XMLAdapter provides a means of converting data between XML and VFP cursors. It has a lot more capabilities than CURSORTOXML() and XMLTOCURSOR(), including support for hierarchical XML and the ability to consume types of XML those functions don't support such as ADO.NET DataSets. XMLTable and XMLField are child objects that provide the ability to fine-tune the schema for the XML data. In addition, XMLTable has an ApplyDiffgram method intended to allow VFP to consume diffgrams.

Before we look at these new classes, note that you need MSXML 4.0 Service Pack 1 or later installed on your system. Although this is installed for you when you install VFP 8, be sure to install it on your client's system if you use the new base classes in an application. If you use the InstallShield Express version that comes with VFP 8, or another installer based on the Windows Installer, include the MSXML4.MSM merge module. You can also download this merge module from the MSDN Web site (go to **http://msdn.microsoft.com** and search for MSXML).

Note that this chapter doesn't discuss XML concepts such as elements and attributes, encoding, XSD and XDR schemas, and so forth. There are a wide variety of sources available for background on XML, including several white papers on the Microsoft web site.

XMLAdapter

XMLAdapter is the main class of the three new ones. As its name implies, it's an adapter between XML and VFP data; it can import XML in a variety of formats into VFP cursors and output XML from VFP cursors. XMLAdapter is much less picky about the XML format it can import and provides you with much more control over both import and output than the XMLTOCURSOR() and CURSORTOXML() functions.

XMLAdapter is a fairly simple class; it consists mostly of properties, has only a few methods, and no events. **Table 1** shows the specific properties of this class.

Table 1. *The properties of XMLAdapter.*

Property	Description
DisableEncode	The default value for the DisableEncode property for new XMLField objects (see Table 3 for a description of this property).
ForceCloseTag	Indicates whether the ToXML method outputs single empty element tags (False, the default) or sets of empty element open and close tags (True) for blank data.
FormattedOutput	Determines whether the ToXML method outputs formatted XML (True, the default) or a single continuous string (False).
IsDiffgram	Indicates whether imported XML is in diffgram format or not, and determines whether ToXML outputs to diffgram format.
IsLoaded	Indicates whether XML has been loaded or not.
IXMLDOMElement	Contains an object reference to an IXMLDOMElement object after XML has been loaded.
MapN19_4ToCurrency	Indicates whether the xsd:decimal data type is mapped to the VFP Currency (True) or Numeric (False, the default) data type when loading XML and the XML properties totalDigits and fractionDigits are 19 and 4, respectively.
NoCpTrans	The default value for the NoCpTrans property for new XMLField objects (see Table 3 for a description of this property).
PreserveWhiteSpace	Indicates whether white space is preserved (True) or removed (False, the default) when XML is loaded or output. This property doesn't apply to data contained in a CDATA section.
RespectCursorCP	Specifies whether the ToXML method creates XML with the default Windows-1252 encoding (False, the default) or with the proper encoding information for the code page of the cursor the XML is created from (True). This property is ignored if UTF8Encoded (see below) is True.
SOM	Contains an object reference to an ISchema (XML Schema Object Model) object after loading XML. This object contains schema information about the XML.
Tables	A collection of XMLTable objects. It has the usual PEMs of the Collection class, such as Count and Item. See Chapter 9, "OOP Enhancements", for a discussion of Collection.
Unicode	The default value for the Unicode property for new XMLField objects (see Table 3 for a description of this property).
UTF8Encoded	Indicates whether the ToXML method creates XML with UTF-8 encoding (True) or uses the RespectCursorCP property (see above) to determine the encoding.

Table 1. Continued

Property	Description
WrapCharInCDATA	The default value for the WrapInCDATA property for new XMLField objects representing Character fields (see Table 3 for a description of this property).
WrapMemoInCDATA	The default value for the WrapInCDATA property for new XMLField objects representing Memo fields.
XMLConstraints	Contains an object reference to an ISchemaItemCollection object after XML has been loaded. This object contains information about any constraints specified in the XML, which may be useful because VFP doesn't make use of any constraints itself.
XMLName	The name of the element used to locate tables in the XML. Contains either a Unicode string or is empty.
XMLNamespace	The XML namespace to which the XML name belongs. Contains either a Unicode string or is blank.
XMLPrefix	The prefix used to reference the XML namespace. Contains either a Unicode string or is blank.
XMLSchemaLocation	The location of the schema when loading or outputting XML. Accepts the same values as the schema location parameter of CURSORTOXML().

Several of these properties contain Unicode values, so if you set these properties manually, you must specify Unicode values; the STRCONV() function can take care of this for you.

XMLAdapter has five methods: LoadXML, AddTableSchema, Attach, ToXML, and ReleaseXML. LoadXML loads XML into an XMLAdapter object. The XML can come from a file or a string. The syntax for this method is:

```
Object.LoadXML( cXML [, lFile [, lValidateOnParse ] ] )
```

cXML is either an XML string or the name of an XML file; if it's the latter, the lFile parameter should be True. The lValidateOnParse parameter, which defaults to True if it isn't passed, indicates whether the XML should be validated as it's parsed. Once LoadXML has finished, the XMLAdapter is fully populated with XMLTable and XMLField objects, and then you can generate VFP cursors (you'll see how to do that when we discuss the XMLTable class). Because LoadXML raises an error rather than returning False if it can't parse the XML (for example, if the XML is invalid), you should wrap calls to it in a TRY structure. See Chapter 12, "Error Handling", for a description of structured error handling and the TRY structure.

AddTableSchema adds a new XMLTable and set of XMLField objects based on an existing VFP cursor. Here's the syntax for this method:

```
Object.AddTableSchema( cAlias [, lElementBased [, cXMLName [, cXMLNamespace
  [, cXMLPrefix [, lWrapMemoInCDATA [, lWrapCharInCDATA ] ] ] ] ] ] )
```

cAlias is the alias of the cursor and lElementBased indicates whether the XML should be element-based (the default if this parameter isn't passed) or attribute-based. cXMLName specifies the name of the table in the XML; it defaults to the alias if it isn't passed, and if it is passed, it must be a Unicode string. cXMLNamespace and cXMLPrefix are the namespace and prefix to use, respectively; they default to blank if not passed and must be Unicode strings if they are passed. The last two parameters indicate whether Memo and Character fields are wrapped in CDATA sections in the XML; if they aren't passed, they default to the WrapMemoInCDATA and WrapCharInCDATA properties, respectively.

The Attach method uses an existing XML DOM document or element to load XML into an XMLAdapter. This is typically used when you receive XML from something as a DOM object rather than an XML string. For example, if you call a Web Service that returns an ADO.NET DataSet, you can't use LoadXML on the result because the DataSet is returned as a DOM object. Instead, use Attach. Here's the syntax for this method:

```
Object.Attach( oDOM [, oSchema ] )
```

This method accepts as a parameter a DOM or IXMLDOMElement object containing the XML, and optionally an ISchema, DOM, or IXMLDOMElement object containing schema information as the second parameter. As with LoadXML, you should wrap calls to Attach in TRY structures to catch any errors Attach will raise if there's a problem.

Here's an example of Attach. In this code, loNWWebService is a proxy for a Web Service that returns an ADO.NET DataSet (for simplicity and because it isn't relevant, how this is set up isn't shown here). The DOM object returned from the Web Service GetAllCustomers method contains two nodes: one for the data and one for the schema information. These nodes are used by the Attach method to load an XMLAdapter.

```
loXML      = loNWWebService.GetAllCustomers()
loSchema = loXML.Item(0)
loData     = loXML.Item(1)
loXMLAdapter = createobject('XMLAdapter')
loXMLAdapter.Attach(loData, loSchema)
```

ToXML generates XML, either to a file or to a string, from the data attached to the XMLAdapter. It can generate complete XML or just a diffgram describing changes in the data. Here's the syntax:

```
Object.ToXML( cXML [, cSchemaLocation [, lFile [, lIncludeBefore
   [, lChangesOnly ] ] ] ] )
```

Like the same parameter for the CURSORTOXML() function, cXML is the name of a file or memory variable to contain the generated XML. In the case of a variable, be sure to put quotes around this parameter (for example, Object.ToXML('lcXML', ... to output to the variable lcXML) or VFP assumes you are passing a variable containing the name of the variable to output the XML to, which would be a pretty rare use. To output to a file, pass True for the lFile parameter. The cSchemaLocation parameter is also similar to its counterpart in CURSORTOXML()—it specifies the location in which to generate external schema information if an internal schema isn't desired. If the IsDiffgram property is True, meaning a diffgram should be generated, pass True for the lIncludeBefore parameter to generate a diffgr:before section in the diffgram. This section contains the original version of each record, even for deleted records. If both IsDiffgram and lIncludeBefore are True, you can pass True for the lChangesOnly parameter to generate XML containing only changes. Note that ToXML won't generate a diffgram unless the cursor is table-buffered; if the cursor is row-buffered, ToXML generates the schema but not the data part of the diffgram. This seems like a bug to us.

ReleaseXML is used when you want to detach the XML (including the IXMLDOMElement object) from the XMLAdapter. This is typically used when you want to load new XML into an existing XMLAdapter rather than creating a new one. In addition to removing the XML, this method also nukes the schema (the Tables collection and SOM object) and resets several other properties to their default values unless you specifically pass False as a parameter.

Here's an example that shows a few of the properties and methods of XMLAdapter. This code creates a cursor, makes some changes in it, attaches it to an XMLAdapter, and shows the different types of XML the XMLAdapter can generate.

```
local loXMLAdapter as XMLAdapter

* Create a cursor from the TESTDATA Customer table, then make some changes.

open database _samples + 'Data\TestData'
select * from Customer into cursor Customers readwrite
set multilocks on
cursorsetprop('Buffering', 5)
replace Company with 'I changed this record'
skip
delete
insert into Customers (Cust_ID, Company, MaxOrdAmt) ;
  values ('XXXXX', 'Test Company', 1000)

* Create an XMLAdapter and attach the cursor to it.

loXMLAdapter = createobject('XMLAdapter')
loXMLAdapter.AddTableSchema('Customers')

* Generate complete XML.

loXMLAdapter.ToXML('Customers.XML', '', .T.)
messagebox('Complete XML', 0, 'XMLAdapter Example')
modify file Customers.xml

* Generate a diffgram of our changes.

loXMLAdapter.IsDiffgram = .T.
loXMLAdapter.ToXML('CustomersDiffgram.XML', '', .T., .T., .T.)
messagebox('Diffgram of changes', 0, 'XMLAdapter Example')
modify file CustomersDiffgram.xml

* Change the encoding and XML properties.

loXMLAdapter.UTF8Encoded   = .T.
loXMLAdapter.XMLName       = strconv('MyCustomers', 5)
loXMLAdapter.XMLNamespace = strconv('MyNamespace', 5)
loXMLAdapter.XMLPrefix     = strconv('mns', 5)
loXMLAdapter.ToXML('CustomersDiffgram.XML', '', .T., .T., .T.)
messagebox('Diffgram showing different encoding and XML properties', 0, ;
  'XMLAdapter Example')
modify file CustomersDiffgram.xml
```

```
* Clean up.

erase Customers.xml
erase CustomersDiffgram.xml
close databases all
```

 *This code is available in XMLAdapterExample.PRG from the Developer Download files for this chapter, available at **www.hentzenwerke.com**.*

We'll look at more complex examples, such as creating cursors from XML, once we've examined the XMLTable class.

Updategrams versus diffgrams

While the XMLUPDATEGRAM() function generates updategrams, XMLAdapter.ToXML generates diffgrams. What's the difference? Mostly just the format of the XML. For example, here's an updategram that describes changes to a single field in a table:

```
<?xml version = "1.0" encoding="Windows-1252" standalone="yes"?>
<root xmlns:updg="urn:schemas-microsoft-com:xml-updategram">
  <updg:sync>
    <updg:before>
      <customers>
        <cust_id>ALFKI</cust_id>
        <company>Alfreds Futterkiste</company>
      </customers>
    </updg:before>
    <updg:after>
      <customers>
        <cust_id>ALFKI</cust_id>
        <company>Bob Jones</company>
      </customers>
    </updg:after>
  </updg:sync>
</root>
```

Here's the same change expressed as a diffgram; schema information was omitted for brevity:

```
<?xml version = "1.0" encoding="UTF-8" standalone="yes"?>
<VFPData>
  <diffgr:diffgram xmlns:msdata="urn:schemas-microsoft-com:xml-msdata"
  xmlns:diffgr="urn:schemas-microsoft-com:xml-diffgram-v1">
    <VFPDataSet xmlns="">
      <Customers diffgr:id="customers_1" msdata:rowOrder="1"
      diffgr:hasChanges="modified">
        <cust_id>ALFKI</cust_id>
        <company>Alfreds Futterkistee</company>
      </Customers>
    </VFPDataSet>
```

```
<diffgr:before>
    <Customers diffgr:id="customers_1" msdata:rowOrder="1" xmlns="">
        <cust_id>ALFKI</cust_id>
        <company>Bob Jones</company>
    </Customers>
  </diffgr:before>
  </diffgr:diffgram>
</VFPData>
```

XMLTable

The Tables property of XMLAdapter contains a collection of XMLTable objects. XMLTable is a new base class that contains schema information for a table in the XML, and provides a way to create a cursor from the XML or to apply changes in a diffgram to local VFP data.

When you first instantiate an XMLAdapter object, the Tables collection is empty. The collection is filled with XMLTable objects when you load the XMLAdapter using the LoadXML or Attach methods or when you attach a cursor using the AddTableSchema method. You can also manually populate the collection if you wish to build an XMLAdapter by hand.

XMLTable is even simpler than XMLAdapter; it only has nine properties and three methods. **Table 2** shows the properties.

Table 2. *The properties of XMLTable.*

Property	Description
Alias	The alias of the table.
ChildTable	Contains an object reference to an XMLTable object that's the child of this one when hierarchical XML is used.
Fields	A collection of XMLField objects. It has the usual PEMs of the Collection class, such as Count and Item. See Chapter 9, "OOP Enhancements", for a discussion of Collection.
ParentTable	Contains an object reference to an XMLTable object that's the parent of this one when hierarchical XML is used.
XMLAdapter	Contains an object reference to the XMLAdapter this object belongs to.
XMLConstraints	Contains an object reference to an ISchemaItemCollection object after XML has been loaded. This object contains information about any constraints specified in the XML, which may be useful because VFP doesn't make use of any constraints itself.
XMLName	The name of the element used to locate tables in the XML. Contains either a Unicode string or blank.
XMLNamespace	The XML namespace to which the XML name belongs. Contains either a Unicode string or blank.
XMLPrefix	The prefix used to reference the XML namespace. Contains either a Unicode string or blank.

The ToCursor method creates a VFP cursor or appends data to an existing one. It has the following syntax:

```
Object.ToCursor( [ lAppend [, cAlias [, Reserved ] ] ] )
```

If lAppend is True, ToCursor appends the data to an existing cursor; otherwise, it creates a new cursor. You'll get an error if a cursor with the name ToCursor uses is already open and lAppend is False. Use cAlias to specify the alias of the cursor to create or append data to. The last parameter is reserved for future use and is ignored if you pass a value for it.

Here's an example that shows how ToCursor works. The NWSchema.XSD and NWDataSet.XML files contain schema and data, respectively, that came from an ADO.NET DataSet.

```
local loXMLAdapter as XMLAdapter, ;
  loTable as XMLTable
close databases all
loXMLAdapter = createobject('XMLAdapter')
loXMLAdapter.XMLSchemaLocation = 'NWSchema.xsd'
loXMLAdapter.LoadXML('NWDataSet.xml', .T.)
loTable = loXMLAdapter.Tables.Item(1)
loTable.ToCursor()
browse
use
```

 You can download the files for this example, ConsumeADODotNet.PRG, NWSchema.XSD, and NWDataSet.XML, from the Developer Download files for this chapter, available at **www.hentzenwerke.com**.

Here's another example showing how VFP deals with hierarchical XML. Hierarchical1.XML contains information about customers and their orders. Here's a customer with one order consisting of two products from this file:

```
<Customers>
  <CustomerID>CACTU</CustomerID>
  <CompanyName>Cactus Comidas para llevar</CompanyName>
  <Orders>
    <OrderID>10521</OrderID>
    <OrderDate>1997-04-29T00:00:00</OrderDate>
    <ShipName>Cactus Comidas para llevar</ShipName>
    <Order_details>
      <ProductID>35</ProductID>
      <UnitPrice>18</UnitPrice>
      <Quantity>3</Quantity>
    </Order_details>
    <Order_details>
      <ProductID>41</ProductID>
      <UnitPrice>9.65</UnitPrice>
      <Quantity>10</Quantity>
    </Order_details>
  </Orders>
</Customers>
```

XMLAdapter deals with hierarchical XML like this depending on how the XML is formatted, which in turn depends on its data source. In the case of XML returned from SQL Server, VFP joins the tables together into a single result set, as if you'd performed a SQL SELECT statement that selects all fields from all tables. It creates individual XMLTable objects for each table in the XML, but only one for the single result set is placed in the Tables collection. The others are accessible as a linked chain via the ChildTable properties of each one, but you cannot use ToCursor to create data from them. On the other hand, if the XML came from an ADO.NET DataSet, each table in the XML results in a separate XMLTable object in the Tables collection.

Hierarchical.PRG loads the XML from Hierarchical1.XML into an XMLAdapter, and then uses the ToCursor method of each XMLTable object to create a VFP cursor. As you'll see when you run this code, only a single table appears in the Tables collection, and the cursor it creates contains all fields from all tables in the XML. That's because Hierarchical1.XML contains data returned from SQL Server via SQLXML. You can access the Orders and Order_Details XMLTables via the ChildTable properties, but will get an error if you try to use ToCursor on them. However, if you comment out the first LoadXML statement and uncomment the second one, so it loads Hierarchical2.XML instead, you'll find it displays three separate cursors: one for Customers, one for Orders, and one for Order_Details. That's because Hierarchical2.XML came from an ADO.NET DataSet.

```
local loXMLAdapter as XMLAdapter, ;
  loTable as XMLTable
close databases all

* Create an XMLAdapter and load some hierarchical XML.

loXMLAdapter = createobject('XMLAdapter')
loXMLAdapter.LoadXML('Hierarchical1.XML', .T.)
*loXMLAdapter.LoadXML('Hierarchical2.XML', .T.)

* If we succeeded, create cursors from the XML.

if loXMLAdapter.IsLoaded
  for each loTable in loXMLAdapter.Tables
    loTable.ToCursor()
    messagebox('Here is the ' + loTable.Alias + ' cursor.' + ;
      iif(vartype(loTable.ChildTable) = 'O', ' It has a child ' + ;
      'named ' + loTable.ChildTable.Alias + '.', '') + ;
      iif(vartype(loTable.ParentTable) = 'O', ' It has a parent ' + ;
      'named ' + loTable.ParentTable.Alias + '.', ''), 0, ;
      'XMLTable Example')
    browse
    do while vartype(loTable.ChildTable) = 'O'
      loTable = loTable.ChildTable
      messagebox('The ' + loTable.Alias + ' table is inaccessible.' + ;
        iif(vartype(loTable.ChildTable) = 'O', ' It has a child ' + ;
        'named ' + loTable.ChildTable.Alias + '.', '') + ;
        iif(vartype(loTable.ParentTable) = 'O', ' It has a parent ' + ;
        'named ' + loTable.ParentTable.Alias + '.', ''), 0, ;
        'XMLTable Example')
    enddo
  next
endif
```

 *Hierarchical.PRG, Hierarchical1.XML, and Hierarchical2.XML are in the Developer Download files at **www.hentzenwerke.com**.*

The ChangesToCursor method is similar to ToCursor, but creates a cursor containing only the changes in the diffgram loaded by the XMLAdapter object. Its syntax is:

```
Object.ChangesToCursor( [ cAlias [, lIncludeUnchangedData [, Reserved ] ] ] )
```

cAlias is the alias of the cursor to create; if it isn't specified, the alias in the Alias property is used. If lIncludeUnchangedData is True, unchanged data is included in the cursor (which means it acts like ToCursor). As with ToCursor, the last parameter is for future use.

Let's look at an example that shows how this method works. XMLWithChanges.XML has both changed and unchanged records. Here's a portion of the contents; the first record has been modified by changing the value of the Num field from 9 to 99 (the diffgr:before section shows the original data) while the second one is untouched.

```
<diffgr:diffgram>
  <NewDataSet>
    <Tbl2 diffgr:id="Tbl21" msdata:rowOrder="0" diffgr:hasChanges="modified">
      <source>Buckner            </source>
      <num>99</num>
      <xdtime>2002-04-03T00:00:00.0000000-08:00</xdtime>
      <xlog>true</xlog>
    </Tbl2>
    <Tbl2 diffgr:id="Tbl22" msdata:rowOrder="1">
      <source>Cohen              </source>
      <num>5</num>
      <xlog>true</xlog>
    </Tbl2>
  </NewDataSet>
  <diffgr:before>
    <Tbl2 diffgr:id="Tbl21" msdata:rowOrder="0" xmlns="">
      <source>Buckner            </source>
      <num>9</num>
      <xdtime>2002-04-03T00:00:00.0000000-08:00</xdtime>
      <xlog>true</xlog>
    </Tbl2>
  </diffgr:before>
</diffgr:diffgram>
```

ChangesToCursor.PRG loads the XML from this file into an XMLAdapter and uses both the ToCursor and ChangesToCursor methods of each XMLTable object to create VFP cursors with complete data and with changes only.

```
local loXMLAdapter as XMLAdapter, ;
  loTable as XMLTable, ;
  lcAlias
close databases all

* Create an XMLAdapter and load some XML.

loXMLAdapter = createobject('XMLAdapter')
loXMLAdapter.LoadXML('XMLWithChanges.XML', .T.)

* If we succeeded, create cursors from the XML, showing the cursor with all
* data and with changes only.

if loXMLAdapter.IsLoaded
  for each loTable in loXMLAdapter.Tables
    loTable.ToCursor()
    messagebox('Here is the ' + loTable.Alias + ;
```

```
        ' cursor with complete data.', 0, 'XMLTable Example')
    select (loTable.Alias)
    browse
    messagebox('Now here it is with changes only.', 0, 'XMLTable Example')
    lcAlias = loTable.Alias + 'Changes'
    loTable.ChangesToCursor(lcAlias)
    select (lcAlias)
    browse
  next
endif
```

 *Both ChangesToCursor.PRG and XMLWithChanges.XML are in the Developer Download files at **www.hentzenwerke.com**.*

ApplyDiffgram fills a gap missing in VFP 7; how to consume a diffgram so local VFP tables are updated with the changes. Here's the syntax for this method:

```
Object.ApplyDiffgram( [ cAlias [, oCursorAdapter [, lPreserveChanges
   [, Reserved ] ] ] ] )
```

cAlias is the alias of the table to update (you're responsible for ensuring the table is already open), and defaults to the Alias property if it isn't specified. If you want to control how the updates are done, create a CursorAdapter object, fill in its properties, and pass it as the second parameter; otherwise, the ApplyDiffgram method will take care of the updates itself. This allows you to specify your own update, insert, and delete commands, or even update non-VFP data. See Chapter 6, "Improved Data Access", for information on using CursorAdapters. lPreserveChanges determine what happens when you pass a CursorAdapter and the update fails. If it's True (the default if it isn't passed), the changes in the cursor attached to the CursorAdapter are preserved. You might use this if you can fix the problem that caused the failure and try to do the update again. Pass False to detach the cursor from the CursorAdapter and revert any changes in it. The last parameter is again reserved for future use. The "Tying it all together" section later in this chapter shows an example using ApplyDiffgram.

XMLField

The Fields property of XMLTable contains a collection of XMLField objects. XMLField is the simplest of the XML classes because it consists of only properties. These properties provide the information necessary to create a field in a table, but also make it possible for you to fine-tune the schema so the cursor created from the XML or the XML generated from the cursor are formatted as you desire. **Table 3** shows the properties of XMLField.

Table 3. The properties of XMLField.

Property	Description
Alias	The name of the field.
DataType	The VFP data type for the field (for example, "C" for Character).
DisableEncode	Indicates whether Memo (binary) or Character (binary) data is encoded.
FractionDigits	For Numeric fields, the number of digits to the right of the decimal. −1 for all other data types or if there are no decimals.
IsAttribute	Indicates whether the field is an attribute (True) or element (False, the default) in the XML document.
IsBase64	Indicates whether the field is encoded as Base64 (True) or hexBinary (False, the default).
IsBinary	Indicates whether the field is defined as Binary in the schema.
IsNull	Indicates whether the field accepts null values or not (the default is False).
KeyField	True if the field is a key field or False if not.
MaxLength	The total length of a Character or Numeric field. See the "Unicode" topic in the VFP Help for information on how the Unicode property affects MaxLength.
NoCpTrans	Indicates whether VFP performs code page translation on this field (the default is False, so code page translation is performed).
Unicode	Specifies whether character fields are handled as Unicode data. Unicode cannot be True if IsBinary is True. NoCpTrans is ignored by the ToCursor, ChangesToCursor, or ApplyDiffgram methods of XMLTable if Unicode is True, because the field is automatically created with the NOCPTRANS flag.
WrapInCDATA	Specifies whether Character and Memo data are wrapped in CDATA sections.
XMLName	The element or attribute name for this field in the XML document.
XMLTable	An object reference to the XMLTable object this field belongs to.
XMLType	An object reference to an ISchemaType object that contains information for the field.
XSDfractionDigits	Contains the XML Schema Definition (XSD) fractionDigits value, which is the number of places to the right of the decimal.
XSDmaxLength	Contains the XSD maxLength value.
XSDtotalDigits	Contains the XSD totalDigits value, which is the total number of digits.
XSDtype	Contains the XSD data type of the field, without the "xsd:" prefix.

If the cursor created from the XML document doesn't have the correct structure, you can set various XMLField properties before calling XMLTable.ToCursor. For example, if you fill an ADO.NET DataSet from a DataAdapter but neglect to set the DataAdapter's MissingSchemaAction property to MissingSchemaAction.AddWithKey, the DataSet won't have complete schema information (in our opinion, this is a bug in .NET), so all character fields in the DataSet will be memo fields in the cursor created by ToCursor. In this case, set each field's DataType and MaxLength properties to the appropriate values before calling ToCursor. Similarly, you can set the properties starting with "XSD" to fine-tune the schema generated by the XMLAdapter ToXML method. For information on how VFP data types map to XSD and XDR data types, see the "Visual FoxPro and XML Schema Data Type Mapping" topic in the VFP Help.

Tying it all together

VFP comes with a great sample that ties most of the features of the new XML classes together. To access this sample, open the new Task Pane from the Tools menu (see Chapter 4, "The Task Pane Manager", for information on the Task Pane), choose the Solution Samples pane, expand the New in Visual FoxPro 8.0 topic, and select the VFP/VB.NET Web Service Samples link. This doesn't actually run the sample; it displays a readme file that describes how to set up and run the sample. This sample is quite complex—it uses SQL Server as a data source, both VB.NET and VFP-based Web Services, and a VFP form as a client of the Web Services. As a result, it has a larger footprint on your system than other samples. It requires SQL Server, the .NET Framework (and probably Visual Studio.NET because you may have to tweak the VB.NET code to specify the correct SQL Server password), and IIS. The setup program for the sample creates a new IIS virtual directory on your system, and installs and registers the various components needed for the sample. If you have the resources and don't mind installing these components on your system, this is a great sample for examining how VFP and .NET can transfer data back and forth, how XMLAdapter can interact with CursorAdapter, and how VFP can be both a data consumer and a data provider in n-tier applications.

However, if you don't have IIS, SQL Server, or .NET available or don't want to pollute your system, here's a much more lightweight example. It calls a simulated Web Service (we'll look at the code later) to return a record for a specific customer as XML, converts the XML to a VFP cursor using an XMLAdapter, and then lets you browse the cursor. If you make changes to the cursor (see the MESSAGEBOX() for some suggestions of changes you can make), it then clears out the XMLAdapter, generates a diffgram from the changes, and sends the diffgram back to the Web Service to apply the changes to the source tables.

```
local loWebService, ;
  lcXML, ;
  loXMLAdapter as XMLAdapter, ;
  lcSchemaLocation, ;
  llIsFile, ;
  llIncludeBefore, ;
  llChangesOnly
close databases all
set multilocks on

* Simulate calling a Web Service to get some data.

loWebService = createobject('WebService')
lcXML = loWebService.GetCustomerByID('ALFKI')

* Create a cursor from the retrieved XML.

loXMLAdapter = createobject('XMLAdapter')
loXMLAdapter.LoadXML(lcXML)
loXMLAdapter.Tables.Item(1).ToCursor(.F., 'Customers')

* Make any changes desired.

select Customers
cursorsetprop('Buffering', 5)
messagebox("Here's the ALFKI customer retrieved from a simulated Web " + ;
  'Service. Make whatever changes you wish (you can even add or delete ' + ;
  'records), then press Ctrl+W to close the BROWSE window and save the ' + ;
  'changes back to the Web Service. ' + chr(13) + chr(13) + ;
  'Try blanking the CUST_ID or COMPANY fields, changing COUNTRY to ' + ;
  '"Pottsylvania", or adding a record with the same CUST_ID as an ' + ;
  'existing record (try "BERGS", for example) and see what happens when ' + ;
```

```
'you save.', 0, 'XMLAdapter Example')
browse

* Now write changes back to the Web Service if there are any. Clean out the
* XMLAdapter first.

if getnextmodified(0) <> 0
  with loXMLAdapter
    .ReleaseXML(.T.)
    .Tables.Remove(-1)

* Attach the Customers cursor to it.

    .AddTableSchema('Customers')

* Set some properties and flags for the ToXML method, then generate a diffgram
* from the cursor.

    .UTF8Encoded     = .T.    && cursor contains international characters
    .IsDiffgram      = .T.    && generate an XML DiffGram
    lcSchemaLocation = ''     && our schema is inline
    llIsFile         = .F.    && our XML is a stream
    llIncludeBefore  = .T.    && include <diffgram:before> format
    llChangesOnly    = .T.    && generate only changes we made
    .ToXML('lcXML', lcSchemaLocation, llIsFile, llIncludeBefore, ;
      llChangesOnly)
  endwith

* Display the diffgram.

  strtofile(lcXML, 'Test.txt')
  messagebox("Here's the diffgram the XMLAdapter created that'll be " + ;
    'sent back to the Web Service to update the data source.', 0, ;
    'XMLAdapter Example')
  modify file Test.txt
  erase Test.txt

* Send the diffgram to the Web Service and display the results.

  lcResults = loWebService.UpdateCustomer(lcXML)
  if empty(lcResults)
    messagebox('The Web Service indicated that the update was ' + ;
      'successful.', 0, 'XMLAdapter Example')
  else
    messagebox('The Web Service indicated that the update was ' + ;
      'unsuccessful. The message from the Web Service is:' + chr(13) + ;
      chr(13) + lcResults, 0, 'XMLAdapter Example')
  endif
endif
close databases all
```

Here's the class that simulates a Web Service. It has a GetCustomerByID method that accepts a customer ID, locates the appropriate record in the TestData Customer table, and returns the record as XML. It also has an UpdateCustomer method that accepts a diffgram and uses XMLTable.ApplyDiffgram to write the changes to the Customer table. UpdateCustomer is fairly complex, because it has to handle both business logic problems (such as a blank customer ID or company name) and data problems (duplicate primary key value, for example).

In a real-world case, this functionality would be split between business and data tier objects. UpdateCustomer returns an error message if it failed or an empty string if it succeeded.

```
define class WebService as Session
  procedure Init
    set multilocks on
    open database (_samples + 'Data\TestData')
  endproc
  procedure Destroy
    close database
  endproc

* Get the customer record for the specified ID and return it as XML.

  procedure GetCustomerByID(CustomerID as String) as String
    local lcXML
    select * from Customer where Cust_ID = ?CustomerID into cursor _Temp
    cursortoxml('_Temp', 'lcXML', 1, 0, 0, '1')
    use
    use in Customer
    return lcXML
  endproc

* Accept a diffgram and try to apply it to the Customer table.

  procedure UpdateCustomer(DiffGram as String) as String
    local lcMessage, ;
      loXMLAdapter as XMLAdapter, ;
      laError[1], ;
      loException as Exception

* First load the diffgram into an XMLAdapter. Then, create a cursor from the
* diffgram so we can do some business rules.

    lcMessage    = ''
    loXMLAdapter = createobject('XMLAdapter')
    try
      loXMLAdapter.LoadXML(DiffGram)
      loXMLAdapter.Tables.Item(1).ToCursor(.F., '_Temp')
      select _Temp
      scan
        do case
          case empty(nvl(Cust_ID, ''))
            throw 'Customer ID cannot be blank or null.'
          case empty(nvl(Company, ''))
            throw 'Company name cannot be blank or null.'
          case upper(Country) = ' POTTSYLVANIA'
            throw "We don't want no stinking Pottsylvanians!"
        endcase
      endscan
      use

* Try to make the changes in the Customer table.

      use Customer
      cursorsetprop('Buffering', 5)
      begin transaction
        loXMLAdapter.Tables.Item(1).ApplyDiffgram('Customer')
        if not tableupdate(.T.)
```

```
      aerror(laError)
      throw laError[2]
   endif
end transaction
messagebox('This is what the Customer table looks like after ' + ;
   'the diffgram was applied.', 0, 'Simulated Web Service')
browse
```

```
* If an error occurred (either a VFP error or one we raised), rollback the
* transaction if we have one and get the error message to return.
```

```
catch to loException
   if txnlevel() > 0
      rollback
   endif
   if loException.ErrorNo = 2071
      lcMessage = loException.UserValue
   else
      lcMessage = loException.Message
   endif
```

```
* Close any tables we opened.
```

```
   finally
      use in select('_Temp')
      use in select('Customer')
   endtry
   return lcMessage
endproc
enddefine
```

 *All of the code for this example is in Updates.PRG, available from the Developer Download files at **www.hentzenwerke.com.***

XMLToCursor and CursorToXML changes

There are a couple of changes in the XMLTOCURSOR() function. First, in VFP 7 Service Pack 1, Microsoft added the ability to import into an existing cursor by adding 8192 to the Flags parameter. This is useful when the XML doesn't have a schema or the schema isn't quite what you want. You can create a cursor with the desired structure, and then use XMLTOCURSOR() to fill that cursor. What's new in Visual FoxPro 8 is this feature is now documented.

The other change is XMLTOCURSOR() now converts Decimal values to Numeric fields with a width of 20 and 19 decimals (that is, N(20,19). In VFP 7, Decimal is mapped to N(8,0).

The VFP 7 version of CURSORTOXML() generates empty tags for fields with blank values, which is invalid XML for non-character fields. This bug is fixed in VFP 8.

Summary

The new XML classes make it possible to work with more types of XML, such as ADO.NET DataSets, than in earlier versions of VFP, and do more with the XML, including creating and consuming diffgrams. As a result, VFP 8 is even better equipped to work with .NET.

Updates and corrections to this chapter can be found on Hentzenwerke's web site, **www.hentzenwerke.com**. Click on "Catalog" and navigate to the page for this book.

Chapter 8
Other Data-Related Changes

The thing that sets VFP apart from every other Microsoft development tool is its built-in database engine. VFP 8 adds features to the engine developers have requested for years.

VFP 8 has more changes in the database engine than any release since 3.0. In earlier chapters, we looked at the new CursorAdapter base class and how it provides a consistent, easy-to-use interface to any data (VFP or otherwise), and at the new XML classes and how they greatly improve VFP's support for XML. In this chapter, we'll look at the rest of the changes in the database engine, including support for auto-incrementing fields, improvements in the Table Designer, changes in SQL, enhancements to data-related commands and functions, improvements in the OLE DB provider, and better use of ODBC resources through shared connections.

Automatically incrementing field values

VFP developers know good database design dictates a table should have a primary key, and the primary key shouldn't be based on anything about the other fields (in other words, it should be a meaningless primary key). Although there are a variety of ways to assign a unique, meaningless primary key, the most common one is to use a series of sequential values.

In some other database engines, such as SQL Server and Access, this is easy to do: you define the primary key field as auto-incrementing. (Auto-incrementing has a different name in each database system—for example, in SQL Server, it's called Identity and in Access, it's called AutoNumber.) This means the database engine has the responsibility of assigning the next available value to the field and ensuring records added simultaneously by different users shouldn't get the same value.

Unfortunately, until version 8, VFP didn't have auto-incrementing fields. The typical way a VFP developer assigned the next available value to the primary key field was by setting the DefaultValue property of the field to call a function (often located in the stored procedures of the database container). To prevent contention problems, the function usually incremented the next available value in a "next ID" table (after locking the record to ensure no one else could do the same thing at the same time) and returned the new value.

Now, assigning unique, meaningless values to primary key fields is a snap thanks to the addition of auto-incrementing fields in VFP 8. These types of fields are available in both free tables and those that are part of a DBC. However, turning this feature on means a table can't be opened in a previous version of VFP or with the VFP ODBC driver; attempting to do so raises error 15, "not a table."

You can define an auto-incrementing field either visually, using the Table Designer, or programmatically, using new clauses in the CREATE TABLE and ALTER TABLE commands. Let's look at how you do it in the Table Designer first.

Figure 1 shows that several changes were made in the Table Designer to support auto-incrementing fields (actually, there were a number of other changes as well; we'll get to those later). First, in the Type drop-down list, a new "Integer (AutoInc)" item appears. This isn't really a new data type (it's still an Integer field), but indicates VFP will automatically increment the values in the field as new records are added. Next, there's a new "AutoIncrement" properties section. Here, you can enter the next value to use for the field and the step value to increment the last used value by. The defaults for a new field are both 1, meaning the first value assigned to the field will be 1, the next value 2, the one after that 3, and so on.

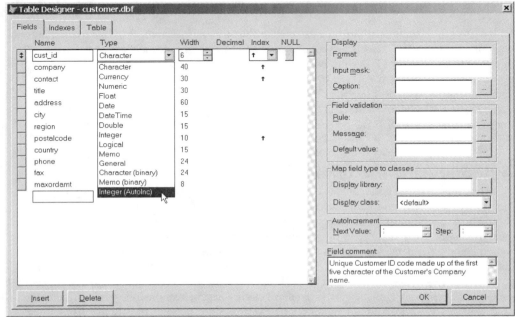

Figure 1. *You can define an auto-incrementing field in the Table Designer.*

Note that defining a field as auto-incrementing doesn't automatically make it a primary key field; you have to create a primary index on the field to do that. In fact, you can have as many auto-incrementing fields in a table as you wish.

To define a field as auto-incrementing programmatically, use the AUTOINC and optional NEXTVALUE and STEP clauses in a CREATE TABLE, ALTER TABLE, or CREATE CURSOR command. Here's an example that defines the ID field as an auto-incrementing primary key:

```
create table MyTable (ID I autoinc primary key, NAME C(40))
```

The next example shows how you might convert an existing table to use an auto-incrementing primary key. Notice it determines what the next available value for the field is and uses it in the NEXTVALUE clause. Also note that making this change automatically removes any existing DefaultValue property for the field, which in this case likely used to call a "next ID" function, because that property doesn't apply to auto-increment fields.

```
use SomeTable exclusive
calculate max(ID) to lnNextValue
alter table SomeTable alter column ID I autoinc nextvalue lnNextValue + 1
```

One important thing to note about auto-incrementing fields is they're read-only. That's perfectly reasonable, but does cause an issue that may break some of your existing code: when you add records to the table, you can't touch auto-incrementing fields. For example, the following code gives a "field ID is read-only" error (error number 1088) because VFP tries to update the ID field from the M.ID memory variable or the ID property of the loData object (we'll discuss the new INSERT ... FROM NAME syntax later in this chapter):

```
scatter memvar
insert into SomeTable from memvar
scatter name loData
insert into SomeTable from name loData
```

The APPEND FROM command is also a problem; you get the same error if the source table contains fields that match the names of auto-incrementing fields in the target table.

You can do one of three things to avoid this error. First, you can use the new SET AUTOINCERROR OFF command (the default is ON) to turn off this error for tables opened in the current data session after the command is used. Second, you can turn the error off for a single cursor using CURSORSETPROP('AutoIncError', .F.). In either of these two cases, VFP ignores any value being inserted into auto-incrementing fields and uses the next available value instead. Third, you can prevent VFP from touching these fields. Add a FIELDS clause to the APPEND FROM command listing all fields except auto-incrementing fields. RELEASE memory variables with the same name as auto-incrementing fields before using INSERT ... FROM MEMVAR. Use the new RemoveProperty() function (described in Chapter 9, "OOP Enhancements") to remove the appropriate properties from the object before using INSERT ... FROM NAME. Regardless of which approach you decide to take, it means examining and updating existing code using INSERT or APPEND FROM commands if you decide to implement auto-incrementing fields in existing applications.

In a similar vein, if you create a view based on a table with an auto-incrementing field, you must not mark the auto-incrementing field as updateable or you'll get an error when you insert new records in the view and those changes are written back to the table.

Here's another complication. Suppose you regularly import parent and child tables (say, orders and order details) from remote offices into the main office's tables using APPEND FROM, and you decide to use an auto-incrementing field as the primary key for the parent table. With AUTOINCERROR turned OFF, APPEND FROM ignores the values of the auto-incrementing fields in the source table and uses the next available values in the target table. As a result, the parent's key values change as they are imported, so the child's foreign key values no longer point to the correct records in the parent table. This is yet another reason to consider carefully all of the ramifications before you implement auto-incrementing fields.

One last issue; it's a little complicated to add an auto-incrementing field to a table with existing records in a single step. The reason is that doing so doesn't automatically populate the values for the new field for existing records. So, for tables in a DBC, add an auto-incrementing field this way:

```
alter table MyTable add column MyField I autoinc nextvalue reccount() + 1 ;
  default recno()
```

Because free tables don't have a DEFAULT property, you have to use a three-step operation: add the field as a regular Integer, populate values for the existing records, and then change the field to be auto-incrementing. Here's an example:

```
alter table MyTable add column MyField I
replace all MyField with recno()
alter table MyTable alter column MyField I autoinc nextvalue reccount() + 1
```

Microsoft updated several commands and functions to support this new feature. The AFIELDS() function now fills an array with 18 columns rather than 16. Column 17 contains the next available value and column 18 contains the step value. There isn't an explicit indication whether a field is auto-incrementing or not, but column 18 contains a non-zero value if it is. The table created by the COPY STRUCTURE EXTENDED command has two additional columns: FIELD_NEXT and FIELD_STEP that contain the next and step values, respectively. As with AFIELDS(), the step value is a non-zero value if the field is auto-incrementing. CREATE FROM, which uses a table created by COPY STRUCTURE EXTENDED to create a new table, creates auto-incrementing fields as necessary using the values in the FIELD_NEXT and FIELD_STEP columns. The COPY TO command preserves the auto-incrementing properties of the source table unless, of course, you specify a FIELDS clause that omits the auto-incrementing fields or if you specify the TYPE clause to output to something other than a VFP table.

A couple of commands are not affected by this new feature. The PACK command doesn't renumber values in auto-incrementing fields, so there may be gaps in the sequence of values where deleted records were removed. A cursor or table created by a SQL SELECT command, even if it's a view, doesn't inherit any auto-incrementing properties.

Microsoft made changes to the DBF file structure to support auto-incrementing fields. Byte 0 in the DBF header contains 0x31 rather than the usual 0x30 if there are any auto-incrementing fields in the table. Byte 18 of an auto-incrementing field's record in the header contains 0x0C, bytes 19 to 22 contain the next value (in least significant byte order), and byte 23 contains the step value. Putting this information into the DBF header rather than into the Properties memo of the database container means auto-incrementing fields can be supported in free tables as well as those in a database. However, as noted earlier, the consequence of this change is a table with auto-incrementing fields cannot be opened in an earlier version of VFP. That's reasonable, however, because doing so would allow someone to write to the auto-incrementing fields without getting an error.

Improved Table Designer

In addition to support for auto-incrementing fields, you may have noticed other changes in the Table Designer shown in Figure 1. The dialog is now larger and field properties appear to the right of the field list rather than below it; these two changes mean the Table Designer can now display up to 20 fields or indexes at one time versus just 6 fields or 16 indexes in VFP 7. An expression builder button now appears beside the Caption property, because in VFP 8, field captions can now contain expressions; see "Caption expressions" later in this chapter for more information. As shown in **Figure 2**, you can also now specify the collate sequence for each index.

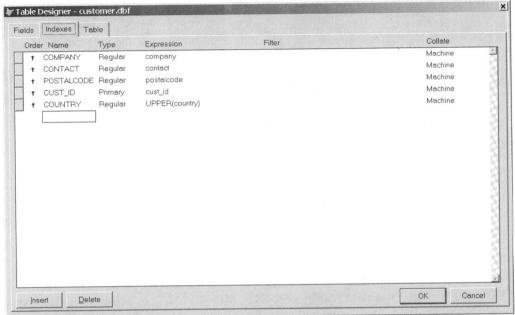

Figure 2. You can specify the collate sequence for each index in the Table Designer.

SQL changes

VFP has never been completely compliant with ANSI-92 SQL standards, partly because of VFP's special requirements and partly because Microsoft just missed some things when they implemented SQL. VFP 8 moves closer to ANSI-92, but like taking cough syrup, this is one of those things that, while you realize it's probably good for you, may leave a bad taste in your mouth for a while. This is because the changes Microsoft made are almost certain to break some code; in fact, some of VFP's own Xbase tools broke during the VFP 8 beta because of these changes. Before you panic, however, be aware that Microsoft was thinking ahead and provided a way for you to tell VFP to do things the old way if necessary.

The first change is you can no longer use the DISTINCT clause in a SQL SELECT statement that contains Memo, General, or Picture fields; attempting to do so causes error 34, "Operation is invalid for a Memo, General or Picture field". Here's an example of a command that worked in VFP 7, but no longer does in VFP 8:

```
select distinct City, Notes from Employee
```

The second change is somewhat similar to the first: you get the same error 34 if you use Memo, General, or Picture fields in a SELECT...UNION statement without including the ALL keyword.

The third change is the one likely to cause the most problems. You now get an error if you use a GROUP BY clause and have any non-aggregate fields in the query that don't appear in the GROUP BY. Here's an example that shows this error; in this case, the To_Name field is the culprit.

```
open database _samples + 'Data\TestData'
select Cust_ID, To_Name, sum(Order_Amt) from Orders group by 1
```

The reason this type of query is no longer legal is it doesn't really make sense to have non-aggregate fields that don't appear in the GROUP BY clause. Although it appears the query would produce meaningful results in this specific example, that's actually due to improper data design: the To_Name field doesn't vary with the Cust_ID field in the sample Orders table that comes with VFP. However, change this query to use the Emp_ID field instead, and what value should VFP retrieve for Emp_ID for each Cust_ID? The value from the first record or from the last one? (In fact, VFP picks the value from the last record.) In most cases, the values in the result set for the non-aggregate fields are meaningless.

This change affects the HAVING clause as well. Here are the rules regarding these clauses:

- If there's a GROUP BY clause, every column in the select list must either be part of an aggregate function (AVG(), COUNT(), MIN(), MAX(), or SUM()) or listed in the GROUP BY clause. Only the second of the following two statements is legal:

  ```
  select Cust_ID, Order_Date from Orders group by Cust_ID
  select Cust_ID, max(Order_Date) from Orders group by Cust_ID
  ```

- If there's an aggregate function in the select list, every column that isn't part of an aggregate function must appear in the GROUP BY clause. While this sounds like it just restates the previous rule, in fact it requires that if you have a mix of columns and aggregate functions, you must have a GROUP BY clause. The first of the following statements breaks this rule and will therefore cause an error:

  ```
  select Cust_ID, max(Order_Date) from Orders
  select Cust_ID, max(Order_Date) from Orders group by Cust_ID
  ```

- If HAVING is used without GROUP BY, the select list must not contain any aggregate functions. For example, the first of the following statements is legal while the second is not:

  ```
  select Company from Customer having Country = 'Brazil'
  select Company, count(*) from Customer having Country = 'Brazil'
  ```

The message for error 1807 changed to "SQL: GROUP BY clause is missing or invalid" ("missing or" was added) to reflect the problem if no GROUP BY is specified when one is now required.

The final change in behavior involves the "_" wildcard. This wildcard character, used with the LIKE operator, matches a single character. Earlier versions of VFP did not consider a trailing space to be a valid match, while VFP 8 does. The following code returns different result sets in VFP 7 and VFP 8:

```
open database _samples + 'Data\TestData'
select * from Employee where Title like 'Sales _____%'
```

VFP 8 contains one additional record—"Sales Manager"—because the space following this title is a valid match for the eighth wildcard character.

If you have existing code that will break because of any of these changes, be sure to use the new SYS(3099) function or SET ENGINEBEHAVIOR command. SYS(3099, 70) or SET ENGINEBEHAVIOR 70 tell VFP to use version 7 behavior while SYS(3099, 80) or SET ENGINEBEHAVIOR 80 (the default settings) use the new behavior. SYS(3099) with no value specified or SET('ENGINEBEHAVIOR') return the current setting. You can use SET ENGINEBEHAVIOR in CONFIG.FPW to set the default preference at startup.

A couple of changes that *won't* cause any controversy are implicit data conversion for the SELECT...UNION command and support for a SELECT clause in the INSERT command.

Working with the UNION clause has sometimes been a little tricky—it is quite strict about the two SELECT statements being UNIONed having identical structures, both in terms of data types and column widths. That often meant doing explicit data type and width conversions in the SELECT statement. In VFP 8, implicit data conversion means VFP automatically converts data types and column widths for you where possible. For example, suppose you want to combine sales figures from two different systems into one cursor. If SALES1.DBF is defined as COMPANY C(40), SALES N(10) and SALES2.DBF as COMPANY C(35), SALES I, the following statement fails in VFP 7 with error 1851, "SELECTs are not UNION compatible", while in VFP 8 it gives the desired results:

```
select * from Sales1 union select * from Sales2
```

 *An expanded version of this example that creates the two tables is included as ImplicitConversion.PRG with the Developer Download files for this chapter, available at **www.hentzenwerke.com**. It also shows the use of the ALL keyword when Memo fields are included.*

The final SQL change is you can now specify a SELECT clause to provide the values in an INSERT statement. Here's the syntax for that form of the command:

```
insert into TableName [ ( FieldName1 [, FieldName2 ... ] ) ] ;
  select FieldName1 [, FieldName2 ... ] from TableName2 ;
  [ additional SQL clauses ]
```

The SELECT clause can be any valid SQL SELECT statement except it cannot contain any non-SQL clauses, such as INTO, TO, and so forth.

This new form of INSERT is useful when you want to put some values from one table into another and can't or don't want to use APPEND FROM. For example, if you want to put summarized sales information into a table (such as for data mining purposes), you can use code similar to:

```
close databases all
open database _samples + 'Data\Testdata'
create table SalesHistory free (Month I, Year I, Cust_ID C(6), ;
   Product_ID C(6), Sales Y)
do UpdateHistory with 1994
do UpdateHistory with 1995
do UpdateHistory with 1996
select SalesHistory
browse

function UpdateHistory(tnYear)
insert into SalesHistory ;
   select month(Orders.Order_Date), year(Orders.Order_Date), Orders.Cust_ID, ;
      OrdItems.Product_ID, sum(OrdItems.Unit_Price * OrdItems.Quantity) ;
      from Orders join OrdItems on Orders.Order_ID = OrdItems.Order_ID ;
      where year(Orders.Order_Date) = tnYear ;
      group by 1, 2, 3, 4
```

 The Developer Download files for this chapter, available at ***www.hentzenwerke.com***, *include this code as InsertSelect.PRG.*

Enhanced language elements

VFP 8 has improvements in several commands and functions related to data. These enhancements include support for expressions in field captions, better use of objects in SCATTER, GATHER, and INSERT, and easier ways to create indexes using non-default collate sequences.

Caption expressions

The caption stored in a database container for a field can now be an expression. This is useful for a variety of situations, such as when you allow users to specify the caption for certain fields (for example, in a project management application, some users may prefer to call projects "jobs") or when your application must display captions in the language specified by the user. To specify that the caption is an expression rather than a literal string, use an "=" for the first character, either in the Table Designer or using the DBSETPROP() function.

You can retrieve the caption using the FIELD() function. The new syntax for this function is:

```
cValue = field( nFieldNumber | cFieldName [, nWorkArea | cAlias [, nFlags ]] )
```

Note a couple of changes here. First, there's a new nFlags parameter: pass 1 to retrieve the caption for the field (for free tables or if the field's caption is empty, FIELD() returns the field name in lowercase), or omit it or pass 0 to get the field name in uppercase, which is the behavior of earlier versions. If the caption is an expression, the expression is evaluated and the result is returned; an error is raised if the expression can't be evaluated. This is a benefit over using DBGETPROP() to retrieve the caption, because that function doesn't evaluate expressions. The second change is the function can now accept a field name instead of a field number. Obviously, this is only useful if you pass 1 for the nFlags parameter.

Here's an example that shows how this function and caption expressions work. FIELD2 uses an expression for its caption; notice FIELD() returns the desired caption while DBGETPROP() returns the unevaluated expression. Comment out the first line, uncomment the second one, and then run the code again to see a different result.

```
gcLanguage = 'English'
*gcLanguage = 'Pig Latin'
close databases all
create database Test
create table TestTable (Field1 C(10), Field2 C(10))
dbsetprop('TestTable.Field1', 'Field', 'Caption', 'My Field Caption')
dbsetprop('TestTable.Field2', 'Field', 'Caption', ;
  "=GetCaption('TestTable.Field2')")
? 'The caption for Field1 is ' + field(1, alias(), 1)
? 'The caption for Field2 is ' + field('Field2', alias(), 1)
? 'The caption for Field2 is ' + dbgetprop('TestTable.Field2', 'Field', ;
  'Caption')
close databases all
erase Test*.*

function GetCaption(tcFieldName)
* Return the caption for the field based on the current language
* In reality, this function would look up the field and language in a table and
* return the caption stored there.
local lcReturn
do case
  case gcLanguage = 'English'
    lcReturn = 'Some Field Caption'
  case gcLanguage = 'Pig Latin'
    lcReturn = 'Omesay Ieldfay Aptioncay'
endcase
return lcReturn
```

 The Developer Download files for this chapter, available at **www.hentzenwerke.com**, *include this code in FieldGivesCaption.PRG.*

In addition to using field caption expressions programmatically, the Form Designer automatically uses them when you drag and drop a field onto a form. The label created for a field has =FIELD(cFieldName, cAlias, 1) for its Caption property. The Report Designer can also use caption expressions if you turn on the Use DBC field captions setting on the Reports page of the Tools | Options dialog (See Chapter 5, "Better Tools", for a description of the other options in this page.) If a field uses an expression for its caption, the Report Designer creates a field object rather than a text object for the label, with FIELD(cFieldName, cAlias, 1) as the field expression.

Data objects

VFP 3 introduced the NAME clause in the SCATTER and GATHER commands. When used with SCATTER, this very useful clause creates an object that has properties matching the names of the fields in the table being scattered from, with each property holding the value of the associated field in the current record. GATHER does the opposite: it replaces the values of the fields in the current record with the values of the properties in the specified object. Many developers use this extensively, because an object is easily passed from one place to another, even to non-VFP applications such as Excel or Word.

However, almost immediately after its introduction, VFP developers wanted more. The first common complaint was you couldn't use an existing object or specify which class to use; SCATTER always creates a new "empty" object (one with no properties other than the ones matching the field names and no events or methods). That means the object can contain data only and not have any behavior. The second complaint was while you can use the object to update an existing record with a single statement (GATHER), it takes two statements to create new record (APPEND BLANK followed by GATHER).

Both of these issues are dealt with in VFP 8. First, the SCATTER command now sports a new ADDITIVE keyword. If this keyword is specified and an object with the name specified in the NAME clause already exists, VFP doesn't create a new object but instead uses the existing one, adding new properties as necessary. This is a tremendous improvement, because now these data objects can be based on other classes and have behavior, such as data validation. Second, the INSERT command now supports the FROM NAME clause, so you can insert a new record using the values from the specified object in a single command.

Here's an example that mimics an n-tier application design. The main routine instantiates a DataManager object and calls its NewCustomer method to return an empty Customer object. It then puts values in the properties of the Customer object, displaying any error that may occur (in fact, an error will occur here because the MaxOrdAmt value isn't the correct data type). Finally, it calls the SaveCustomer method to save the Customer object. The NewCustomer method of the DataManager object instantiates a Customer object that has the behavior we desire (in this simple example, an assign method in the Customer class ensures the MaxOrdAmt value is Currency) and uses SCATTER BLANK NAME ADDITIVE to properly set up the new object as a container for the data values for the Customer table. The SaveCustomer method saves the data in the passed object into the Customer table, either using GATHER or INSERT, depending on whether the customer ID already exists or not. Although the code here is all in one PRG, the DataManager object could easily be a COM component that can be used by any application, such as Excel or a Web page, to serve up VFP data as objects.

```
close databases all
loManager = createobject('DataManager')
loData = loManager.NewCustomer()
try
  loData.Cust_ID   = 'XXXXX'
  loData.Company   = 'New Customer'
  loData.MaxOrdAmt = 'Test'
catch to loException
  wait window 'Error updating data: ' + loException.UserValue
endtry
loManager.SaveCustomer(loData)

define class DataManager as Session
  function Init
    open database _samples + 'Data\TestData'
```

```
   endfunc

   function Destroy
* DELETE and PACK only used in this demo so we can clean up on exit
      delete
      pack
      close databases all
   endfunc

   function NewCustomer
      if used('Customer')
         select Customer
      else
         select 0
* EXCLUSIVE only used in this demo so we can clean up on exit
         use Customer exclusive
      endif
      loData = createobject('Customer')
      scatter name loData blank additive
      return loData
   endfunc

   function SaveCustomer(toData)
      select Customer
      if seek(toData.Cust_ID, 'Customer', 'Cust_ID')
        gather name toData
      else
         insert into Customer from name loData
      endif
* BROWSE only used in this demo so we can see results
      browse
   endfunc
enddefine

define class Customer as Custom
  MaxOrdAmt = $0
  procedure MaxOrdAmt_Assign(tuValue)
     if vartype(tuValue) = 'Y'
        This.MaxOrdAmt = tuValue
     else
        throw 'MaxOrdAmt can only contain currency values'
     endif
  endproc
enddefine
```

 *DataObjectWithBehavior.PRG, available with the Developer Download files at **www.hentzenwerke.com**, has the code for this example.*

Better support for collate sequences

FoxPro has had support for languages other than English since the 2.x days. However, until version 8, creating indexes using a collate sequence other than the default MACHINE required extra code: saving the current SET COLLATE setting, changing it to the desired value, creating the index, then restoring the former setting. The addition of the COLLATE clause to the CREATE TABLE, ALTER TABLE, and INDEX commands reduces this to a single step.

Here are some examples that show the use of this clause (this code expects a database is already open and a table called TypesTable exists):

```
create table MyTable (ID I primary key collate 'GENERAL', NAME C(40), TYPE I)
index on NAME tag NAME collate 'GENERAL'
alter table MyTable add foreign key TYPE tag TYPE collate 'GENERAL' ;
  references TypesTable
```

As with the SET COLLATE command, if the specified collate sequence isn't valid, you'll get error 1915, "collate sequence is not found."

Odds and ends

There are a few more data-related language improvements, including fixes to a long-standing problem exporting to Excel and changing the direction of an index.

The SET DATABASE command now accepts an empty string (that is, SET DATABASE TO ""), which has the same effect as SET DATABASE TO with no database specified: no database is selected. In earlier versions, this gave a "Database '' is not open" error. That made it more complicated to write generic code that saved the current database, opened or selected a different one, did something, and then restored the former database upon exit. Such code had to specifically handle the case where no database was initially selected to avoid the error upon trying to restore the database at the end.

A long-overdue change in the COPY TO and EXPORT commands is they now export up to 65,535 rows to Excel. Earlier versions only output a maximum of 16,384 records.

Before VFP 8, if a table was open more than once (for example, with USE AGAIN and a different alias or in different data sessions), and the direction of an index was set with the ASCENDING or DESCENDING keyword in USE or SET ORDER commands, all open instances of the table used that direction for the index. This "last one wins" situation could cause problems; suddenly, a form that was open would access data in the opposite order just because something else changed the direction. VFP 8 now works the way you'd expect: the direction of an index isn't dependent on other open copies of the table.

Finally, TABLEUPDATE() now always returns True if the BatchUpdateCount property for a cursor, which specifies the number of update statements sent to the remote data source at one time, is more than 1. According to the Help, this is because VFP can't detect a conflict occurred when an update fails due to no row matching the WHERE clause VFP generated for the update. This could happen if another user changed one of the underlying values matching the WHERE clause.

OLE DB provider changes

The OLE DB provider for VFP, first available with VFP 7, received a few improvements.

- The OLE DB provider is more compatible with .NET. In particular, it now works with the ADO.NET CommandBuilder class, which determines information about an ADO data source and uses that information to build SQL statements for updating purposes. The Visual Studio.NET visual design tools still don't work properly with the VFP provider, but this is actually a VS.NET problem, not a VFP problem. Microsoft has plans to fix this in a future release of VS.NET.

- If your stored procedures are bumping into VFP's default limit of memory variables (which is unlikely, considering it has been increased in VFP 8 to 16,384 from 1,024), you can now place a CONFIG.FPW file into the OLE DB provider's directory (by default, C:\Program Files\Common Files\System\OLE DB) with an MVCOUNT= line in it to increase the number of variables allowed.

- You can now specify a VFP ODBC data source name (DSN) instead of a data source directory in the connection string. When you open the connection, the OLE DB provider gets the data source directory to use from the DSN and puts it into the connection string. Here's an example:

```
loConn = createobject('ADODB.Connection')
loConn.ConnectionString = 'provider=vfpoledb;dsn=My VFP DSN'
```

- The GETENV() function is no longer supported.

- This seems odd to us: you can no longer determine the setting of ANSI using SET('ANSI') but you can set it using SET ANSI.

Microsoft also changed the distribution policy for the OLE DB provider. Instead of having to buy Visual FoxPro just to obtain the provider, you can now download it from the MSDN Web site.

ODBC changes

VFP 8 makes better use of ODBC resources than before. In earlier versions, every time you use SQLCONNECT() or SQLSTRINGCONNECT() to connect to an ODBC data source, VFP opens a new connection to the database engine. Connections are expensive resources: they are time-consuming to open, take up resources on both the workstation and server, and may be limited by the number of licenses available for the database engine. In VFP 8, you can declare a connection as shared.

ODBC-related functions in previous versions of VFP use connection handles. For example, the return value of SQLCONNECT() and SQLDISCONNECT() is a connection handle, which you can then use in a SQLEXEC() statement. In VFP 8, rather than connection handles, statement handles are used instead. A statement handle is like a child of a connection handle—every connection handle, which indicates a unique connection to a database engine, can have multiple statement handles associated with it, but every statement handle has a single connection handle associated with it. Think of an ODBC connection as analogous to a shared Internet connection in an office. Each workstation in the office can connect to a Web site (a statement handle) but there's only one actual connection to the Internet for the whole office (a connection handle). Obviously, the more people that try to do things on the Internet over the shared connection, the slower results are returned, but it provides a great way to share an expensive resource.

There are several changes in existing functions to implement this. First, all functions either return or accept a statement handle rather than a connection handle. Don't worry—this won't affect any of your code because the handles returned by these functions were always internal VFP handles rather than true ODBC handles anyway. In other words, this is really an internal change rather than one that affects us. Second, the SQLSTRINGCONNECT() function accepts a new parameter to indicate whether the connection should be shareable:

```
nHandle = sqlstringconnect( [ lShared ] | [ cConnectionString [, lShared ] ] )
```

If lShared is True, SQLSTRINGCONNECT() creates a new connection and returns a new statement handle for that connection, but flags the connection as being shareable.

The next change is SQLCONNECT() can also create a new shared connection if you pass True for the lShared parameter, and can also create a new statement handle for an existing connection if you pass the statement handle for an existing shared connection. Here's the new syntax:

```
nHandle = sqlconnect( [ lShared ] )
```

or

```
nHandle = sqlconnect( nHandle )
```

or

```
nHandle = sqlconnect( cConnectionName | cDataSourceName [, cUserID [, cPassword
    [, lShared ] ] ] )
```

This looks confusing, so let's break it down:

- You can pass nothing, False, or True (the first syntax) to get a "Select Connection or Data Source" dialog. Passing True results in a connection that's shareable.

- You can pass an existing statement handle to create a new statement handle on the same shared connection (the second syntax).

- You can pass either the name of a Connection object defined in a database container or an ODBC DSN to create a new ODBC connection using the third syntax. In either case, you can optionally pass a user name and password; this was previously not documented in the case of a Connection object. Pass True for the lShared parameter to make the connection shareable. Note that if you specify a Connection object and lShared is True, and the connection is already open in shared mode, the user name and password must be the same as those previously used or you'll get a "Connection is busy" error.

Finally, the CONNSTRING clause in the USE command can now accept either a connection string (as it can in VFP 7) or a statement handle. This means your remote views can now share connections with SQL Pass-Through (SPT) functions like SQLEXEC().

Here's an example that demonstrates the changes in SQLSTRINGCONNECT() and SQLCONNECT() and shows how shared connections work. It displays the VFP statement handle, the real ODBC connection handle, and the real ODBC statement handle for several "connections."

```
close databases all
create database Remote
create connection NWConnection connstring 'driver=SQL Server;' + ;
  'server=(local);uid=sa;pwd=;database=Northwind'
create sql view NWCustomers remote connection NWConnection share as ;
  select * from Customers
create sql view NWOrders remote connection NWConnection share as ;
  select * from Orders

* Create a shareable ODBC connection, and then another one it's shared with.

lnHandle1 = sqlstringconnect('dsn=Northwind;uid=sa;pwd=;' + ;
  'trusted_connection=no', .T.)
lnHandle2 = sqlconnect(lnHandle1)

* Create a shareable connection from the DBC Connection object.

open database Remote
lnHandle3 = sqlconnect('NWConnection', .T.)

* Open the remote views; they should share the connection with lnHandle3.

use NWCustomers
use NWOrders in 0

* Display connection information.

clear
ShowConnection(lnHandle1)
ShowConnection(lnHandle2)
ShowConnection(lnHandle3)
ShowConnection(cursorgetprop('ConnectHandle', 'NWCustomers'))
ShowConnection(cursorgetprop('ConnectHandle', 'NWOrders'))
close databases all
erase Remote.d*
sqldisconnect(0)

function ShowConnection(tnHandle)
? 'VFP handle=' + transform(tnHandle) + ;
  ' ODBC connection=' + transform(sqlgetprop(tnHandle, 'ODBChdbc')) + ;
  ' ODBC statement=' + transform(sqlgetprop(tnHandle, 'ODBChstmt'))
```

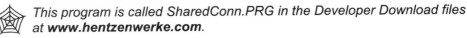 *This program is called SharedConn.PRG in the Developer Download files at **www.hentzenwerke.com**.*

We show the following results (the actual values will differ on your system but the pattern should be the same):

```
VFP handle=1 ODBC connection=104545824 ODBC statement=104548616
VFP handle=2 ODBC connection=104545824 ODBC statement=104542648
VFP handle=3 ODBC connection=104542136 ODBC statement=104549824
VFP handle=4 ODBC connection=104542136 ODBC statement=104539896
VFP handle=5 ODBC connection=104542136 ODBC statement=104547480
```

Note that while every connection has a different VFP statement handle and ODBC statement handle, the first two have the same connection handle, as do the last three. Thus, although it appears we have five connections to SQL Server, SQL Server only sees two connections.

With shared connections, it's possible for one query to block another using the same shared connection. For example, if you run the following code, you'll get a "Connection is busy with results for another hstmt" error for the first SQLEXEC() statement. (Now that's an error message we'll avoid showing to our users!) This is because it shares the same connection as the NWCustomers remote view, the FetchAsNeeded property of the remote view is True, and not all records for the view have been returned yet. By default, VFP doesn't allow another process to simultaneously retrieve data over the same connection. However, if you set the new AllowSimultaneousFetch property for the view, either permanently using DBSETPROP() or for the current instance using CURSORSETPROP(), VFP allows this. So, the second SQLEXEC() succeeds in this example.

```
close databases all
create database Remote
create connection NWConnection connstring 'driver=SQL Server;' + ;
  'server=(local);uid=sa;pwd=;database=Northwind'
create sql view NWCustomers remote connection NWConnection share as ;
  select * from Customers
dbsetprop('NWCustomers', 'View', 'FetchAsNeeded', .T.)
dbsetprop('NWCustomers', 'View', 'FetchSize',      10)

* Open the NWCustomers view, then open a shared connection and try to get
* records from the connection. If it failed, show the error message.

use NWCustomers
lnHandle = sqlconnect('NWConnection', .T.)
lnResult = sqlexec(lnHandle, 'select * from Employees')
if lnResult < 0
  aerror(laError)
  messagebox(laError[2])
endif
sqldisconnect(lnHandle)
use in NWCustomers

* Now set the AllowSimultaneousFetch property to .T. and try again.

dbsetprop('NWCustomers', 'View', 'AllowSimultaneousFetch', .T.)
use NWCustomers
lnHandle = sqlconnect('NWConnection', .T.)
lnResult = sqlexec(lnHandle, 'select * from Employees')
if lnResult < 0
  aerror(laError)
  messagebox(laError[2])
endif
sqldisconnect(lnHandle)
close databases all
erase Remote.dbc
```

 *This code is available by downloading SimultaneousFetch.PRG from the Developer Download files at **www.hentzenwerke.com**.*

One last ODBC-related change: SQLEXEC() now evaluates expressions used as parameter values before passing them to ODBC. To indicate you want an expression evaluated, surround it with parentheses. In earlier versions, you had to evaluate an expression yourself, store it in a variable, and use the variable in the SQLEXEC() statement. For example, in the following code, SQLEXEC() calls the GetCustomer function and passes the result as the parameter value for the SQL SELECT statement.

```
lnHandle = sqlstringconnect('dsn=Northwind;uid=sa;pwd=;' + ;
  'trusted_connection=no')
sqlexec(lnHandle, 'select * from Customers where CustomerID=?(GetCustomer())')
browse

function GetCustomer
return inputbox('Customer ID', 'Select Customer', 'ALFKI')
```

This code is available in the Developer Download files at **www.hentzenwerke.com** *by downloading SQLExecExpression.PRG.*

Detecting table corruption

Earlier versions of VFP have a very serious bug: if a table header is slightly corrupted in that the record count in the header doesn't match the actual number of records in the table, VFP doesn't give an error opening the table but loses records as new ones are added.

VFP 8 doesn't fix a table with this problem, but does prevent data from being lost. When it opens a table, VFP checks that the record count is correct and if not, raises error 2091, "Table 'tablename' has become corrupted. The table will need to be repaired before using again." Most table repair utilities, including free ones available from places such as the Universal Thread (**http://www.universalthread.com**), will fix this problem.

VFP locks the DBF header while this record count check is performed, so there may be an impact on performance or scalability in some environments. Microsoft added a new SET TABLEVALIDATE command that controls how checking is done. The syntax for this command is:

```
set tablevalidate to [ nLevel ]
```

The values for nLevel are shown in **Table 1**. Omitting the value is the same as specifying 3.

Table 1. *The values specified in the SET TABLEVALIDATE command specify how record count validation is performed.*

Value	Description
0	No table validation.
1	The record count is checked when the table is opened.
2	The record count is checked when records are added and written to disk.
3	Both types of validation is performed (the default).

A related change prevents files from becoming corrupted when they grow too large. FoxPro has always had (and will almost certainly always have) a limitation of 2 GB on a file's size. In earlier versions, when a change (addition or edit) caused the DBF or FPT files to become more than 2 GB in size, the table or memo became corrupted, and it was very difficult to repair this corruption. In VFP 8, this situation causes a new error, error 1190, to occur, and the changes are not written to disk.

Other changes

In addition to the changes already discussed, there are a just a few other data-related changes in VFP 8.

GENDBC.PRG has been updated to handle new data features. This utility, located in the TOOLS\GENDBC subdirectory of the VFP home directory, creates a PRG that can regenerate a database container and its tables and views (although not the contents of the tables). In VFP 8, it now supports auto-incrementing fields and filtered primary keys (support for filtering on primary keys was actually added in VFP 6, but this is the first update to GENDBC in a while), and uses INDEX ON … COLLATE and ALTER TABLE … COLLATE rather than SET COLLATE TO statements.

The Referential Integrity (RI) Builder is also updated. It no longer requires the database container be packed before running the builder, you're now only prompted once rather than twice when you click on the OK button, and saving existing stored procedure code to a file called RISP.OLD before generating new code is now optional. More importantly, however, a couple of nasty bugs are fixed. One bug, in the generated stored procedures, could cause orphaned child and grandchild records in the case of a delete trigger with an update rule from parent to child and a restrict rule from child to grandchild. (For details on this bug, see the "Error Handling in Visual FoxPro" and "Building and Using VFP Developer Tools" white papers, available from the Technical Papers page of **http://www.stonefield.com**.) The second bug resulted in an invalid trigger expression when you used the RI Builder and a table already had a trigger that referenced some function which was ANDed or ORed with the appropriate RI function. For example, if the delete trigger for a table was MyProc() AND __RI_DELETE_Customers(), earlier versions of the RI Builder mangled this to __RI_DELETE_Customers() AND (MyProc() AND), which is invalid.

VFP 7 Service Pack 1 introduced a bug causing the size of CDX files to be double the size they had been in earlier versions. Since portions of the CDX file are transferred from the server over the network to the workstation and are cached in memory on the workstation, this obviously could cause performance problems. In VFP 8, CDX files are now the proper size.

Because of the new AllowSimultaneousFetch property for views (discussed in the "ODBC changes" section earlier in this chapter), using VALIDATE DATABASE in earlier versions of VFP results in "Bad property types or lengths" errors for any views created in VFP 8 or that have this property set with DBSETPROP().

One last change: opening and closing offline views within a transaction is now prohibited.

Summary

VFP 8's list of enhancements to the database engine is so extensive it took three chapters to cover. These changes make VFP developers more productive, improve reliability, and make VFP a better player in the database sandbox.

Updates and corrections to this chapter can be found on Hentzenwerke's web site, **www.hentzenwerke.com**. Click on "Catalog" and navigate to the page for this book.

Chapter 9
OOP Enhancements

Visual FoxPro 8 introduces a variety of enhancements to the object-oriented portion of the language. Two key changes are the ability to specify the class to use within a number of container objects, and a new base class for collections. Many controls sport new properties as well.

VFP's OOP sub-language is one of the main things distinguishing it from earlier FoxPro versions. Each new version of VFP enhanced this part of the language, adding new classes, new properties, new events, and new methods. VFP 8 is no exception. It offers a variety of changes, some major, some minor. Quite a few changes are aimed at making user interfaces built with VFP more attractive and easier to use.

Defining member classes

VFP has two types of container classes: those that can hold a variety of objects (such as forms and pages) and those that can hold only a specific object type (such as option groups and grids). Working with the more general containers has always been fairly simple—you could subclass them visually and add whatever controls you wanted. The specific containers, though, have been limited to containing only members of the appropriate base class. While you can replace the members programmatically at run-time, working with these objects in the Class Designer and Form Designer is difficult.

VFP 8 changes all that. Each of the specific container classes now has a pair of properties that let you specify the class to use for its members. For example, you can indicate a page subclass to use in a page frame and an option button subclass to use in an option group. **Table 1** lists the classes affected and the names of the relevant properties.

Table 1. Specifying member classes. Each of the container classes that requires a specific type of member has properties to let you indicate what subclass to use.

Container class	Member type	Member class properties
CommandGroup	CommandButton	MemberClass, MemberClassLibrary
Form	DataEnvironment	DEClass, DEClassLibrary
Column	Header	HeaderClass, HeaderClassLibrary
Grid	Column	MemberClass, MemberClassLibrary
OptionGroup	OptionButton	MemberClass, MemberClassLibrary
PageFrame	Page	MemberClass, MemberClassLibrary

The DEClass and DEClassLibrary properties are discussed in Chapter 6, "Improved Data Access." We'll look at the rest of this group here.

In each case, you can set these properties at design time or at run time. When you set them at design time, all the member objects of the container are replaced with members based on the specified class. (You're warned that you'll lose any PEMs you've already set.)

At run time, the behavior is different. In that case, existing members are left alone and only new members are based on the currently specified class. This means, at run time, you can actually create containers where each member is based on a different class.

Along with the ability to specify the member class, each of the members, except for columns and headers, can now be subclassed in the Class Designer. So you can, for example, create a Page subclass, and then create a page frame with your page subclass specified via MemberClass and MemberClassLibrary.

For columns and headers, you're still restricted to a PRG-based class. However, you can still specify your column or header class at design time.

The Solutions Samples that come with VFP include an example that demonstrates both the design time and run time behavior of these properties. Look for the "Member Class" example in the "New to Visual FoxPro 8.0" category.

New base classes

VFP 8 includes quite a few new base classes. Most of them are discussed in other parts of the book. (See Chapter 6, "Improved Data Access" for CursorAdapter, Chapter 7, "XML Classes" for XMLAdapter, XMLTable and XMLField, and Chapter 12, "Error Handling" for Exception.) However, two of the new classes are really designed for object-oriented programming: Collection and Empty.

A built-in collection class

Collections are widely used in object-oriented programming. A collection is much like an array; it holds references to a group of items, usually items of the same sort. Most often, the items are objects. VFP has a number of native collections such as Pages and Forms, as well as several COM collections like Projects and Files. The object models for the Office products are loaded with collections. For example, Word includes Documents, Tables, and Paragraphs collections, while Excel includes Workbooks, Worksheets, and Cells collections. Until VFP 8, there was no direct way to create collections in VFP (although several people designed very credible simulations using the tools at hand.)

The new Collection base class allows you to create and use collections in your applications without having to resort to any tricks. **Table 2** and **Table 3** show its significant properties and methods, respectively.

Table 2. Collection properties. The new Collection base class has only a few collection-specific properties.

Property	Purpose
Count	The number of items currently in the collection.
KeySort	Determines whether FOR EACH goes through the collection in index order or in key order, and ascending or descending.

Table 3. Collection methods. Most of the real action for collections is in the methods. The Item method can be treated much like an array property.

Method	Parameters	Purpose
Add	eItem [, cKey] [, eBeforeItem | , eAfterItem]	Add eItem to the collection with optional key cKey. eBeforeItem and eAfterItem determine the position of the item in the collection.
GetKey	eIndex	Return the key of the item with index eIndex or the index of the item with key eIndex.
Item	eIndex	Return the item with index or key eIndex.
Remove	eIndex	Remove the item with index or key eIndex.

A collection is composed of items. Each item in a collection has a value (whatever you assign it) and an index based on its position in the list (beginning with 1 for the first item). You can also assign each item in the collection a character key to identify it. The value of an item can be any of the types supported for variables in VFP, including a reference to another object.

The Count property always tells you how many items are in the collection. It's read-only and is managed by the collection itself.

To put an item into a collection, you call the collection's Add method, passing the value for the item and, optionally, a character key. You can specify the position of the new item in the collection by passing either the index or the key for another item. The interpretation of this index or key depends on whether you pass it as the third or the fourth parameter. If you pass the index or key as the third parameter, the new item is placed before the specified item; if you pass the index or key as the fourth parameter (omitting the third), the new item is placed after the specified item. Be aware that keys are case-sensitive.

This example creates a collection and adds a list of names to it, without specifying keys. The last name added is placed between the second and third items.

```
oNames=CREATEOBJECT("Collection")
WITH oNames
    .Add("Lucy")
    .Add("Ricky")
    .Add("Fred")
    .Add("Ethel")
    .Add("Little Ricky",,3)
ENDWITH
```

This example creates a collection of US states. A State class is used for each, and each is assigned its abbreviation as a key. (A few lines of the data file, statedata.txt, are also shown here.)

```
LOCAL oStates as States

oStates = CREATEOBJECT("States")
oStates.LoadStates("statedata.txt")

* Manipulate the collection here
```

```
RETURN

DEFINE CLASS State AS Custom

StateName = ""
Abbreviation = ""
OrderJoined = 0
Population = 0

PROCEDURE Init( tcName, tcAbbrev, tnOrder, tnPopulation )

WITH This
   .StateName = EVL(tcName,"")
   .Abbreviation = EVL(tcAbbrev,"")
   .OrderJoined = EVL(tnOrder,0)
   .Population = EVL(tnPopulation,0)
ENDWITH
ENDPROC

ENDDEFINE

DEFINE CLASS States AS Collection

PROCEDURE LoadStates( cDataFile as Character)
* Populate the collection by reading the data
* from a specified file

LOCAL cData, aStateInfo[1], nStateCount
LOCAL aOneState[1], nItemCount, oState, oException

TRY
   cData = FILETOSTR( cDataFile )
   nStateCount = ALINES(aStateInfo,cData)
   FOR nState = 1 TO nStateCount
      nItemCount = ALINES(aOneState, aStateInfo[ nState ], ",")
      cState = EVALUATE(aOneState[1])
      IF NOT EMPTY(aOneState[2])
         cAbbrev = EVALUATE(aOneState[2])
      ELSE
         cAbbrev = ""
      ENDIF
      IF NOT EMPTY(aOneState[3])
         nOrder = EVALUATE(aOneState[3])
      ELSE
         nOrder = 0
      ENDIF
      IF NOT EMPTY(aOneState[4])
         nPopulation = aOneState[4]
      ELSE
         nPopulation = 0
      ENDIF

      oState = CREATEOBJECT("State", cState, cAbbrev, ;
                            nOrder, nPopulation )
      This.Add(oState, oState.Abbreviation)
   ENDFOR

CATCH TO oException
   MESSAGEBOX("Problem reading data from " + ;
```

```
                cDataFile + CHR(13) + ;
                oException.Message + " on line " + ;
                TRANSFORM(oException.LineNo))
ENDTRY

RETURN This.Count
ENDPROC


PROCEDURE SaveStates( cDataFile as Character)
* Save the state info to a comma-delimited file

LOCAL oState, lReturn, oException as Exception

TRY
    lReturn = .T.
    CREATE CURSOR StateInfo (cName C(30), cAbbrev C(2), ;
                            nRank N(2), nPopulation N(9))

    FOR EACH oState IN This
        WITH oState
            INSERT INTO StateInfo VALUES ;
                (.StateName, .Abbreviation, .OrderJoined, .Population)
        ENDWITH
    ENDFOR

    COPY TO (cDataFile) TYPE DELIMITED
    USE IN StateInfo

CATCH TO oException
    MESSAGEBOX("Problem writing state data to " + ;
                cDataFile + CHR(13) + ;
                oException.Message + " on line " + ;
                TRANSFORM(oException.LineNo))

    lReturn = .F.
ENDTRY

RETURN
ENDPROC



PROCEDURE FillArray
* Fill an array with the names of the states
LPARAMETERS aStatesArray

LOCAL oState, nItem

DIMENSION aStatesArray[ This.Count ]
nItem = 0

FOR EACH oState IN This
    nItem = nItem + 1
    aStatesArray[ nItem ] = oState.StateName
ENDFOR

RETURN This.Count
ENDPROC


ENDDEFINE
```

```
* StateData.Txt
"Alabama","AL",22,4447100
"Alaska","AK",49,626932
"Arizona","AZ",48,5130632
"Arkansas","AS",25,2673400
"California","CA",31,33871648
"Colorado","CO",38,4301261
"Connecticut","CT",5,3405565
"Delaware","DE",1,783600
"District of Columbia","DC",0,0
"Florida","FL",27,15982378
"Georgia","GA",4,8186453
```

The methods other than Add that address the members of the collection allow you to refer to an individual member by its position or its key, if keys were specified. For example, to remove the District of Columbia from the collection of states, you can use either of the following forms:

```
oStates.Remove(8)     && Specify either the index (position)
oStates.Remove("DC")  && or the key
```

Remove can also accept –1 as a parameter to remove all items from the collection.

Be aware that, like record numbers in a VFP table, the item number for an item can change as the collection is modified. Therefore, it's generally better to include a key with each item and use the key to locate the item as needed. The GetKey method lets you convert an index into a key or a key into an index. For example:

```
? oStates.GetKey(5)     && Returns "CA"
? oStates.GetKey("CA")  && Returns 5
```

The Item method lets you address the contents of the collection. Pass it an index or key, and it returns the item at that position or with that key. If the item is a scalar value (as in the first example above), you can use it directly. If the item is a reference to another object (as in the states example), you can address the object's properties and methods.

The Item method is Collection's default method, a concept not shared by other VFP classes. The name of the default method for a class can be omitted in code, so the following all refer to the same item:

```
oStates.Item(3)
oStates.Item("AZ")
oStates(3)
oStates("AZ")
```

Because Item is a method rather than a property, unfortunately, IntelliSense doesn't help you drill into the properties of a contained item.

When you want to process all the items in a collection, use a FOR EACH loop. For example, this code lists all the states in the oStates collection:

```
FOR EACH oState IN oStates
   ?oState.StateName
ENDFOR
```

By default, FOR EACH processes the items in a collection in ascending index order. You can change the order of FOR EACH processing by setting the KeySort property. Specify 0 for the default order, 1 for descending index order, 2 for ascending key order, and 3 for descending key order. This code lists the states in abbreviation order:

```
oStates.KeySort = 2
FOR EACH oState IN oStates
  ?oState.StateName
ENDFOR
```

Collections are extremely useful for a variety of framework tasks. In particular, we imagine many VFP developers will use subclasses of collection for the various manager objects a framework needs, such as a form manager.

We recommend you follow what seems to be a standard in other environments and name collection subclasses and instances in the plural (as with the examples, oNames and oStates) and use the singular for items within a collection.

 *Code to build a collection of states is included as StatesCollection.PRG in the Developer Downloads available at **www.hentzenwerke.com**. The states data file is StateData.txt.*

An ultra-lightweight base class

The new Empty base class is really easy to describe. It has no properties, no events, and no methods. Not only that, but it can't be subclassed.

Although the Empty class sounds pretty useless, it's not. It provides a very resource-friendly way to create certain kinds of items at run time. Because it has no PEM's, the memory footprint of an Empty object is extremely small. You add to it exactly what you need and no more.

How can you add anything to a class with no methods, in particular, no AddObject or AddProperty methods? The new AddProperty() and RemoveProperty() functions, described in "Adding and removing properties on the fly" later, let you manage the contents of an object.

We see two principal uses for the Empty class. You can use it with the new ADDITIVE clause of SCATTER NAME (described in Chapter 8, "Other Data-Related Changes") to create objects based on data, but give them properties beyond the fields of the table. (In fact, SCATTER NAME without the ADDITIVE clause bases the objects it creates on the Empty class.) For example, the following code creates a Customer object.

```
USE _SAMPLES + "TasTrade\Data\Customer"
oCust = CREATEOBJECT("Empty")
ADDPROPERTY(oCust, "Name", "Customer")
SCATTER NAME oCust ADDITIVE
```

The second use we see for Empty is creating objects to hold data on the fly. For example, you could use an Empty object for passing parameters between methods.

```
oParams = CREATEOBJECT("Empty")
ADDPROPERTY( oParams, "FirstParam", "Some value")
ADDPROPERTY( oParams, "SecondParam", DATE())
oSomeOtherObject.SomeMethod( oParams )
```

This approach has several advantages over creating a subclass of Custom (or another class) to hold parameters and using the subclass when needed. The first is that an Empty subclass uses fewer resources. Second, you don't have to worry about making sure your subclass is in the path; the Empty class is always available. Finally, you needn't worry about the names of the properties you create conflicting with intrinsic properties of the base class, because it doesn't have any.

Adding and removing properties on the fly

The ability to add properties to an object on the fly was added in VFP 6, with the AddProperty method. However, there was no corresponding RemoveProperty method and, in fact, no way to remove a property from an instantiated object. It's likely that wouldn't have changed in VFP 8, except the new Empty base class needed a way to let us manage its members.

Enter AddProperty() and RemoveProperty(). As their names suggest, these functions add and remove properties from objects, respectively.

AddProperty() accepts three parameters: the object, the name of the property, and the initial value for the property. If the value is omitted, the property is initialized to False.

RemoveProperty() accepts two parameters: the object and the name of the property. RemoveProperty() can only remove properties added after instantiation. That limits it to those added with AddProperty() and those created by SCATTER NAME.

Both functions return a logical value indicating success or failure.

Here's an example that shows both functions in use:

```
USE _SAMPLES + "TasTrade\Data\Customer"
oCust = CREATEOBJECT("Empty")
ADDPROPERTY(oCust, "Name", "Customer")
SCATTER NAME oCust ADDITIVE
REMOVEPROPERTY( oCust, "Max_Order_Amt" )
REMOVEPROPERTY( oCust, "Min_Order_Amt" )
```

AddProperty() is reasonably well-behaved if you attempt to add a property that's already a member of the object. If it possibly can, it simply updates the value of the property without triggering an error. One case it can't handle is specifying an array property when there's already a scalar property with the same name. In that case, the function returns False.

Fewer errors with DoDefault

The DoDefault keyword allows you to call up the class hierarchy. When issued, it executes the method of the parent class with the same name as the calling method. It's typically used when extending the behavior of a method.

In earlier versions, issuing DoDefault when the parent class didn't have a method of the same name caused an error. VFP 8 eliminates that error, so you can use DoDefault without worrying whether the method you're coding is inherited or not. In addition, there's no longer an error if the method DoDefault calls is designated as a hidden method in the parent class.

Delayed binding

When controls have a value specified for ControlSource or a grid has a RecordSource specified, VFP normally binds the value of the control to the specified variable, field, property, or table as a form is initialized. There are a couple of reasons why this might not be a good choice in some situations. First, binding each control takes some time, so a form that has a lot of bound controls may take quite a while to instantiate. Second, and more compelling, is sometimes the right data source is not known or is not available at the time a form instantiates.

The new BindControls property of the Form class provides a solution. If BindControls is False when a form instantiates, the controls are not bound to their ControlSources at that time. When BindControls is later set to True, the controls are bound.

One common situation is for an application to use multiple databases with identical structure. The databases might be production data and test data or data for different divisions of a company or for different years. Handling this situation has always been a little tricky in VFP because the Init method receives parameters, but generally tables are opened and controls bound before the Init method fires. BindControls offers a solution. Here's code from the Init method of a form that accepts a single parameter, the path and filename of the database to use. The form has BindControls set to False; after the Init method swaps in the right database, BindControls is set to True.

```
LPARAMETERS cDatabase
   * cDatabase - indicates which database to use. Must include path.

* Loop through DE and change database
* for each table
IF NOT EMPTY(cDatabase)
   This.DataEnvironment.CloseTables
   FOR EACH oObject IN This.DataEnvironment.Objects
     IF UPPER(oObject.BaseClass) = "CURSOR"
       oObject.Database = cDatabase
     ENDIF
   ENDFOR
   This.DataEnvironment.OpenTables
ENDIF


* Now bind
This.BindControls = .T.

RETURN
```

 *An example form using this technique, LateBind.SCX, is included in the Developer Downloads available at **www.hentzenwerke.com**. The downloads also include programs to set up the test data (MakeBindControlsData.PRG) and clean it up afterwards (DeleteBindControlsData.PRG), as well as a program (RunBindControls.PRG) that uses the others to set up the data, run the form a couple of times, and clean up. Be sure you've created the data before you attempt to open the form in the Form Designer.*

Improved performance with objects

VFP's blazing speed in processing data has spoiled us, so we expect it to do everything quickly. Fortunately, the Fox team shares our feelings. In VFP 8, they made changes to the object manager that handles the creation and destruction of objects to speed it up.

In our tests, it appears the changes apply to situations where many objects are being created and destroyed, not to the creation and destruction of individual objects. In particular, object destruction seems to be much faster; for many base classes, when dealing with 5,000 objects, we're seeing improvements in destruction speed of more than an order of magnitude. Also notable is our tests show creating 5,000 instances of Session is three orders of magnitude faster in VFP 8 than in VFP 7. (We suspect there's more going on here than just the changes to the object manager.)

 *The program for testing the creation and destruction of objects, ObjectManagerSpeed.PRG, is included in the Developer Downloads available at **www.hentzenwerke.com**. To compare results, you need to run it in both VFP 8 and VFP 7, and save the results. Be careful when running this program. We were able to test 5,000 instances of each class without too much difficulty, but 10,000 brought our machines to their knees.*

Another change isn't about performance in the speed sense, but is about how objects perform in applications. The COMPOBJ() function compares objects and returns True if they're identical in structure and values. In VFP 7 and earlier, if two objects have the same properties, and have the same values for all properties, but at least one property of both objects is null, the function returns False. In VFP 8, having the null value for the same property of each object no longer keeps them from comparing as the same. For example:

```
CREATE CURSOR Test (cField C(3), nField N(3) null)
INSERT INTO Test VALUES ("abc",.null.)
SCATTER NAME Object1
SCATTER NAME Object2
?COMPOBJ( Object1, Object2)
```

Support for Windows XP

Sometimes, a good thing is also a bad thing. We were delighted when VFP 7 finally shipped, but it happened before the release of Windows XP, and thus didn't provide support for new Windows XP features. VFP 8 catches up on that front.

Support for themes comes in the form of two properties and a SYS() function. The Themes property applies to some controls (see the Help topic "Themes Property" for the list). When Themes is set to True and the operating system supports themes (for the moment, that means Windows XP set to use the Windows XP style), the current theme is applied to the control and the SpecialEffect property is more or less ignored. (A setting of Hot Tracking for SpecialEffect does still apply, but the object uses the theme when the mouse is over it.)

For the remaining visible controls that do not support Themes (see Help for the Style property for this list), the Style property has been added along with a new setting for it. The value 3-Themed indicates the control uses the current theme (when appropriate). Several other properties are ignored when a control uses the theme; the list varies with the control. (The one visible control that offers no way to turn themes on and off is Line. We presume that's because there's no difference in a Line's appearance with and without themes.)

The availability of themes depends on a number of factors. First, you have to be using Windows XP and have themes turned on. Second, you need to have themes turned on for Visual FoxPro. There are two ways to turn on themes in VFP. The new SYS(2700) function tells you about themes at the Windows level and also lets you control VFP's use of themes. Querying SYS(2700) always tells you whether themes are supported in Windows at this time; it returns 1 if they are, and 0 if not. Passing an optional second parameter of 0 or 1 to SYS(2700) lets you turn themes off and on for VFP. Note, though, regardless of what you last passed to SYS(2700), the function always tells you about the Windows setting. Changing SYS(2700) doesn't affect the Windows setting or any other applications.

_SCREEN has a Themes property; you can also use it to control VFP's use of themes. It's True by default, but setting the property to False turns off themes within VFP. Once you've set this property, it returns your current setting. Be aware that SYS(2700) and _SCREEN.Themes are independent of each other. Changing one doesn't affect the other, so your best bet is probably to use one or the other exclusively. We recommend reserving SYS(2700) for checking whether you have themes available in Windows, and using _SCREEN.Themes (which lets you check the current setting) to control VFP's behavior.

The setting of Themes for forms and toolbars determines whether controls they contain are permitted to use themes. If Themes is False, controls on the form or toolbar do not use themes at all. If Themes is True for the form or toolbar, the Themes or Style property of the individual controls determines their appearance.

Figures 1 and **2** show the same form (from the Solutions Samples) with themes turned on and off.

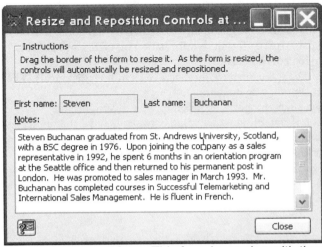

Figure 1. Themed form. This form is running with themes turned on in VFP.

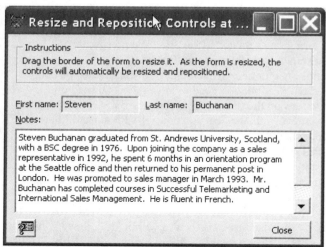

Figure 2. No themes. This is the same form as in Figure 1, but support for themes has been turned off in VFP. Note the shapes of the buttons and the styling of the text boxes and edit box.

Improved image support

Each new version of VFP has supported more formats for images than the one before it. VFP 8 takes a bold step to ensure that will continue to be true. Rather than just adding support for new formats that have become popular since VFP 7 was released, VFP 8 supports a new graphics API, GDI+, which is included with Windows XP and supported for older versions of Windows back to Windows 98 and NT 4.

GDI+ provides an intermediate layer between the graphics and the hardware that needs to render them. By calling on GDI+, VFP can use images in any format GDI+ supports. See the Help topic "Graphics Support in Visual FoxPro" for more information on GDI+ and for details on adding GDI+ support to older versions of Windows.

As a consequence of using GDI+, VFP 8 can show animated GIFs in Image controls. VFP 7 and earlier can display such images, but they're not animated.

In addition, the Image control has a new property, RotateFlip, that determines the positioning of the image in the control. RotateFlip takes a value between 0 and 7 that indicates how much to rotate the image (in increments of 90 degrees) and whether to flip the image around the Y axis. **Figure 3** shows a form that demonstrates each of the 8 values.

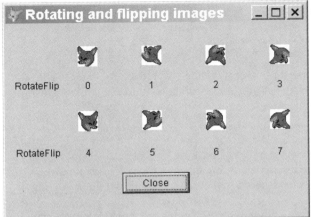

Figure 3. Manipulating images. The new RotateFlip property lets you determine the orientation of the picture shown in an image control. Because VFP caches pictures, each of the image controls on this form uses a separate copy of the fox bitmap.

 *The form shown in Figure 3 is included in the Developer Downloads available at **www.hentzenwerke.com** as ImageFlip.SCX.*

Better tooltips and status information

VFP 8 brings several changes to tooltips. First, tooltips can now hold up to 4,095 characters. Of course, it is not very useful if they all appear in a straight line, so tooltips now wrap their text.

The expansion of tooltips brings a couple of caveats. First, a tooltip that is actually 4,095 characters long would be useless. Keep the word "tip" in mind and keep your tooltips to the minimum length necessary to deliver the message. Also, remember users can set the tooltip font in Windows, so tips may not be sized as you expect.

The second warning is that VFP doesn't allow you to specify a tooltip longer than 255 characters in the Property Sheet. You can't solve the problem by using a builder either—assigning a long tooltip with a builder results in the entire tooltip being discarded.

You don't have control over how VFP wraps your tips. It appears the maximum width of the rectangle containing a tooltip is fixed, and the number of characters per line is determined by the Windows tooltip font. For example, we found that using 9-point Arial, we see about 46 characters per line, but with 12-point Arial, it goes down to about 33 characters per line. You can use CHR(13) to force a line break in a tooltip.

Not only can you write longer tooltips, but you can use them in more places. The ToolTipText property has been added to the base classes for visible controls that previously didn't have it. The Help topic for the ToolTipText Property explains the priority rules for displaying tooltips in container situations.

In addition, the same list of controls now all support the StatusBarText property. However, for controls that don't get the focus (like shapes, containers, and labels), the specified text appears in the status bar only if ShowTips is True for the form and only when the mouse passes over the control. (Note, though, once the status bar changes, it keeps that value until something else triggers a change.)

Grid enhancements

Grids are the best of controls and the worst of controls. They provide an easy way to show a lot of data at once, but making them behave as you'd like can be very tricky. VFP 8 adds several capabilities to grids that make them easier both to configure and to use.

Locking columns

One feature users (and therefore, developers) have been asking for since grids appeared in VFP 3 is the ability to keep some columns from scrolling when you scroll horizontally in a grid. This is a standard feature of spreadsheet software and users tend to look at grids as spreadsheets.

VFP 8 finally adds locking capability with the LockColumns and LockColumnsLeft properties. Since you'll probably use LockColumns far more than LockColumnsLeft, we'll look at that property first. You specify the number of columns in the grid you want to stay fixed when scrolling horizontally. The divider between the rightmost column specified and the column to its immediate right is slightly thickened. **Figure 4** shows a grid with two columns locked. LockColumns can also be set interactively by right-clicking between columns.

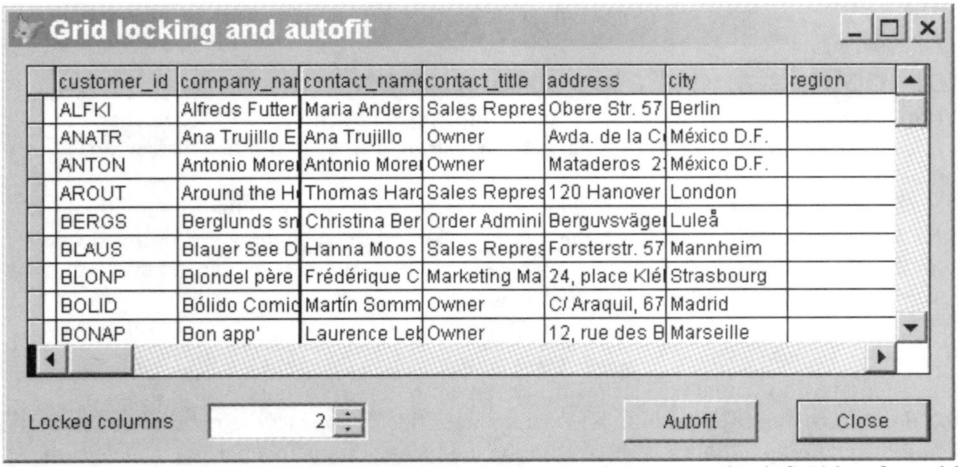

Figure 4. Locking grid columns. You can set up columns on the left side of a grid so they don't scroll.

LockColumnsLeft is used for cases where you've partitioned the grid into two sections (either using the Partition property or by dragging the split bar). In that case, it controls the number of columns that don't scroll horizontally in the left partition. (By definition, the section of the grid you see when it's not split is the right partition.)

Sizing columns to fit

One of the most tedious of all grid tasks is resizing the columns so data looks right. VFP 8 takes out all the tedium by providing both an interactive and a programmatic way to size individual columns or all columns to fit the displayed data.

Programmatically, you resize a grid or an individual column by calling its AutoFit method. The form shown in Figure 4 has an Autofit button that calls the grid's AutoFit method.

Interactively, a user can resize an entire grid by double-clicking the box in the upper left corner of the grid (component 11 from GridHitTest) or resize an individual column by double-clicking in the header row on the grid line that separates the column from the one to its right. The column to the left of the mouse is resized. For performance reasons, only visible rows are used when determining the size for a column, so it's possible to autofit a column, scroll, and then find some data that doesn't fit. (You may also find columns not fitting properly if DynamicFontBold is set, so that some cells are bold some of the time.) For interactive fitting of all columns to be available, at least one of RecordMark and DeleteMark must be True; when both are False, the corner box of the grid isn't displayed.

You can control the user's ability to resize the grid and its columns. The AllowAutoColumnFit property determines what the user is allowed to do. **Table 4** shows the possible values.

Table 4. *May the user fit columns? The AllowAutoColumnFit property determines whether the user can resize the whole grid, individual columns, or nothing at all.*

Value	Meaning
0	The user can auto-resize individual columns or all columns at once.
1	The user can auto-resize only individual columns and cannot auto-resize all columns at once.
2	The user cannot auto-resize columns.

The same interactive techniques work with BROWSE windows, making life much nicer for developers. Better yet, once you autofit columns, BROWSE LAST retains those settings.

*The form shown in Figure 4, which allows you to experiment with locking columns and auto-fitting, is included in the Developer Downloads available at **www.hentzenwerke.com**, as LockGrid.SCX.*

A real row highlight

Another feature both users and developers have been asking for in grids for a long time is the ability to highlight a whole row and have the highlight stick when focus leaves the grid. In VFP 8, several new properties make this possible.

The key to the whole thing is the new HighlightStyle property. It offers three choices as shown in **Table 5**. HighlightStyle interacts with AllowCellSelection, which determines whether individual cells are allowed to get focus. If you're using a grid as a picklist, setting

AllowCellSelection to False keeps the data in whichever cell the user happens to click on from being highlighted. When AllowCellSelection is True (the default) and HighlightStyle is set to 1 or 2, the cell that has focus looks different than the rest of the cells in the row.

Table 5. *Highlighting rows. The new HighlightStyle property determines whether the whole row is highlighted and whether the highlight persists when the grid loses focus.*

Value	Meaning
0	The row is not highlighted. This is the default and backward-compatible setting.
1	The entire row is highlighted as long as the grid has focus.
2	The entire row is highlighted and the highlight persists, even when the grid loses focus.

HighlightBackColor and HighlightForeColor let you set the colors used for the highlighted row. By default, they use the Selected Items colors from the current Windows appearance scheme. In that case, HighlightBackColor is the Selected Items back color, but at a 50% gradient fill, and HighlightForeColor is the Selected Items fore color. You can set these properties to use different colors. When you do so, there's no gradient effect for the back color. (Regardless of these settings, when AllowCellSelection is true, the selected cell uses SelectedItemBackColor and SelectedItemForeColor.)

If you choose to change these colors, it's wise to set them to colors from the user's current color scheme. Applying your favorite colors can lead not only to forms that may be unattractive with the user's chosen color scheme but far more importantly, to forms some users can't read.

Figure 5 shows a grid with HighlightStyle set to 2 and AllowCellSelection set to False. The default highlight colors are in use.

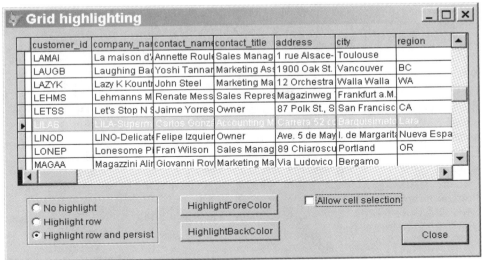

Figure 5. *Highlight a whole row. Combining HighlightStyle=2 with AllowCellSelection=False turns a grid into a good picklist.*

 The form shown in Figure 5 is included in the Developer Downloads available at **www.hentzenwerke.com** as GridHighlight.SCX.

Other Grid changes

As if the items above weren't enough to make grids far more useable, there are some other changes to grids in VFP 8.

In earlier versions of VFP, checkboxes in a grid column can't be centered horizontally. VFP 8 eliminates this restriction.

In VFP 7 and earlier, resizing a grid column fires the Click event of the Header. That's no longer true in VFP 8, which makes it easier to tell when a user clicks or double-clicks on a header. Unfortunately, this change means the only events that fire on a column resize are the mouse events—MouseEnter, MouseMove, and MouseLeave.

Headers now have a Picture property, so you can add an image to the text there. By default, the specified image appears to the right of the caption (unless the column isn't wide enough, in which case the image overwrites the caption from the right). You can put the image to the left of the caption by setting Alignment for the header to one of the settings that includes "right," such as 1-Middle Right. You might use this ability to put an arrow in the header to show the column on which the grid is sorted.

 The Developer Downloads available at **www.hentzenwerke.com** include a form named SortGrid.SCX that shows a very rudimentary example of this technique. In this form, only the first column is sortable—double-clicking on the header changes the sort order and changes the arrow icon.

The last change to grids is one many developers have requested for a long time, the ability to make a column disappear. In earlier versions of VFP, setting a column's Visible property to False blanked the column, but left its allocated space in the grid. In VFP 8, when you set Visible to False for a column, the column entirely disappears, both at design time and run time.

Controlling picture position

Several controls have the ability to hold both a caption and a picture: command buttons, option buttons, and check boxes. In VFP 8, these controls have a new property, PicturePosition, that lets you determine the orientation of the picture and the caption when both are supplied.

The property controls two characteristics of the picture, where it appears relative to the caption, and how the two are aligned. The default (which is the behavior of earlier versions) is for the picture to be centered in the control, with the caption beneath it a fixed distance from the bottom of the control.

Figure 6 shows a form with 14 buttons containing an image and a caption. Each one uses a different setting for PicturePosition, as noted in the Caption. Position 13 is the VFP 7 behavior.

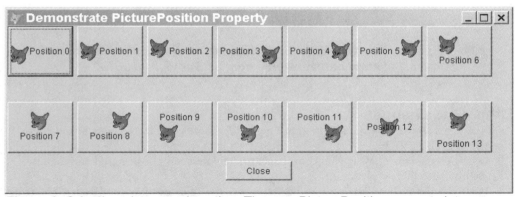

Figure 6. Orienting picture and caption. The new PicturePosition property lets you determine where the picture appears on a graphical button or checkbox, and how it's aligned with the caption.

 *The form shown in Figure 6 is included in the Developer Downloads available at **www.hentzenwerke.com** as PicturePos.SCX.*

Control tab orientation

From the day VFP 3 appeared with the ability to create page frames, FoxPro developers have been asking for a way to specify where the tabs appear. Finally, in VFP 8, we have the TabOrientation property.

Not surprisingly, TabOrientation has four possible settings: 0-Top, 1-Bottom, 2-Left, and 3-Right. You can change the setting on the fly (though it's hard to imagine when you'd want a form that does so, other than for testing purposes.)

There is one (documented) glitch with TabOrientation. Although you can specify hot keys for the tabs, when you use left or right orientation the hot keys are not underlined, though they work. We suspect it has to do with the technique used to display the characters sideways.

Figure 7 shows a form that lets you manipulate the tabs of a page frame on the fly. In the figure, the tabs are set to left orientation.

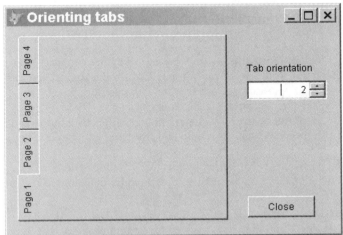

Figure 7. Changing tab orientation. The new TabOrientation property controls the position of tabs on a page frame. When tabs are side-oriented (left or right), hot keys are not underlined.

 *The form shown in Figure 7 is included in the Developer Downloads available at **www.hentzenwerke.com** as Tabs.scx.*

Odds and ends
There are a number of other changes that affect controls or their properties.

Keep output off of forms
VFP has a number of commands (including all the DISPLAY and LIST commands and the ? operator) that send their output to the active window. While you can turn some of this output off in various situations (as with SET TALK OFF), it's always been a bit of a struggle to keep some of these items from landing on forms where they don't belong. VFP 8 solves this problem neatly with a new AllowOutput property for forms.

When AllowOutput is False (the default is True for backward compatibility), none of this output lands there. We suspect this property was added as much for Microsoft's benefit as for ours; quite a few of VFP's tools are based on VFP forms, and they've always needed special code to work around this issue.

There is one trap involving this new property. MROW() and MCOL() may return different results than you expect when AllowOutput is False for the form where the mouse is positioned. If you don't pass a parameter to MROW() and MCOL(), they return information relative to the active, user-defined window. However, a form with AllowOutput set to False is never the active, user-defined window.

Hyperlinks in controls

The TextBox and EditBox controls have a new property, EnableHyperlinks. When this property is True (the default is False), the control makes any contained hyperlinks active. Unlike ordinary hyperlinks, you need to use Ctrl-Click to follow these links. When this property is True, text that looks like it should be a hyperlink is displayed as a hyperlink as it's entered.

If ShowTips is True for the containing form, there's a tooltip to tell the user to use Ctrl-Click; there's even reasonable interaction between the tooltip specified for the control and this special tip. When the mouse is over the hyperlink, you see the Ctrl-Click tooltip; when it's anywhere else over the control, you see the control's ToolTipText.

It's worth noting the hyperlink need not be the only content in the textbox or editbox and the controls can handle all kinds of hyperlinks (such as mailto and ftp specifications), not just web addresses.

Finally, be aware that EnableHyperlinks is controlled by the _VFP.EditorOptions setting—if hyperlinks are turned off globally, they're not available in individual controls.

Combo box improvements

Two enhancements affect combo boxes. First, they now have a MaxLength property that controls the amount of text you can enter into the textbox portion, when Style is set to 0-drop-down combo. MaxLength doesn't affect the items in the drop-down list, regardless of the Style setting, and is irrelevant when Style is set to 2-drop-down list. In addition, as with text boxes, an InputMask overrides the MaxLength setting.

The second change to combos doesn't require you to do anything. Combo boxes have always supported the addition of pictures for the items in the drop-down list. In VFP 8, the picture for the currently chosen item appears in the textbox portion of the combo, as well.

Button coloring

Command buttons feature one of the most commonly requested changes, a BackColor property. As with the grid highlight colors, we recommend using this property with caution—keep in mind that about 10% of the population has some form of color blindness and may have chosen their Windows colors for more than just aesthetic reasons.

Refresh methods for static objects

The Label and Shape controls now have Refresh methods. As far as we can tell, calling these methods doesn't have any default action because they are not bound to data. However, by adding the method to these two controls, all of the form controls except line and image now have it, making it a place to put code in your base classes and know it'll be called whenever the form is refreshed.

More control over moverbar actions

Until VFP 8, there was no way, other than brute force, to know when a user was moving items around in a list box and no programmatic way to move items. VFP 8 addresses both of these issues.

The MoveItem method lets you move items in a list programmatically. You pass the index (position) of the item to move, and the number of positions it should move, using positive numbers to move downward in the list and negative numbers to move upward. For example, to move the third item in the list to the first position from another method of the list, you'd issue:

```
This.MoveItem(3, -2)
```

The OnMoveItem method fires whenever an item is moved, whether interactively or programmatically. It receives four parameters, as shown in **Table 6**.

Table 6. You move me. The OnMoveItem event receives four numeric parameters to tell it what was moved and how.

Parameter	Meaning
nSource	Indicates what triggered the move (keyboard, specific mouse button, or programmatic). See Help for the list of values.
nShift	Indicates whether any of the special keys (Shift, Ctrl, Alt) were pressed. This is an additive value between 0 and 7.
nCurrentIndex	The index (position) of the item being moved.
nMoveBy	The number of positions the item is being moved: positive to move downward, negative to move upward.

Ordinarily, when an item is moved interactively, nMoveBy is always 1 or −1 and the event fires for each position the item is moved. However, if the user moves the item by dragging it off the list box and then dropping it into a different position in the list, OnMoveItem fires only once and nMoveBy indicates the total distance of the move. In that situation, OnMoveItem doesn't fire at all if the item is dropped back into the same position.

When an item is moved programmatically with MoveItem, OnMoveItem fires only once, and nMoveBy indicates the total distance of the move.

Return False from OnMoveItem to prevent an item from being moved. For example, if you have a list with headings of some sort, you might not want the user to be able to move them. So you can put code in OnMoveItem that determines whether the selected item is a heading and, if so, returns False. Be aware that, even in this situation, such an item might change its position in the list because other items are moved around it.

One more mouse pointer

The list of available mouse pointers is another of those items that gets enhanced now and then. VFP 8 adds a new setting for the "hand" pointer (set MousePointer to 15). Because the hand is the default pointer in many situations, you may not notice the change, but the new setting allows you to explicitly choose the hand, even when it's not the default.

Keep in mind the actual pointer a user sees at any time is based not just on the MousePointer setting, but on the user's choice of pointers in Windows.

Summary

There are a wide variety of changes affecting the object-oriented portion of VFP. The ability to define member classes and the many changes to PEM's will make it possible to give users better applications with less code.

Updates and corrections to this chapter can be found on Hentzenwerke's web site, **www.hentzenwerke.com**. Click on "Catalog" and navigate to the page for this book.

Chapter 10
COM and Web Services
Enhancements

While VFP can work well in a COM environment, there's always room for improvement. Fortunately, VFP 8 provides additional capabilities to VFP COM servers and clients. It also greatly improves the ability to work with Web services.

Each new version improves the way VFP interacts with other objects in a COM environment. VFP 7 in particular made great strides in how VFP COM servers work. VFP 8 fine-tunes VFP's COM support even more. VFP 7 also added several tools making it easier to work with Web services than earlier versions. VFP 8 puts those tools on steroids and adds several new ones, making it much easier to register, explore, consume, and publish Web services.

COM enhancements
There are three COM-related improvements in VFP 8: the default instancing of EXE servers, improvements in what's written to the type library for a COM server, and support for byte arrays.

Default instancing for EXE servers
In earlier versions of VFP, when you create an EXE from a project that contains any classes marked as OLEPUBLIC, VFP uses Multi Use as the default value for the Instancing property in the Servers page of the Project Information dialog. In VFP 8, the default is Single Use, which is more appropriate for EXE servers. The default is still Multi Use for DLL servers.

Type library improvements
When you build a COM server, VFP automatically creates a type library. A type library is binary information that lists all the classes marked as OLEPUBLIC in your server and provides information about them, such as the type of parameters their methods expect and what type of values they return. Clients of the COM server use this information so they know what the interface of the server is and how to call its various methods. VFP 8 has four improvements in how it creates type libraries.

The first is Character type is now treated the same as String: it's marked as BSTR, a COM string type, in the type library rather than Variant. So, methods like FUNCTION MyFunction as Character will now appear properly to COM clients.

The second improvement regards how VFP treats arrays passed to a COM component. You can now specify the data type of the elements in an array by using the new AS clause in the DIMENSION command. Previous versions of VFP treated arrays as containing Variant values. Here's an example:

```
dimension laValues[5] as String
oCOMServer.SomeMethod(@laValues)
```

Another array-related improvement: you can specify a parameter received by a method should be an array by placing "[]" after the parameter name, and that the array elements are of a specific data type by using the AS clause. In the following example, MyArray is expected to be an array of strings passed by reference.

```
function MyFunction(MyArray[] as String @) as Boolean
```

When you specify an array this way, VFP defines the parameter in the type library as a "safe array". A safe array is one that contains its own lower boundary and size, and supports locking and unlocking so updates are handled correctly.

The final improvement is you can now specify the ProgID of a COM class as a data type. For example, a method that returns an ADO Recordset object can be defined as:

```
function GetData() as ADODB.Recordset
```

A method passed a Recordset as a parameter would be defined as:

```
function SaveData(DataSet as ADODB.Recordset @) as Boolean
```

In all of these cases, the data types are not enforced by VFP, but are simply written to the type library so strongly typed languages such as Visual Basic can ensure methods of the VFP COM server are called properly.

Byte array support

VFP has issues passing arrays to COM objects. By default, it passes them by value; some COM servers expect arrays to be passed by reference. Second, VFP arrays are one-based, meaning the first element is considered to be 1, whereas some languages use zero-based arrays. To eliminate these problems, Microsoft added the COMARRAY() function in VFP 6. It allows you to specify whether arrays are passed to COM objects by value or reference, whether they should be zero- or one-based, and whether they can be redimensioned.

In VFP 8, COMARRAY() supports a new value for the second parameter: add 1000 to this parameter's value to prevent byte arrays from being converted to strings.

Web services enhancements

Microsoft's vision of software development strongly embraces Web services (now called XML Web services). A Web service is nothing more than a component that sits on a Web server somewhere. A client calls a function on the component, using SOAP (Simple Object Access Protocol) as the transport mechanism for the function call, parameters, and return value, and does something with the results, which are usually in the form of XML. The reason Web services are becoming more important for application development is they can form the building blocks of distributed applications.

Although you can use Web services in VFP 6 using Microsoft's SOAP Toolkit, VFP 7 makes it much easier by providing some wrapper classes and providing IntelliSense for Web services you register in VFP. Version 8 greatly extends the use of Web services in VFP, making it easier than ever to register, explore, consume, and publish Web services.

Registering Web services

Although you can use a Web service in VFP without first registering it, IntelliSense and some new tools in VFP 8 make it much easier to work with Web services if you register them first.

The XML Web Services Registration dialog is totally revamped in VFP 8. The new dialog, shown in **Figure 1**, lets you search for Web services to register. The dialog can be accessed in a variety of ways:

- Clicking on the Web Services button in the Types page of the IntelliSense Manager (itself accessed from the Tools menu).

- Clicking on the Register link in the My XML Web Services category of the Toolbox (see Chapter 2, "The Toolbox", for information on this new tool).

- Choosing the Register an XML Web Service link in the XML Web Services pane of the Task Pane Manager. Chapter 4, "The Task Pane Manager", discusses this tool in detail.

- Selecting the New button in the XML Web Services Manager, which is also available from the XML Web Services pane of the Task Pane Manager.

Figure 1. Registering a Web service. The new dialog lets you search for Web services rather than having to know the URL.

If you know the URL for the WSDL of the Web service you want to register, you can simply type it into the combo box, making sure to include the http:// prefix. (A WSDL is a Web Services Definition Language document that describes the Web service's interface.) If you don't know it, you can search for it. When you click the UDDI Search button, the dialog shown in **Figure 2** appears. Type a name and click the Search button. The combo box is populated with a list of matching Web services from the UDDI database. To select a particular

Web service, choose it from the combo box and click the Select button. Choose Cancel to close the dialog without selecting a Web service.

> *Universal Description, Discovery, and Integration (UDDI) is a public registry of Web services. For information on UDDI, check the links at the bottom of the XML Web Services pane in the Task Pane Manager.*

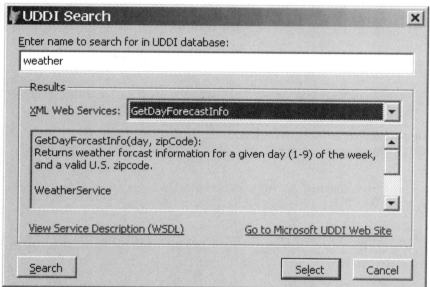

Figure 2. Searching for Web services. This dialog lets you search the UDDI database for Web services.

Click Register in the Registration dialog to register the Web service by adding a record to the table FoxWS3.DBF in the HOME(7) directory.

Registered Web services appear in the XML Web Service Manager (**Figure 3**), accessed from the XML Web Services task pane of the Task Pane Manager. It lists all registered Web services and allows you to control them in various ways. Highlight a Web service to "manage" it. You determine whether it's displayed in any Web services categories in the Toolbox with the Show in Toolbox checkbox. You can delete the Web service, thus unregistering it. The View button shows the record for the Web service in the FoxWS3 table where registered Web services are stored. Less obvious is the hyperlink text "View Web service description (WSDL)" that you click to open your browser displaying the WSDL file for this Web service. The New button displays the XML Web Services Registration dialog, so you can add Web services.

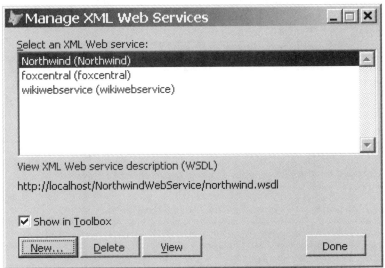

Figure 3. *The XML Web Service Manager. This dialog lets you work with registered Web services.*

Exploring Web services

Once you have registered a Web service, you'll probably want to find out how it works. The Explore an XML Web Service section of the XML Web Services pane in the Task Pane Manager lets you see what a Web service offers without leaving VFP. Choose a Web service from the drop-down list and the pane expands to show documentation for the Web service. (**Figure 4** shows an example.)

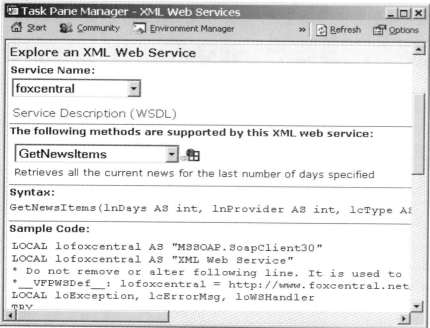

Figure 4. *Exploring a Web service. When you choose a Web service from the Service Name drop-down list, documentation appears in this pane.*

Choose a method from the methods drop-down list and the syntax and an example are shown. If that isn't enough, the little button next to the combo box lets you test a method. When you click it, a dialog appears (**Figure 5**) asking you to specify parameters. Fill in the parameters you want to pass (the Zoom button displays a larger dialog in which to enter the values if you wish) and click OK. The method is executed and the results displayed (see **Figure 6**).

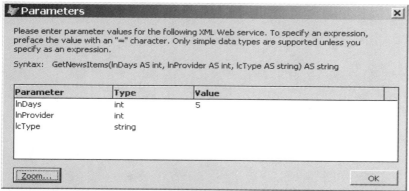

Figure 5. *Specifying parameters. When you test a Web service method, this dialog appears for you to specify parameters.*

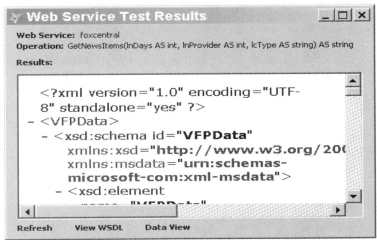

Figure 6. Method results. After running the specified method, this dialog shows you the results. Click Data View to make them more readable.

The Results dialog has several options. The Refresh link prompts for parameters and runs the method again. View WSDL displays the Web service's description in a new browser instance. If the results can be converted into a VFP cursor, the Data View link is available; selecting it switches the dialog to a grid showing the results returned, as in **Figure 7**. When the data view is displayed, the button changes to XML View, which, of course, restores the display in Figure 6. If a test page is available (as it is when the Web service was created with ASP.NET), a Web Test Page link also appears. Click on that link to launch the test page for the Web service in your browser.

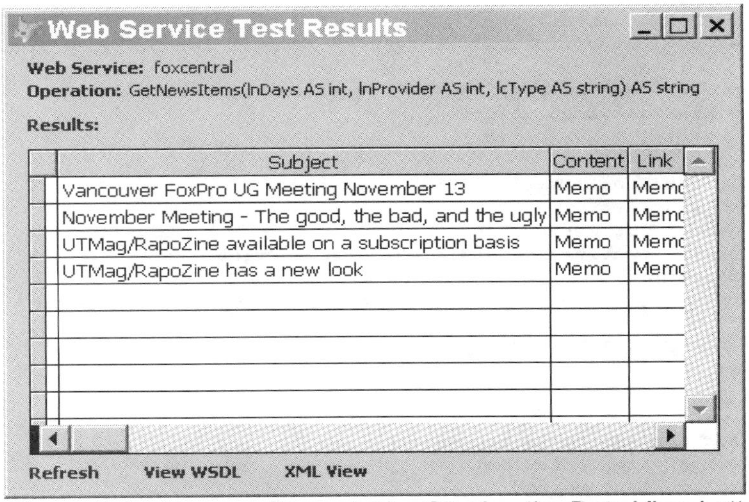

Figure 7. Making results readable. Clicking the Data View button in the Results dialog shows a grid.

If something goes wrong during the test (most likely because of a problem with the parameters), a message box appears. After you clear it, the Results dialog shows all error messages.

To shrink the Explore an XML Web Service section of this pane back to a minimal size, choose "<select a service>" from the Service Name drop-down list.

Using Web services

VFP 7 provides a convenient way to use a registered Web service: through IntelliSense. Once you register both the name and WSDL URL for a Web service, you can type "local MyVariable as" in a code window and select the Web service by its name from the type list IntelliSense provides to generate code similar to the following:

```
local loWiki as FoxWiki
LOCAL loWS
loWS = NEWOBJECT("Wsclient",HOME()+"ffc\_webservices.vcx")
loWS.cWSName = "FoxWiki"
loWiki = loWS.SetupClient("http://fox.wikis.com/wikiwebservice.wsdl", ;
  "wikiwebservice", "wikiwebserviceSoapPort")
```

In VFP 8, the way you use registered Web services is totally different because they're no longer included in the type list IntelliSense displays. (We suspect the only reason you can still access the XML Web Services Registration dialog from the IntelliSense Manager is because you can in VFP 7.) Instead, you drag a Web service from the Toolbox to either a code window or a container (such as a form) in the Form or Class Designers. If you drag to a code window, VFP generates code. Dragging to the Form or Class Designer adds an object to the container.

Here's the code generated in a code window for the same Web service as the VFP 7 example (formatted slightly different to fit the printed page):

```
LOCAL lowikiwebservice AS "MSSOAP.SoapClient30"
LOCAL lowikiwebservice AS "XML Web Service"
* Do not remove or alter following line. It is used to support IntelliSense for
* your XML Web service.
*__VFPWSDef__: lowikiwebservice = http://fox.wikis.com/wikiwebservice.wsdl ,
*    wikiwebservice , wikiwebserviceSoapPort
LOCAL loException, lcErrorMsg, loWSHandler
TRY
  loWSHandler = NEWOBJECT("WSHandler", IIF(VERSION(2) = 0, "", ;
    HOME() + "FFC\") + "_ws3client.vcx")
  lowikiwebservice = loWSHandler.SetupClient( ;
    "http://fox.wikis.com/wikiwebservice.wsdl", "wikiwebservice", ;
    "wikiwebserviceSoapPort")
* Call your XML Web service here.  ex: leResult = lowikiwebservice.SomeMethod()
CATCH TO loException
  lcErrorMsg = "Error: " + TRANSFORM(loException.Errorno) + " - " + ;
    loException.Message
  DO CASE
    CASE VARTYPE(lowikiwebservice)#"O"
      * Handle SOAP error connecting to web service
    CASE !EMPTY(lowikiwebservice.FaultCode)
      * Handle SOAP error calling method
      lcErrorMsg = lcErrorMsg + CHR(13) + lowikiwebservice.Detail
    OTHERWISE
      * Handle other error
```

```
ENDCASE
* Use for debugging purposes
MESSAGEBOX(lcErrorMsg)
FINALLY
ENDTRY
```

There are several things to note about this code. First, it uses the new TRY structure (see Chapter 12, "Error Handling") to make the code handle errors more gracefully. More importantly, it uses a different class, WSHandler in _WS3Client.VCX rather than WSClient in _WebServices.VCX, to act as the Web service proxy.

Dragging a Web service from the Toolbox to the Form or Class Designers provides a brand new capability in VFP 8: visual use of a Web service. The Toolbox adds an instance of the same WSHandler class used for code to the container you dropped the Web service on and fills in several properties with information about the selected Web service. Now for the cool part: right-click on the object and choose Builder from the context menu to launch the new XML Web Service Builder for the object. This builder provides a way to configure the WSHandler object so it not only calls a particular method of the Web service, but also obtains any parameters needed for the method in a variety of ways (such as prompting the user or from controls in the form) and binds the results to other controls.

WikiSearch.SCX, shown in **Figure 8**, demonstrates the use of WSHandler. This form uses the FoxWiki Web service to search for a specific string in the FoxWiki. The results are shown in a grid that auto-fits the columns to its contents and provides hyperlinks to the Wiki articles (see Chapter 9, "OOP Enhancements", for information on the new Grid.AutoFit and TextBox.EnableHyperlink properties).

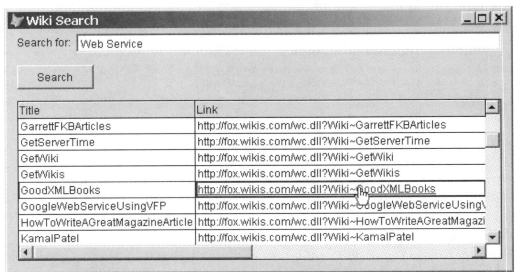

Figure 8. WikiSearch.SCX provides a practical example of using Web services in VFP 8: searching the FoxWiki for a specific string. Use Ctrl-Click to follow the hyperlinks.

*The downloads at **www.hentzenwerke.com** include WikiSearch.SCX. However, instead of running this form directly, run WikiSearch.PRG, also available in the downloads. This PRG ensures the path to the WSHandler object in WikiSearch.SCX is correct for your system.*

The WSHandler object is based on Custom, so it doesn't appear in Figure 8. When you select it in the Form Designer and invoke the builder for it, the XML Web Service Builder, shown in **Figure 9**, appears. Page 2, Operations, is automatically selected because the Web service has already been defined. This page allows you to define the operations (which methods of the Web service are called) and which clients (other controls) will consume the results of each operation.

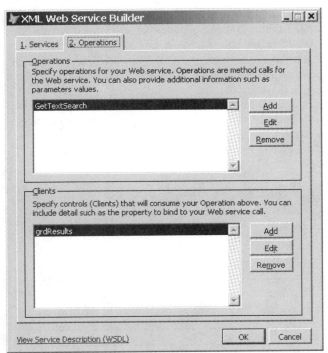

Figure 9. *The XML Web Service Builder allows you to define which methods of a Web service are called and which other objects in the container will use the results of the Web service.*

To define an operation, click on the Add button. This adds a new operation and displays the dialog shown in **Figure 10**. This dialog is also displayed if you select an existing operation and click on Edit. To remove an operation, select it and click on the Remove button.

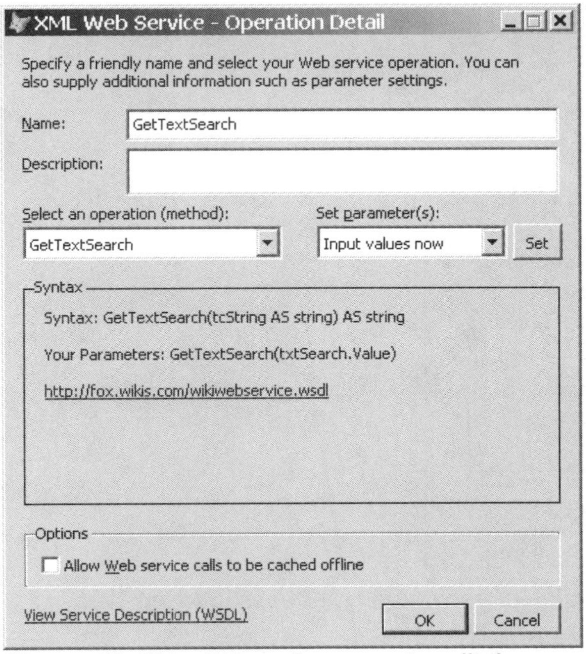

Figure 10. *This dialog allows you to edit the properties of an operation, including which method to call and what parameters to pass to it.*

There are several properties you can set for an operation. You can enter a friendly name and description in the appropriate controls. To select the Web service method to call, choose it from the Select an operation (method) combo box. The syntax for the selected method is shown in the Syntax area. You can also view the WSDL file for the Web service if you wish. If you turn on the Allow Web service calls to be cached offline option, WSHandler will cache the results of a Web service call and use those results when the Web service isn't available for a future call.

Use the Set parameter(s) combo box to specify how the values for the parameters passed to it are obtained. The choices are Input values now, Programmatically set at run-time, and Prompt at run-time. Programmatically set at run-time means you will set the value in code. Use Prompt at run-time if you want VFP to display a dialog in which the user can enter the values (likely only useful for developer tools rather than end-user applications). The term "Input values now" is somewhat misleading, since it doesn't necessarily mean you enter hard-coded values (although you certainly can do that). When you select that choice, the Set button is enabled. Click on it to display the dialog shown in **Figure 11**.

Figure 11. You can specify how the value of each parameter passed to the Web service method is obtained.

To specify a value for a parameter, select it in the Select parameter list, choose Value (expression) as the parameter type, and enter the value into the edit box below this option. To indicate the value is an expression that should be evaluated at runtime, precede it with "=". To obtain the parameter value from another control, choose Control/Property, put a checkmark in front of the appropriate control, and select the property that holds the value from the combo box below the control list. In Figure 11, the tcString parameter is obtained from the Value property of the txtSearch text box in the WikiSearch form.

To define a client for an operation, click on the Add button beside the Clients list in the Operations page of XML Web Service Builder. This adds a new client and displays the dialog shown in **Figure 12**. This dialog is also displayed if you select an existing client and click on Edit. Use the Remove button to remove the selected client.

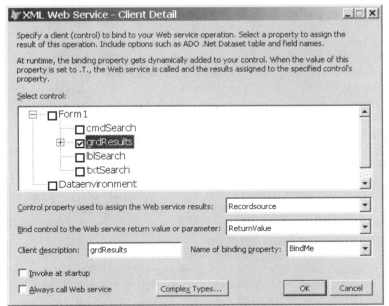

Figure 12. *Use this dialog to set the properties of a client of a Web service operation. This allows you to bind the results of the operation to a control and define when the operation is invoked.*

Use the client dialog to specify which control in the container is the client for the operation. Select the desired control by putting a checkmark beside its name in the control list. You can then indicate which property of the control receives the result, and whether the property is bound to a parameter or the return value of the Web service method. The Client description setting is used as a friendly name for the client; it's displayed in the dialog shown in Figure 9, for example.

If you turn on the Invoke at startup option, the operation executes when the container instantiates. Otherwise, you'll have to invoke it manually. If the client object is a CursorAdapter and you turn on Invoke at startup, you're warned you should set the form's BindControls property to False. That way there won't be any problem with controls bound to the CursorAdapter. WSHandler automatically sets BindControls to True after the CursorAdapter has been filled with data from the Web service so data binding can occur.

If you turn on the Always call Web service option, the client will always call the Web service method. Otherwise, WSHandler will reuse the results when it detects multiple clients call the same operation at the same time (such as when the container instantiates).

The property you specify in the Name of binding property control is interesting. WSHandler adds this property to the client control at runtime if it doesn't already exist. The property acts like a switch: setting its value to True causes the WSHandler object to call the Web service method and put the results into the client control. (WSHandler uses BINDEVENTS() so it's notified when the property's value changes. See Chapter 11, "Event Binding", for information on how this new feature works.) Custom properties or methods in the client control appear in the combo box for this option, as does a default "BindMe" property.

Not all Web services return simple XML, such as a value. Some, such as the Google search Web service, return objects serialized as XML. Others may return ADO.NET DataSets or VFP cursors converted to XML via CURSORTOXML(). If the Web service you want to call returns complex XML, click on the Complex Types button to display the dialog shown in **Figure 13**. Click on the Query button to call the Web service method immediately; the builder will then examine the return value and fill in the rest of the controls. For example, if the Web service returns an ADO.NET DataSet, the Dataset option is selected, the Dataset tables combo box is filled with the names of the tables in the DataSet, and the Table fields combo box shows the fields in the selected table. (In the case of a grid client, Table fields is ignored and the grid is bound to the selected table.) If the Web service returns an XML string that can be converted into a VFP cursor (as is the case with the WikiWebService used in these examples), you'll be informed of that and asked if you want to view the cursor's schema. If you choose Yes, the Dataset tables and Table fields combo boxes are filled in. The Use existing cursor if already opened option tells WSHandler to create a new cursor with a new alias if an existing cursor with the same name as the Dataset table is open. The Reset button clears the choices. The Attach button is only enabled if the client object is a CursorAdapter and you click on Query to query the Web service. Under those conditions, if you click on the Attach button and choose Yes in the subsequent dialog, the builder will update the CursorSchema property of the CursorAdapter object to match the schema of the selected table in the DataSet. (See Chapter 6, "Improved Data Access", for information on CursorAdapter.)

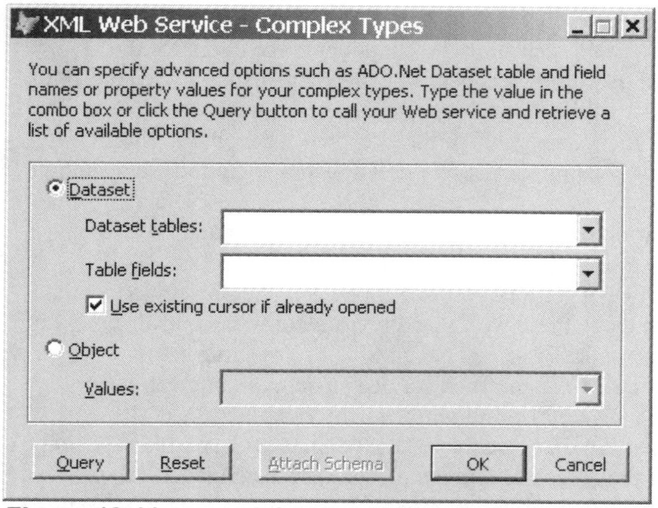

Figure 13. You can define how XML containing complex types such as ADO.NET DataSets or objects is treated using this dialog.

As you can see from Figures 9 through 12, the WSHandler object in the WikiSearch form calls the GetTextSearch method of the FoxWiki Web service, passing it the contents of the Value property of the txtSearch text box, and putting the results into the RecordSource property of the grdResults grid. This operation is not invoked at startup, so we have to start it somehow. That's done when you click on the Search button; the Click method of that button has the following code:

```
Thisform.grdResults.BindMe = .T.
Thisform.grdResults.AutoFit()
```

Setting the BindMe property of grdResults to True starts the operation because that was the property specified as Name of binding property in Figure 12. When it's finished, the cursor will be created and the grid bound to it (assuming everything worked). The grid's AutoFit method ensures the grid columns are adjusted to fit the received data.

So, we now have a fully functional form that searches the FoxWiki for all articles containing a certain text string and displays the results in a grid, complete with hyperlinks back to the articles. Not bad for just two lines of code!

The XML Web Service Builder has an additional page: Services (**Figure 14**). Use this page to specify the Web service to invoke if you drag the Generic Handler item from the Toolbox to a form instead of a specific Web service item, or if you wish to change the Web service you originally selected (using the "Change XML Web service" link). The View operations section allows you to see the various methods of the Web service and the syntax for the selected method.

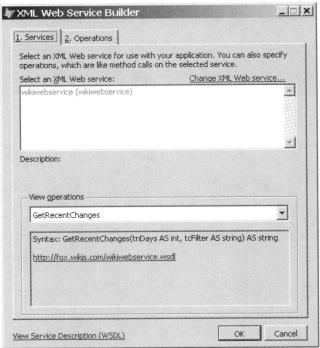

Figure 14. *The Services page of the XML Web Service Builder allows you to select a Web service to use.*

Publishing Web services

VFP 7 added a Web Services Publisher dialog that makes it easy to publish a VFP COM DLL as a Web service. VFP 8 adds a new STK3 Wizard button to this dialog (**Figure 15**). It opens the Soap Toolkit 3.0 WSDL Generator, which provides an alternate way to publish a Web service. There's also a new way to get to the dialog besides Tools | Wizards | Web Services: through the Publish your XML Web Service link in the XML Web Services pane of the Task Pane Manager.

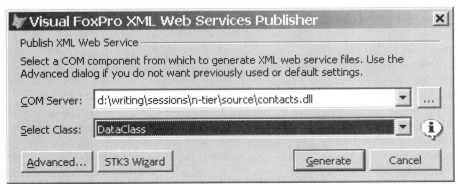

Figure 15. Publishing a Web service. Specify the DLL containing the Web service class and choose Generate.

The options dialog launched when you click on the Advanced button has been expanded significantly. Instead of the single set of options in VFP 7, the dialog (**Figure 16**) now has three pages of options. New in VFP 8 is the ability to specify the methods exposed through the Web service (the Methods page) and the namespaces used in the files generated by the Web Services Publisher. Also, since XML Web services are now registered in the Toolbox rather than IntelliSense, the IntelliSense scripts option was removed.

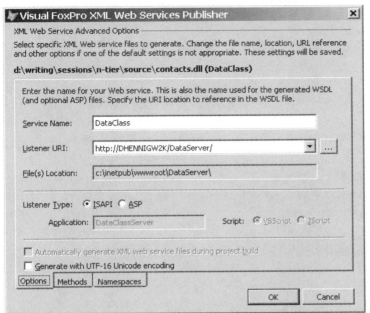

Figure 16. The advanced options dialog in VFP 8 has more choices than its VFP 7 counterpart, including options to select which methods to expose and namespaces to use.

Summary

VFP has been able to serve as a COM client since VFP 3 and a COM server since VFP 5. However, every new version has improved VFP's COM support, and the enhancements in VFP 8 are a welcome change for developers working in a COM environment. The extra capabilities VFP 8 has in working with Web services make it easier than ever for developers to develop applications that use these building blocks to create distributed applications.

Updates and corrections to this chapter can be found on Hentzenwerke's web site, **www.hentzenwerke.com**. Click on "Catalog" and navigate to the page for this book.

Chapter 11
Event Binding

VFP 7 gave us the ability to bind our code to events of COM objects. VFP 8 goes a step farther, allowing us to bind code to events of VFP objects. In addition, this version gives us the ability to fire events.

Programming Windows applications is all about events. Things happen and our code responds to them. The more events we can respond to, the more control our applications have.

Since Visual FoxPro was introduced (and even, to some extent, in earlier versions of FoxPro), we've been able to write code that executes when the user acts or when something happens elsewhere on the system. Initially, we could respond only to events exposed in the VFP environment. That changed in VFP 7 with the addition of the EVENTHANDLER() function, which lets you attach VFP code to an event of a COM object.

VFP 8 gives us a similar capability for native objects—we can attach code to any property, event or method of a FoxPro object. Your first reaction might be to wonder why you'd want to do this—after all, if you want code to fire when a VFP event happens, you can just put code in the event method. However, there are situations where you can't do that. The most obvious is when you're using objects for which the source code isn't available, such as a third-party tool. In addition, event binding lets you determine at runtime what you bind to a particular event, and lets you bind the same code to a number of events without having to modify all the objects in question. You can also bind several different methods to the same event. (Consider things like updating a progress bar by binding to the events whose progress you're tracking.)

Another new feature of VFP 8 provides a totally new capability. In earlier versions of VFP, while you can run the code that's associated with an event, there's no way to actually fire the event itself. The new RAISEEVENT() function lets you fire the event, executing not just that event method, but any other methods bound to that event.

Binding events

Two objects are involved in any case of event binding. The object whose event is bound is called the *event source*. The object containing the code to run when the event occurs is called the *event handler*. The method of the event handler that's bound to the event is called the *delegate*. So what's happening is the delegate method of the event handler executes whenever the specified method of the event source fires.

The way you make that happen is by calling the BINDEVENT() function. The syntax is:

```
BINDEVENT( oEventSource, cMethod, oEventHandler, cDelegate, nFlags )
```

BINDEVENT() is for VFP objects, not COM objects, so both oEventSource and oEventHandler must be native VFP objects. Use EVENTHANDLER() to bind VFP code to COM objects. You also need to be aware of the scope of the methods involved. You can only bind to a method that's visible from the bound object. For instance, you can't bind a method of one object to a protected method of another.

For example, to bind the RightClick method of a text box referenced by oTextbox to the HandleRightClick method of a form referenced by oForm, you'd use this call:

```
BINDEVENT( oTextbox, "RightClick", oForm, "HandleRightClick" )
```

The nFlags parameter lets you determine two things: whether the delegate method fires before or after the event method code of the event source, and whether the delegate code is executed when the bound event is run programmatically or only when the event actually fires. (Actually, it's a little more complicated. See "Firing events" later in this chapter.) **Table 1** shows the four possible settings of nFlags.

Table 1. Event binding flags. The nFlags parameter determines the order in which methods fire, and whether bound code fires on a regular method call.

nFlags	Meaning
0	Run delegate code before event method code. Run delegate code when event method is called programmatically. (Default)
1	Run event method code before delegate code. Run delegate code when event method is called programmatically.
2	Run delegate code before event method code. Do not run delegate code when event method is called programmatically.
3	Run event method code before delegate code. Do not run delegate code when event method is called programmatically.

So, in the example above, when the text box's RightClick event fires (whether from an actual right click or because it was called programmatically), the form's HandleRightClick method executes, and then any code in the text box's RightClick method is run. If you want to execute the text box's RightClick method code first, change the call to this:

```
BINDEVENT( oTextbox, "RightClick", oForm, "HandleRightClick", 1 )
```

To run the HandleRightClick method only when an actual right click occurs (and run it before the RightClick method code), use this call:

```
BINDEVENT( oTextbox, "RightClick", oForm, "HandleRightClick", 2 )
```

If you call BINDEVENT() twice with the same parameters, the delegate method is bound only once. If you pass the same parameters, but change the nFlags parameter, the binding is changed to respect the new value of nFlags.

There are some timing issues when you're binding. Obviously, both objects involved must exist, but you can also run into some issues if you're binding in Load or Init. You can't bind events of controls on a form in the form's Load because the controls haven't been instantiated at that point. The bottom line is you need to make sure objects exist before you use them on either side of a binding relationship.

VFP has some events that are handled like methods internally. They include GotFocus, LostFocus, InteractiveChange, ProgrammaticChange, Refresh, Valid, and When. To bind to those events, you must specify 0 or 1 for nFlags.

You can bind to properties as well as to events and methods. When you do so, the delegate method fires when the property receives a new value. If the property has an Assign method, the delegate method may fire twice; first, when the assignment statement for the property runs, and again, when a value is assigned to the property in the Assign method. Make sure your code can handle this case.

The delegate method receives the parameters passed to the original event or method. Make sure your code is prepared to receive them. This can seem a little tricky if a single method is serving as a delegate for several different events that receive different parameters. Just receive the parameters and sort out their meanings once you know what event invoked the delegate method. (See "Finding out what's bound" later in this chapter.)

When nFlags is 1, the return value from a method call is the value returned by the delegate, not that of the source method.

 *The Developer Downloads available at **www.hentzenwerke.com** include a form called EventBindDemo.SCX that demonstrates the various nFlags values, as well as dealing with parameters passed to an event handler. The About method of the form contains a detailed explanation of what it does.*

BINDEVENT() returns the number of bindings in effect for the specified method, including the new binding.

You can bind the same source event to multiple delegate methods. When the source event fires, the delegate methods are run in the order they were bound. To change that order, you have to unbind them (see "Turning off event binding" later in this chapter), then use BINDEVENT() to bind them in the order you want them to execute.

You can also bind an event to a method that is, in turn, bound to another method. When the original event occurs, its delegate method fires, as does the delegate method's delegate method. For example, consider this series of bindings:

```
BINDEVENT(oTextBox, "RightClick", oGrid, "RightClick")
BINDEVENT(oGrid, "RightClick", oForm, "HandleRightClick")
```

When a right-click occurs on the text box, first the form's HandleRightClick method fires, and then the grid's RightClick method, and finally the textbox's RightClick method. You can change the order of firing by passing 1 for the nFlags parameter.

Calls to events created by this kind of chain are considered programmatic calls. That means if you pass 2 or 3 for the nFlags parameter in bindings after the first, the chain is broken. Here's the same example as above, except for the nFlags parameter:

```
BINDEVENT(oTextBox, "RightClick", oGrid, "RightClick")
BINDEVENT(oGrid, "RightClick", oForm, "HandleRightClick", 2)
```

In this case, a right-click on the textbox fires the grid's RightClick method and the text box's RightClick method, but the form's HandleRightClick method does not fire.

> You can bind code to events of the _SCREEN object, giving you significant control over VFP's main window.

Turning off event binding

The UNBINDEVENTS() function lets you turn off one or more bindings. There are several ways to call the function. The simplest approach is to pass a single object. When you do so, all bound events involving that object are unbound, whether the object is the event source or the event handler. For example, this line unbinds all events involving the active form, whether the form is the event source or the event handler:

```
UNBINDEVENTS( _SCREEN.ActiveForm )
```

The second approach is to release a specific binding. To do so, you pass the same parameters as you do to create the binding, except for the nFlags parameter. For example, to unbind the RightClick event of oTextbox from oForm's HandleRightClick method, you can issue:

```
UNBINDEVENTS( oTextbox, "RightClick", oForm, "HandleRightClick" )
```

UNBINDEVENTS() returns the number of event bindings released.

Finding out what's bound

It's likely the code you write in the delegate method will need to know what event fired to call it. Fortunately, there's a way to find out. The AEVENTS() function fills an array with information about bound events. There are two ways to call this function:

```
nEventCount = AEVENTS( aArrayOfEvents, 0 )
nEventCount = AEVENTS( aArrayOfEvents, oObject )
```

The first form is intended for use in event handler code; the second offers you a bigger picture regarding what's bound.

Pass 0 for the second parameter to AEVENTS() to find out what binding got you to the call. If you're in a delegate method (or a routine called by the delegate), the array passed as the first parameter is filled with three elements: an object reference to the event source, the name of the event, and an indication of how the event was fired. The third element of the array contains a numeric value. When the event comes from the system (as when a user clicks a button or a timer fires), the value is 0. When the event was fired by RAISEEVENT() (see "Firing events" later in this chapter), this column contains 1. When the event was fired by calling the source method directly, the column contains 2. (Note that the last case can occur only when the nFlags parameter to BINDEVENT() is 0 or 1.)

For example, the EventBindingDemo form mentioned earlier in this chapter includes this code in the delegate method:

```
* Find out who called
AEVENTS(aCallingEvent, 0)

* Put together the message
cMessage = "EventHandler called by " + aCallingEvent[1].Name + "." ;
           + aCallingEvent[2] + CHR(13)
```

 *The Developer Downloads available at **www.hentzenwerke.com** include a form (BoundRightClicks.SCX) that demonstrates binding all right-click events to a single delegate method. The form also binds use of the context menu shortcut key (and its equivalent, Shift-F10) to the same method. The downloads include Chapter11.VCX, which contains the class on which the form is based. The About method of the class explains what's going on.*

For the second form of AEVENTS(), you can pass any object reference as the second parameter. In that case, the resulting array is two-dimensional; it has one row for each binding involving the passed object, whether the object is the event source or the event handler. The columns are described in **Table 2**.

Table 2. Examining event bindings. By passing an object reference to AEVENTS(), you can find out about all bindings involving that object. Each row of the resulting array has five columns, representing one binding.

Column	Contents
1	.T. if the second column represents the event source; .F. if the second column represents the event handler.
2	Object reference to the other object involved in this binding. ("Other" here means the one not passed to the function.)
3	Name of the bound event.
4	Name of the delegate method
5	The nFlags value used to create this binding.

For example, suppose you have a form that contains code to handle all right clicks by calling a form-level method called HandleRightClick. Suppose further the form contains two textboxes and their RightClick methods are bound to the HandleRightClick method, as is the form's RightClick method. The code to set this up might look like:

```
BINDEVENT( THIS.txtTextBox1, "RightClick", THIS, "HandleRightClick")
BINDEVENT( THIS.txtTextBox2, "RightClick", THIS, "HandleRightClick")
BINDEVENT( THIS, "RightClick", THIS, "HandleRightClick")
```

After making these bindings, a call to AEVENTS(), passing the form as the second parameter returns 4. Here's the call, assuming it's made in a method of the form:

```
nEventCount = AEVENTS( aBoundEvents, THIS )
```

Table 3 shows the array contents after this call. As with the other "A" functions, AEVENTS() returns the number of rows in the resulting array. The array is created or resized as needed; if 0 is returned, the array is unchanged.

Table 3. AEVENTS() results. When you pass an object reference as the second parameter, each row represents one binding. The third row in this example considers the binding of the form's RightClick method from the point of view of the event source, while the fourth row looks at it from the event handler perspective.

Column 1	Column 2	Column 3	Column 4	Column 5
.T.	Object reference to txtTextBox1	"RIGHTCLICK"	"HANDLERIGHTCLICK"	0
.T.	Object reference to txtTextBox2	"RIGHTCLICK"	"HANDLERIGHTCLICK"	0
.T.	Object reference to the form	"RIGHTCLICK"	"HANDLERIGHTCLICK"	0
.F.	Object reference to the form	"RIGHTCLICK"	"HANDLERIGHTCLICK"	0

Firing events

Events happen, but they don't always happen when we want them to, so VFP 8 provides a way to fire event handler code even when the underlying event hasn't occurred. The new RAISEEVENT() function let you fire events programmatically.

When you call the method associated with an event, the method code is executed, but the event doesn't actually fire. By default, when you have additional code bound to an event, the additional code (the delegate method) is also executed in that case. However, if you pass 2 or 3 to BINDEVENT() for the nFlags parameter, calling the method directly does not execute the delegate code. So, in that situation, issuing:

```
oForm.cmdClose.Click()
```

runs the code in the Click method, but not any delegate code bound to the Click event.

The RAISEEVENT() function ensures all bound code is executed, regardless of the nFlags parameter to BINDEVENT(). The syntax is:

```
RAISEEVENT( oObject, cEvent [, uParms ] )
```

uParms lets you pass parameters to the method; it's a comma-separated list of parameters.

The event you want to raise must be in scope in the method that's raising it. So a method of one object can't raise a protected event of another object, but an object can raise its own protected event.

In the previous example, when you issue:

```
RAISEEVENT( oForm.cmdClose, "Click" )
```

both the Click method's code and any delegate code is executed (in the order specified in the call to BINDEVENT()). However, even in this case, the Click event itself doesn't fire—the button doesn't visually depress and, if you use Event Tracking, you won't see a Click event in the results.

The bottom line is RAISEEVENT() along with the nFlags parameter of BINDEVENT() lets you decide whether to handle a call to method code differently than actually firing the event method. You can use these functions with custom methods, not just native events, so you can make your own methods behave exactly like events.

For example, you probably want use of the context menu key (or Shift-F10) to be handled just like a right click. The BoundRightClicks form mentioned earlier in the chapter handles this by binding each control's KeyPress method to the HandleRightClick delegate method, and then checking to see what key was pressed. A better approach is probably to use a separate delegate method for KeyPress, and if the appropriate keystroke is encountered, raise the RightClick method. Here's the code for the delegate method for KeyPress:

```
LPARAMETERS nKeyCode, nShiftAltCtrl

* Do any generic keypress handling
DO CASE
CASE nKeyCode = 93 AND nShiftAltCtrl = 1
   AEVENTS(aBoundEvent, 0)
   RAISEEVENT( aBoundEvent[1], "RightClick")

OTHERWISE
   * Handle other generic cases
ENDCASE

RETURN
```

 *The Developer Downloads available at **www.hentzenwerke.com** includes this version of the form as AlternateBoundRightClicks.SCX; the underlying form class is in Chapter11.VCX. The About method of the class explains the strategy.*

Using event binding

Even after reading about these capabilities, you may have trouble seeing where you'd use them. Here are a few examples of the situations where binding and raising events offer new opportunities, or result in simpler, more maintainable code.

One case where event binding allows new abilities is binding to the main VFP window. While _SCREEN has the same events as other forms, there's never been a way to add code to those events. You still can't subclass _SCREEN and add code to its methods, but event binding lets you write code that responds when things happen. For example, you could bind a custom context menu to _SCREEN's RightClick event or keep an image you're using as wallpaper centered by binding to the Resize event.

More generally, enabling resizing of forms lends itself to the event binding model very well. Most resize controls work by looping through all the controls on a form. With event binding, each control can bind to the Resize event of its container. Then, when a form is resized, all the resize code fires automatically; there's no need to add special code to the form beyond what it needs to resize itself.

Another situation where event binding simplifies code is in keeping a toolbar in synch with application activities, especially, keeping the right buttons enabled and disabled. It's common now to use a timer on the toolbar that interrogates the application and the active form, and then enables and disables buttons. A simpler architecture defines a set of events (such as OnNavigate or BeginEdit), and then binds toolbar methods to those events. (Of course, form methods can also be bound to the same events.) Then, as the user works with the application, the appropriate events are raised and every button is updated as needed.

Grids offer some opportunities for using event binding. Consider binding the events of controls in the grid to the corresponding grid events. This avoids having to put code like This.Parent.Parent.DblClick in the DblClick method of each control in the grid.

Finally, you can use event binding to keep track of changes to properties. Although you can get the same effect with an Assign method in classes you design, event binding gives you the same capability with objects you can't modify.

Summary

The ability to bind code to events and to raise events provides an easier way to handle a variety of situations. It's especially useful in retrofitting functionality into applications, dealing with third-party code, or adding behavior you want only under certain circumstances.

Updates and corrections to this chapter can be found on Hentzenwerke's web site, **www.hentzenwerke.com**. Click on "Catalog" and navigate to the page for this book.

Chapter 12
Error Handling

VFP 8 now has structured error handling. This powerful new feature provides a third layer of error handling and allows you to eliminate a lot of code related to passing and handling error information.

VFP 3 greatly improved the error handling ability of FoxPro by adding an Error method to objects. This allowed objects to encapsulate their own error handling and not rely on a global error handler.

However, one of the downsides of putting code in the Error method of your objects is it overrides the use of the ON ERROR command. That makes sense, because to do otherwise would break encapsulation. Unfortunately, one hole in this strategy is if an object with code in its Error method calls procedural code (such as a PRG) or a method of an object that doesn't have code in its Error method, and an error occurs in the called code, the Error method of the calling object is fired, even if the called code set up a local ON ERROR handler. There are two problems with this mechanism:

- Many types of errors can be anticipated in advance, such as trying to open a table someone else might be using exclusively. However, since the ON ERROR handler set up by the called routine isn't fired, the routine doesn't get a chance to handle its own error.

- Since the calling object has no idea what kind of errors the called routine might encounter, how can it possibly deal with them except in a generic way (such as logging it or displaying a generic message to the user)?

Another issue is because you can't use a local ON ERROR handler in an object if you're using the Error method, that method must handle all errors in all methods of the object. That often leads to code in Error that looks like this:

```
lparameters tnError, tcMethod, tnLine
do case
  case tcMethod = 'OpenCursor' and tnError = 1
    * handle "file not found" in OpenCursor method
  case tcMethod = 'OpenCursor' and tnError = 15
    * handle "not a table" in OpenCursor
  case tcMethod = 'OutputResults' and tnError = 1102
    * handle "cannot create file" in OutputResults
  * more cases here
endcase
```

Clearly, a better mechanism is needed. Fortunately, VFP 8 gives it to us: structured error handling.

Structured error handling

C++ has had structured error handling for a long time. .NET adds structured error handling to languages that formerly lacked it, such as VB.NET. So what is structured error handling? Structured error handling means code in a special block, or structure, is executed, and if any errors occur in that code, another part of the structure deals with it.

VFP 8 implements structured error handling in the following way:

- A new TRY ... ENDTRY structure allows you to execute code that may cause an error and handle it within the structure. This overrides all other error handling, so it provides true local error handling (meaning errors aren't sent to some other routine or method).

- A new THROW command lets you pass errors up to a higher-level error handler.

- A new Exception base class provides an object-oriented way of passing around information about errors.

Let's take a look at these improvements.

TRY ... ENDTRY

The key to structured error handling is the new TRY ... ENDTRY structure. Here's its syntax:

```
try
   [ TryCommands ]
[ catch [ to VarName ] [ when lExpression ]
   [ CatchCommands ] ]
   [ exit ]
   [ throw [ uExpression ] ]
[ catch [ to VarName ] [ when lExpression ]
   [ CatchCommands ] ]
   [ exit ]
   [ throw [ uExpression ] ]
[ ... (additional catch blocks) ]
[ finally
   [ FinallyCommands ] ]
endtry
```

TryCommands represents the commands VFP will attempt to execute. If no errors occur, the code in the optional FINALLY block is executed (if present) and execution continues with the code following ENDTRY. If any error occurs in the TRY block, VFP immediately exits that block and begins executing the CATCH statements.

If TO *VarName* is included in a CATCH statement, VFP creates an Exception object, fills its properties with information about the error, and puts a reference to the object into the *VarName* variable. *VarName* can only be a regular variable, not a property of an object. If you previously declared the variable, it'll have whatever scope you declared it as (such as LOCAL); if not, it will be scoped as PRIVATE. We'll look at the Exception base class later in this chapter.

The CATCH statements can act like CASE statements if the optional WHEN clause is used. The expression in the WHEN clause must return a logical value so VFP can decide what to do. If the expression is True, the code in this CATCH statement's block is executed. If not, VFP moves to the next CATCH statement. This process continues until a CATCH statement's WHEN expression returns True, a CATCH statement with no WHEN clause is hit, or there are no more CATCH statements (we'll discuss the last case later). Normally, the WHEN expression will look at properties of the Exception object, such as ErrorNo, which contains the error number. Here's a typical example:

```
try
  * some code
catch to loException when loException.ErrorNo = SomeErrorNum
  * handle this type of error
catch to loException when loException.ErrorNo = AnotherErrorNum
  * handle this type of error
catch to loException
  * handle all other errors
endtry
```

Once VFP finds a CATCH statement to use, the commands in that block are executed. After the block is done, the code in the optional FINALLY block is executed (if present) and execution continues with the code following ENDTRY.

The following example shows how CATCH statements are evaluated, and that the TRY structure overrides any ON ERROR setting.

```
on error llError = .T.
llError = .F.
try
* This will cause error #12 since xxx is not defined:
  wait window xxx
catch to loException when loException.ErrorNo = 1
  wait window 'Error #1'
catch to loException when loException.ErrorNo = 2
  wait window 'Error #2'
catch to loException
  messagebox('Error #' + transform(loException.ErrorNo) + chr(13) + ;
    'Message: ' + loException.Message)
finally
  messagebox('Finally')
endtry
on error
messagebox('ON ERROR ' + iif(llError, 'caught ', 'did not catch ') + ;
  'the error')
```

 *This code is included in SimpleTry.PRG in the Developer Download files for this chapter, available at **www.hentzenwerke.com**.*

If VFP doesn't find a CATCH statement to use, then an unhandled exception error (error 2059) occurs. You don't really want this to happen for a variety of reasons, the biggest one being the problem that caused the original error isn't handled, and now you have a new error to deal with. Here's an example of this:

```
on error do ErrHandler with error(), program(), lineno()
try
* This will cause error #12 since xxx is not defined:
  wait window xxx
catch to loException when loException.ErrorNo = 1
  wait window 'Error #1'
catch to loException when loException.ErrorNo = 2
  wait window 'Error #2'
finally
  messagebox('Finally')
endtry
on error

procedure ErrHandler(tnError, tcMethod, tnLine)
local laError[1]
aerror(laError)
messagebox('Error #' + transform(tnError) + ' occurred in line ' + ;
  transform(tnLine) + ' of ' + tcMethod + chr(13) + 'Message: ' + ;
  message() + chr(13) + 'Code: ' + message(1))
```

 The Developer Download files for this chapter, available at
www.hentzenwerke.com, include this code in UnhandledException.PRG.

When you run this code, you'll see the message shown in **Figure 1**. Notice the error number, line number, error message, and code are all for the unhandled exception error, not the original error, and the error is caught by the ON ERROR handler rather than the TRY structure. Although the error message includes information about the original error, you'd have to parse it to obtain that error number and message. Also note the FINALLY block executed before the message appeared. That's because the error didn't occur until the ENDTRY statement was reached, at which point VFP realized the error hadn't been handled.

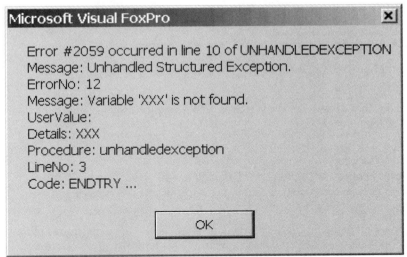

Figure 1. *An unhandled exception error muddies things because it's a new error on top of the original one.*

As you can see from this example, it's good practice to always include a final CATCH with no WHEN clause. It's like the OTHERWISE in a CASE structure, ensuring all possible cases are handled.

Less is more

One of the benefits of structured error handling is it allows you to reduce the amount of code related to handling and propagating errors. One source estimates up to half of the code in an application is related to dealing with errors.

Here's some code that might be used to output the contents of a table to a Word document:

```
lcOnError = on('ERROR')
on error llError = .T.
llError = .F.
use MyTable
if not llError
  loWord = createobject('Word.Application')
  if not llError
* process the table, sending the results to Word via Automation
  else
* handle the error instantiating Word
  endif
else
* handle the error opening the table
endif
on error &lcOnError
```

In VFP 8, this code can be reduced to:

```
try
  use MyTable
  loWord = createobject('Word.Application')
* process the table, sending the results to Word via Automation
catch
* handle the errors in CATCH blocks
endtry
```

Because it has fewer lines of code, fewer variables, and a simpler structure, this code is much easier to read and maintain.

You can't go back

One important difference between structured error handling and the other types of VFP error handling is you can't go back to the code that caused the error. In an Error method or ON ERROR routine, there are a few ways to continue:

- RETURN (or an implied RETURN by having no RETURN statement) returns to the line of code following the one that caused the error. This typically gives rise to further errors, because the one that caused the error didn't complete its task (such as initializing a variable or opening a table).

- RETRY returns to the line of code that caused the error. Unless the problem was somehow magically fixed, it's almost certain to cause the same error again.

- QUIT terminates the application.

- RETURN TO returns to a routine on the call stack, such as the one containing the READ EVENTS statement. This is very useful if you want to stay in the application and not go back to the routine that caused the error. Of course, that doesn't mean all is well, but frequently allows the user to do something else if the error wasn't catastrophic (for example, a simple resource contention issue while trying to get into a form).

In the case of a TRY structure, once an error occurs, the TRY block is exited and you can't return to it. If you use RETURN or RETRY in the CATCH block, you'll cause error 2060 to occur. You can, of course, use QUIT to terminate the application.

Try, try again

It may not be obvious, but you can nest TRY structures. In other words, your code can have a TRY structure that itself is wrapped in a TRY structure. You wouldn't necessarily do that in a single routine. However, you might do this in code that calls another routine that uses a TRY structure. For example:

```
try
  do SomeFunction
catch to loException
* handle error
endtry

function SomeFunction
```

```
try
* do something here
catch to loException when loException.ErrorNo = SomeNumber
* handle anticipated error
catch to loException
   throw
endtry
```

The reason for using the "outer" TRY structure is the code being called may raise an error using the THROW command, which we'll look at later in this chapter, and you may want to handle that error locally rather than in a global error handler.

Exception object

VFP 8 includes a new Exception base class to provide an object-oriented means of passing around information about errors. As we saw earlier, Exception objects are created when you use TO *VarName* in CATCH commands. They're also created when you use the THROW command, which we'll discuss next.

Besides the usual properties, methods, and events (Init, Destroy, BaseClass, AddProperty, and others), Exception has a set of properties containing information about an error; these properties are shown in **Table 1**. All of them are read-write at runtime.

Table 1. The properties of an Exception object contain information about an error.

Property	Type	Description	Similar Function
Details	Character	Additional information about the error (such as the name of a variable or file that doesn't exist); NULL if not applicable.	SYS(2018)
ErrorNo	Numeric	The error number.	ERROR()
LineContents	Character	The line of code that caused the error.	MESSAGE(1)
LineNo	Numeric	The line number.	LINENO()
Message	Character	The error message.	MESSAGE()
Procedure	Character	The procedure or method where the error occurred.	PROGRAM()
StackLevel	Numeric	The call stack level of the procedure.	ASTACKINFO()
UserValue	Variant	The expression specified in a THROW statement.	Not applicable

THROW

VFP 8 provides a new way to raise an error in a higher-level error handler: the THROW command. THROW is like the ERROR command in that it causes an error to be passed to an error handler, but it works quite differently. Here's the syntax for this command:

```
throw [ uExpression ]
```

uExpression can be anything you wish, such as a message, a numeric value, or an Exception object.

If *uExpression* is specified, THROW creates an Exception object, sets its ErrorNo property to 2071, its Message to "User Thrown Error", and its UserValue to *uExpression*. If *uExpression* isn't specified, the original Exception object (the one created when an error occurred) is used if it exists and a new Exception object is created if not. In either case, it then passes the Exception object to the next higher-level error handler (typically a TRY structure that wraps the TRY structure from which the THROW was called).

Here's an example. It uses nested TRY structures so the outer TRY catches the Exception object thrown by the inner one.

```
messagebox('First example: THROW loException throws a new Exception ' + ;
   'object with the original one in its UserValue property.', 0, 'Example')
try
   try
* This will cause error #12 since xxx is not defined:
      wait window xxx
   catch to loException when loException.ErrorNo = 1
      wait window 'Error #1'
   catch to loException when loException.ErrorNo = 2
      wait window 'Error #2'
   catch to loException
      throw loException
   endtry
catch to loException
   messagebox('Error #' + transform(loException.ErrorNo) + ;
      chr(13) + 'Message: ' + loException.Message, 0, ;
      'Thrown Exception')
   messagebox('Error #' + ;
      transform(loException.UserValue.ErrorNo) + chr(13) + ;
      'Message: ' + loException.UserValue.Message, 0, ;
      'Original Exception')
endtry

* Now do the same thing, but use THROW without any expression

messagebox('Second example: THROW with no parameter throws the existing ' + ;
   'Exception object.', 0, 'Example')
try
   try
* This will cause error #12 since xxx is not defined:
      wait window xxx
   catch to loException when loException.ErrorNo = 1
      wait window 'Error #1'
   catch to loException when loException.ErrorNo = 2
      wait window 'Error #2'
   catch to loException
      throw
   endtry
catch to loException
   messagebox('Error #' + transform(loException.ErrorNo) + chr(13) + ;
      'Message: ' + loException.Message, 0, 'Thrown Exception')
endtry
```

 *This code is available by downloading TestThrow.PRG from the Developer Download files at **www.hentzenwerke.com**.*

Although you might think the THROW loException command in the first part of this code throws loException to the next higher error handler, that isn't the case. THROW creates a new

Exception object and throws it, putting loException into the UserValue property of the new object. Thus, the code in the outer TRY structure shows the Exception object it receives is about the user-thrown error. To retrieve information about the original error, you need to get the properties of the Exception object referenced by the UserValue property.

The second part of this example shows THROW by itself will rethrow the Exception object if there is one. In this case, we have the same object, so the outer error handler doesn't have to reference the UserValue property.

You can use a THROW statement outside a TRY structure, but it doesn't really provide any benefit over the ERROR command, because in either case, an error handler must be in place to catch it or the VFP error handler will be called. In fact, if something other than a TRY structure catches a THROW, it will likely be somewhat confused about what the real problem is, because only a TRY structure can catch the Exception object that's thrown. In the case of an Error method or ON ERROR routine, the parameters received and the results of AERROR() will be related to the THROW statement and the unhandled exception error rather than the reason the THROW was used. Some of the Exception object's properties are placed into columns 2 and 3 of the array filled by AERROR(), so the error handler could parse those columns. However, that doesn't seem like the proper way to do things. Instead, make sure THROW is only used when it can be caught by a TRY structure.

The FINALLY clause

A common question about structured error handling is why the FINALLY clause is necessary. After all, the code following the ENDTRY statement is executed regardless of whether an error occurs or not. It turns out this isn't actually true; as you'll see, errors can "bubble up" to the next highest error handler, and you may not return from that error handler. That means you can't guarantee the code following ENDTRY will execute. However, the code in the FINALLY block will always execute.

Here's an example that shows this. The call to the ProcessData function is wrapped in a TRY structure. ProcessData itself has a TRY structure, but it only handles the error of not being able to open the table exclusively; any other errors are thrown to the next highest handler. As a result, the error caused by WAIT WINDOW XXX error will bubble up to the outer TRY structure in the main routine, and therefore the code following ENDTRY in ProcessData won't be executed. Comment out the FINALLY block in ProcessData and run this code. You'll see the Customers table is still open at the end. Uncomment the FINALLY block and run it again; you'll see this time, the Customers table was closed, so the code properly cleaned up after itself.

```
try
  do ProcessData
catch to loException
  messagebox('Error #' + transform(loException.ErrorNo) + ' occurred.')
endtry
if used('customer')
  messagebox('Customer table is still open')
else
  messagebox('Customer table was closed')
endif
close databases all
```

```
function ProcessData
try
  use (_samples + 'data\customer') exclusive
* do some processing
* This will generate error # 12:
  wait window xxx

* Handle not being able to open table exclusively.

catch to loException when loException.ErrorNo = 1705
* whatever

* Throw any other errors.

catch to loException
  throw

* Clean up code. Comment/uncomment this to see the difference.

finally
  if used('customer')
    messagebox('Closing customer table in FINALLY...')
    use
  endif
endtry

* Now cleanup. This code won't execute because the error bubbles up.

if used('customer')
  messagebox('Closing customer table after ENDTRY...')
  use
endif
```

 This code is available as UsingFinally.PRG in the Developer Download files available at ***www.hentzenwerke.com***.

There is one exception to the rule that the FINALLY block will always execute: if a VFP COM object's error handler calls COMRETURNERROR(), execution immediately returns to the COM client.

Errors within errors

One of the biggest issues in error handling in VFP is preventing errors while in an error condition. An "error condition" is defined as the situation in which an error has occurred, it has been trapped by the Error method of an object or an ON ERROR handler, and the handler hasn't yet issued a RETURN or RETRY. If anything goes wrong while your application is in an error condition, there is no safety net to catch you; instead, the user gets a VFP error dialog with a VFP error message and Cancel and Ignore buttons. Bad news! That means your entire error handling mechanism must be the most bug-free part of your application, plus you have to test for things that may not be bugs but environmental issues.

For example, suppose your error handler logs an error to a table called ERRORLOG.DBF. What happens if that file doesn't exist? You have to check for its existence using FILE() and create it if it doesn't exist. What if something else has it open exclusively? You could minimize that by never opening it exclusively, but to be absolutely safe, you should use

FOPEN() first to see if you can open it, since FOPEN() returns an error code rather than raising an error. What if it exists and you can open it using FOPEN(), but it's corrupted? You can't easily test for that, unfortunately.

See the problem? Your error handler can start becoming so complex by testing for anything that can possibly go wrong while in the error condition, you actually introduce bugs in this complex code!

In earlier versions of VFP, there was no solution to this problem. You just wrote some reasonable code, tested it as much as possible, and then hoped for the best. Fortunately, we have a solution in VFP 8: wrapping your error handler in a TRY structure. Because any errors that occur in the TRY block are caught by the CATCH blocks, we now have a safety net for our error handling code.

Here's a simple (albeit contrived) example:

```
on error do ErrHandler with error(), program(), lineno()
use MyBadTableName && this table doesn't exist
on error

procedure ErrHandler(tnError, tcMethod, tnLine)

* Log the error to the ErrorLog table.

try
  use ErrorLog
  insert into ErrorLog values (tnError, tcMethod, tnLine)
  use

* Ignore any problems in our handler.

catch
endtry
return
```

 WrappedErrorHandler.PRG, available in the Developer Download files at ***www.hentzenwerke.com***, *has this code.*

If the ErrorLog table doesn't exist, can't be opened, is corrupted, or for any other reason can't be used, the CATCH block will execute. In this case, there's no code, so the error within the error is ignored.

What happens if there's an error in the CATCH block of an error handler? There are four places where an error could occur: in the CATCH statement, in any function or method called by the CATCH statement, in the CATCH block, or in any function or method called by the CATCH block. Here's an example showing the first two cases:

```
loObject = createobject('MyClass')
try
* This will cause error #12 since xxx is not defined:
  wait window xxx
* Error in CATCH statement (ErrorNo is numeric): skipped
catch to loException when loException.ErrorNo = '12'
* Error in CATCH statement (DoWeHandleError returns string): skipped
catch to loException when DoWeHandleError()
* Error in procedural code called by CATCH statement: skipped
```

```
catch to loException when AnotherHandler()
* Error in method called by CATCH statement: loObject.Error handles it
catch to loException when loObject.Handler()
* This CATCH isn't taken because loObject.Error was fired
catch
  messagebox('Final catch')
endtry

function DoWeHandleError
return 'Yes'

function AnotherHandler
* This will cause error #12 since xxx is not defined:
wait window xxx

define class MyClass as Custom
  function Handler
* This will cause error #12 since xxx is not defined:
    wait window xxx
  endfunc
  procedure Error(tnError, tcMethod, tnLine)
    messagebox('MyClass.Error caught the error')
  endproc
enddefine
```

 This code for this example is provided in BadCatch1.PRG in the Developer Download files at **www.hentzenwerke.com***.*

This code shows a couple of things:

- An error in a CATCH statement, in procedural code called from a CATCH statement, or in the method of an object lacking code in its Error method that's called from a CATCH statement is "eaten" and the CATCH statement is ignored. Execution continues with the next CATCH statement.

- An error in the method of an object with code in its Error method that's called from a CATCH statement is handled by the object's Error method. Notice the original error isn't actually dealt with in this case; the final CATCH block doesn't execute as you might expect, nor do you get an unhandled exception.

The next example shows the second two cases, errors in the CATCH block:

```
try
* This will cause error #12 since xxx is not defined:
  wait window xxx
* Error in CATCH block (ErrorNo is numeric so can't concatenate with string)
catch to loException when loException.ErrorNo = 12
  messagebox(loException.ErrorNo + ' ' + loException.Message)
* You might think this would catch the error in the above CATCH, but it doesn't
catch to loException
  messagebox(transform(loException.ErrorNo) + ' ' + loException.Message)
finally
  messagebox('An unhandled exception error is about to occur because ' + ;
    'there is an error in the CATCH block and no higher-level error ' + ;
    'handler to catch that.', 0, 'Finally Block')
```

```
endtry

* Show error in procedural code called from CATCH block

try
* This will cause error #12 since xxx is not defined:
  wait window xxx
* Error in CATCH block (AnotherHandler has an error)
catch to loException
  AnotherHandler()
finally
  messagebox('An unhandled exception error is about to occur because ' + ;
    'there is an error in a function called from the CATCH block and ' + ;
    'no higher-level error handler to catch that.', 0, 'Finally Block')
endtry

* Show error in an object method called from CATCH block

try
* This will cause error #12 since xxx is not defined:
  wait window xxx
* Error in CATCH block (loObject.Handler has an error)
catch to loException
  loObject.Handler()
endtry

* Now show an outer TRY.

try
  try
* This will cause error #12 since xxx is not defined:
    wait window xxx
  catch to loException when loException.ErrorNo = 12
    messagebox(loException.ErrorNo + ' ' + loException.Message)
  finally
    messagebox('The outer TRY structure will catch the error in the ' + ;
      'CATCH block.', 0, 'Finally Block')
  endtry
* Gotcha!
catch to loException
  messagebox(transform(loException.ErrorNo) + ' ' + loException.Message)
endtry
```

> *This code for this example is provided in BadCatch2.PRG in the Developer Download files at **www.hentzenwerke.com**.*

We can see a couple of things from this example:

- An error in a CATCH block, in procedural code called from a CATCH block, or in the method of an object lacking code in its Error method that's called from a CATCH block bubbles up to the next level of error handler, such as the VFP error handler (shown in this case when an "unhandled exception error" occurs), the Error method of an object (if the TRY was performed within a method of the object), an ON ERROR handler, or an outer TRY (also shown in this example).

- An error in the method of an object with code in its Error method that's called from a CATCH statement is handled by the object's Error method.

So, what does all this mean? First, wrap your error handling code in a TRY structure to ensure any errors that occur won't cause a VFP error dialog to appear. Second, if you're doing anything at all in the CATCH statements or blocks (in other words, not just an empty CATCH statement with no code in the block), wrap the TRY structure in an outer TRY structure. Here's an example:

```
procedure Error(tnError, tcMethod, tnLine)
try
   try
      * error handling code goes here
   catch to loException
      * handle an error in the error handling code
   endtry
* This is the error handler of the error handler of the
* error handler (does your brain hurt yet? <g>): we'll just
* ignore any errors
catch
endtry
```

Note that the outer CATCH statement and block should be empty, or you'll have to use yet another layer of TRY structure around it; that would get ridiculous very quickly!

Wrap your app?

One thing you may be wondering is whether you should wrap your entire application in a TRY structure. Our opinion is you shouldn't do this. The reason is there's no way for the user to stay within the application as soon as an error that bubbles up to this level occurs. VFP seems to do an implicit CLEAR EVENTS if a READ EVENTS statement is wrapped in a TRY structure and an error occurs anywhere. Thus, VFP will exit the TRY block, and the application will terminate once the CATCH and FINALLY blocks have been executed.

Other error-related changes

VFP now handles errors in two places that were previously untrappable: in reports and when tables have invalid DBC backlinks. This is a welcome change because untrappable errors always display the VFP error dialog to the user.

SYS(2410) is a new function that returns a numeric value indicating how an error will be handled at this point in the code. **Table 2** shows the possible values.

Table 2. The return values of SYS(2410) indicate how an error will be handled.

Value	Description
0	VFP's error handler
1	TRY structure
2	Error event
3	ON ERROR

Note that this function isn't perfect. For example, if it's called from within a TRY structure without any CATCH blocks that will execute in the case of an error, SYS(2410) still returns 1.

Summary

The structured error handling features added in VFP 8 provide us with three levels of error handling: local, object, and global. Structured error handling allows you to reduce the amount of code related to propagating error information, making your applications simpler, easier to read, and more maintainable. In addition, some thorny issues, such as one object inadvertently catching errors raised in another, are now neatly dealt with. For more information on error handling strategies, see the "Error Handling in Visual FoxPro" white paper on the Technical Papers page of **http://www.stonefield.com**.

Updates and corrections to this chapter can be found on Hentzenwerke's web site, **www.hentzenwerke.com**. Click on "Catalog" and navigate to the page for this book.

Chapter 13
Language Improvements

Visual FoxPro's programming language is a hybrid of Xbase, SQL, OOP, and a variety of other components. Thanks to its long life, it's a rich, full language. But there's always room for improvement. Beyond the major enhancements described in other chapters, VFP 8 includes a variety of small changes in the language that make it easier to get the results you need.

VFP 8 features some major enhancements in the programming language, such as structured error handling (see Chapter 12, "Error Handling") and the ability to bind code to native events (see Chapter 11, "Event Binding"). Beyond those, however, there are a number of changes that are smaller in scope, but make life easier for VFP developers.

Files and directories

Quite a few of the changes relate to working with files and directories. VFP 8 improves support for hidden files, gives you quick access to the default project directory, and takes better advantage of built-in dialogs.

Where is it?

There are two changes to the HOME() function. In VFP 6 and 7, HOME(5) pointed to the Visual Studio MSDN Samples directory. That made sense for VFP 6, since VFP was part of Visual Studio, and its examples were installed through MSDN. It didn't make sense in VFP 7, and fortunately, has changed in VFP 8. HOME(5) now returns the Visual Studio MSDN directory, if the Visual Studio version of MSDN is installed; if not, it returns the empty string.

It seems every new version of VFP offers new values through HOME(), and VFP 8 is no exception. This version introduces HOME(8), which contains the default directory for new files created by VFP. By default, this is a subdirectory of "My Documents" called "Visual FoxPro Projects." However, we can't find any situation where this directory is used by default, nor can we find a way to change this setting.

Working with hidden files

Addressing hidden files in VFP is a hit-or-miss proposition. Some commands can see them, while others can't. Some commands trigger errors when applied to hidden files, while others simply fail silently. VFP 8 improves this situation somewhat by adding support for hidden and system files to the FILE() and DIRECTORY() functions, and letting the CD/CHDIR command see hidden directories.

FILE() and DIRECTORY() each have a new nFlags parameter. Passing the default value of 0 for this parameter indicates only visible, non-system files and directories should be found. Pass 1 to search for any files, regardless of attributes. For example, the following call checks for the file Desktop.INI in the Windows directory, whether it's visible or hidden.

```
? FILE( "C:\WINDOWS\DESKTOP.INI", 1)
```

Similarly, the following line looks for a directory called C:\BigSecrets, regardless of its status:

```
? DIRECTORY( "C:\BigSecrets", 1)
```

The CD (or CHDIR) command and the nearly equivalent SET DEFAULT also support hidden directories in VFP 8. In earlier versions, specifying a hidden directory in a CD or SET DEFAULT command resulted in error 202, "Invalid path or file name." In VFP 8, they change to the specified directory.

Displaying paths

The DISPLAYPATH() function was added in VFP 7 to provide a way to shorten paths when display space is at a premium. The function takes a path and a number and substitutes an ellipsis for a portion of the path, so the returned value is no longer than the specified number of characters. In VFP 7, the function always returns the path in lower case.

VFP 8 changes DISPLAYPATH() to return its results in the same case passed to it. For example, this call:

```
? DISPLAYPATH( HOME(7), 50 )
```

gives this result:

```
C:\...\Application Data\Microsoft\Visual FoxPro 8\
```

Using system dialogs

VFP has a number of functions that let you call on the system Open and Save dialogs. For example, the GETFILE() and LOCFILE() functions display the Open dialog, while PUTFILE() displays the Save As dialog. In addition, many file-related system dialogs are used throughout the VFP interface. In VFP 8 under Windows 2000 or Windows XP, both the IDE and the functions call on newer, resizable versions of these dialogs that include a Places bar, and a Thumbnails option on the View menu.

In one case, this is a change for the worse, not the better. The version of the Open dialog used by GETPICT() no longer includes a preview option. Instead, you have to choose Thumbnails from the View menu.

Improved management of text merge

VFP 7 brought major improvements in text merge functionality, making it possible to store text merge results in a variable and cutting down the amount of code needed to set up text merge. VFP 8 adds one improvement, increased control over what comes at the beginning of each generated line.

When you perform text merge using the TEXT command, by default, any white space at the beginning of a line is carried through to the results. The new PRETEXT clause lets you indicate whether to keep those characters or to remove them. The same clause also lets you add a character string at the beginning of each line. However, you can't combine the two functionalities in a single command.

Let's look at them one by one. First, when you're generating output with TEXT, you may want to remove certain characters from the beginning of each line. PRETEXT gives you three choices (shown in **Table 1**), and you can specify any combination of the three.

Table 1. Removing white space. The new PRETEXT clause of TEXT… ENDTEXT allows you to remove spaces, tabs, and/or returns. The values are additive.

PRETEXT value	Meaning
1	Remove spaces at the beginning of each line.
2	Remove tabs at the beginning of each line.
4	Remove extra returns at the beginning of each line.

The second use of PRETEXT gives you the functionality of the _PRETEXT system variable right in the TEXT command. You can specify any string and it's placed in front of each line in the result. One place this is really useful is in writing IntelliSense scripts, where you may want to indent every line in a block to the position of the triggering keystrokes for the script. For example, you might have the following as part of a script to insert an IF-ENDIF block:

```
lcLine = oFoxcode.FullLine
lnPos = ATC(ALLTRIM(oFoxcode.Abbrev),lcLine)
lcSpace = SUBSTR(lcLine,1,lnPos-1)
TEXT TO myvar TEXTMERGE NOSHOW PRETEXT lcSpace
IF ~

ELSE

ENDIF
ENDTEXT
```

This example doesn't behave exactly as you want because the indentation is added to the first line, as well, but that line is already indented. In fact, you don't need this script because the VFP 8 FoxCode table includes scripts for all of the VFP control structures, including IF with and without an ELSE clause. (See Chapter 1, "Interactive Development Environment" for details.)

Unfortunately, neither the PRETEXT clause nor the _PRETEXT variable affects every line merged in via text merge. So, you can't use this feature to insert a block of code from a memo field and have it properly indented.

As noted above, you can't combine the two uses of PRETEXT in a single command. However, you can use the _PRETEXT system variable together with a numeric PRETEXT setting. So, to strip away existing white space and substitute something else, you can use code like this:

```
_PRETEXT = "*** TEG ***"
TEXT TO cResult TEXTMERGE NOSHOW PRETEXT 7
   This line will have its blanks removed and the comment inserted.
   So will this one.
ENDTEXT
```

Checking for empty values

FoxPro's EMPTY() function tests whether an expression is empty. But sometimes what you really need is the ability to test an expression and return a default value if the expression is empty. That is, you need code something like this:

```
uVariable = <<Some expression>>
IF EMPTY(uVariable)
   uVariable = <<Some default non-empty value>>
ENDIF
```

We've probably all written similar code hundreds or thousands of times. VFP 8 reduces it to one line with the EVL() function. EVL() does for empty values what NVL() does for nulls. In VFP 8, you can replace the code above with:

```
uVariable = EVL(<<Some expression>>, <<Some default non-empty value>>)
```

Both parameters to EVL() can be expressions of any type. (In fact, they can be of different types, but that's probably not a good idea in most cases.)

One obvious place to use this function is with optional parameters, so you might have code like:

```
LPARAMETERS tcFileName

LOCAL lcFileName
lcFileName = EVL(tcFileName, THIS.cFileName)
```

Finally, keep in mind EVL() replaces only empty values, not nulls. For nulls, you still need NVL(). In some cases, you might need to combine the two, like this:

```
uResult = NVL( EVL(uVariable, uDefaultValue), uDefaultValue)
```

Better output at design time and run time

There are a number of changes related to the way VFP displays things, either in the development environment or at run time.

First, the DEBUGOUT command can now handle a list of expressions rather than just a single expression. It behaves like the ? command, evaluating each expression separately, and then sending all the results as a single line to the Debug Output window. Consecutive values are separated by a single space.

This change is most useful when using DEBUGOUT as a tracing mechanism. While debugging, we often use code like this:

```
DEBUGOUT PROGRAM() + ": At start, value = " + TRANSFORM(nValue)
```

In VFP 8, we don't have to make sure all those values are character. Instead, we can separate them with commas, and omit the call to TRANSFORM():

```
DEBUGOUT PROGRAM(), ": At start, value = ", nValue
```

In VFP 7 and earlier, handing an object to the various display commands and functions (TRANSFORM(), MESSAGEBOX(), DEBUGOUT, WAIT WINDOW, and ?) generates an error. In VFP 8, the string "(Object)" is displayed instead. While that's still not terribly informative, it's a major improvement because the code won't crash.

The WAIT command gets a feature in VFP 8 that was added to MESSAGEBOX() in VFP 7; the ability to automatically transform the value you pass it into a character string for display. You no longer have to make sure that whatever you pass to WAIT is character. So, for example, the following works in VFP 8, but not in VFP 7:

```
WAIT WINDOW DATETIME()
```

As with MESSAGEBOX(), if you want to combine expressions of different types, you do have to convert them all to character. For example:

```
WAIT WINDOW "It's now " + TRANSFORM(DATETIME())
```

In addition, in Windows XP, WAIT WINDOWs appear with a shadow.

Finally, VFP 8 offers control over status bar messages that relate to open tables. By default, when a table is open in the current work area, the status bar shows the name and alias of the table, the current position of the record pointer, the number of records, and the exclusive/locking status of the table or record. (See **Figure 1** for an example.) The new SET NOTIFY CURSOR command lets you turn this display off and on. Use SET NOTIFY CURSOR OFF to prevent table information from showing in the status bar, and SET NOTIFY CURSOR ON to restore the display.

| Customer (Tastrade!Customer) | Record: 1/92 | Record Unlocked | NUM |

Figure 1. *Table information in status bar. By default, the status bar tells you all about the table open in the current work area. VFP 8 lets you turn that information off.*

You can check the current setting using SET("NOTIFY",1).

Font control

Each version of Visual FoxPro has included some improvements for those building international or multi-lingual applications. VFP 8 continues the pattern with increased support for multiple character sets.

The AFONT() function has changed in two ways. First, the function no longer puts every font in a font family into the array it creates. In previous versions, every single variation of a font was listed, even though many of the variants weren't available for use under most circumstances. For example, on Tamar's machine, in VFP 7, the array created by AFONT() (when only an array is passed) includes five entries for "Courier New":

- "Courier New"
- "Courier New CE"
- "Courier New CYR"
- "Courier New Greek"
- "Courier New TUR"

However, GETFONT() and the font list in the Property Sheet include only "Courier New." In VFP 8, the array created by AFONT() includes a single listing for "Courier New."

The second change to AFONT() lets you check whether a particular font exists in a particular character set. A new nFlags parameter changes the behavior of the third parameter. The new syntax is:

```
lResult = AFONT( FontArray [, cFontName, [, nFontSize | nFontCharSet
             [, nFlags ] ] ] )
```

When nFlags is omitted or 0, the third parameter is treated as the font size, and the function determines whether the specified font exists in that size. When nFlags is 1 (or, in fact, anything other than 0), the function treats the third parameter as a character set number and determines whether the font exists in that character set. So, for example, to see whether Arial is available in a Hebrew character set, issue this call:

```
lResult = AFONT( aFontResult, "Arial", 177, 1 )
```

Support for a variety of character sets has also been added to individual controls. The new FontCharSet property lets you specify which character set should be used to display the Caption or Value of the control. This allows you to have some controls display text in languages that use a different character set than the other currently in use. For example, you might turn on a Greek character set to enable display of mathematical formulas using Greek letters. Interestingly, you don't need to have installed support for these character sets to use them in your forms. Be aware that the characters that use the specified character set are in the higher range (CHR(128) and higher); regular Latin characters can also be displayed.

For forms, the FontCharSet property affects text placed on the form with the Print method or with the ? operator. However, it doesn't change the form's Caption or tooltips for the controls on the form. Note also that setting FontCharSet for a control doesn't affect the tooltip for that control.

The FontCharSet for a control is specified as a number with the default value 1 indicating Western. The list of values is documented in Help. Choosing to set this property in the Property Sheet brings up the Font dialog; you choose the character set from the Script drop-down list. The choices you make in the dialog also affect the other font properties (FontName, FontSize, FontBold, and FontItalic).

Forcing event processing

The DOEVENTS command was added in VFP 5 to provide a way to interrupt processes that aren't usually interruptible. DOEVENTS tells VFP to check for any Windows events that may have fired since the last wait state or call to DOEVENTS and process them before continuing execution. VFP 8 introduces two changes to DOEVENTS, one minor, one major.

The minor change is you can no longer add parentheses to a DOEVENTS call. That is, in VFP 7 and earlier, the following is a legal statement, while in VFP 8 it generates an error:

```
DOEVENTS ()
```

The new Code References tool (see Chapter 3, "Code References") should help you find and clean up any calls in that format.

The major change is the addition of a new FORCE keyword. In VFP 5 and 6, using DOEVENTS could slow your application down considerably because VFP waited until a Windows event occurred before continuing execution. In VFP 7, the wait for an event was removed, giving DOEVENTS less impact on performance.

However, there was a side effect of this change. In VFP 6, DOEVENTS allowed various items to be repainted during the wait. For example, ordinarily, when you change the caption of a label in a tight loop, the form isn't updated until the loop finishes. In VFP 6, DOEVENTS allowed the form to be updated. The VFP 7 behavior of DOEVENTS meant the form wasn't repainted in that situation.

Enter the new FORCE clause. When you issue DOEVENTS FORCE, you get the VFP 6 behavior. DOEVENTS without FORCE gives the VFP 7 behavior. We'd really prefer a way to combine the two behaviors so you could process whatever events are waiting, and repaint as needed, without having to wait for a Windows event. (Incidentally, DOEVENTS FORCE is one of the rare places where a user's perception that the application runs more quickly when he moves the mouse around is correct.)

SYS() function changes

What would a new version of VFP be without some new or enhanced SYS() functions? VFP 8 enhances two existing SYS() functions and adds several new ones.

SYS(602) was added in VFP 6 Service Pack 3 to work together with the new BITMAP=OFF configuration setting. Ordinarily, VFP keeps a bitmap in memory for each form it runs, and then updates the forms by copying the bitmap into visible space. This has the advantage of appearing to update in one fell swoop. Putting BITMAP=OFF into the configuration file tells VFP not to do that. It's useful when running applications remotely such as with Terminal Server. In that case, the bitmap technique for updating forms can be extremely slow.

In VFP 6 SP3 and later and in VFP 7, SYS(602) simply lets you find out the current setting. It returns "0" to indicate bitmap is off or "1" to indicate it's on. VFP 8 lets you change the setting dynamically. Pass 0 to turn off-screen bitmaps off, or 1 to turn them on. For example:

```
cNewSetting = SYS(602, nNewSetting)
```

Be aware that the new value affects only forms run after it's changed. Once a form is open, it uses the setting in effect at the time it was run.

Changes to an existing function plus a new function give you more options in computing checksums, numeric values that let you check the validity of a value. (For example, VFP uses checksums in the resource file to ensure values haven't been changed.)

SYS(2007), which has been in FoxPro for many versions, computes checksums. Pass it a string and it returns a value. The same string always gives the same result. However, there's no guarantee two different strings won't return the same result. So, a checksum is useful for validating data, but can't replace it.

In VFP 7 and earlier, this function is restricted to a 16-bit return value, limiting its results to the range 0 to 65335. There are situations where 65K values aren't enough. To handle that situation, VFP 8 has a new nFlags parameter that lets you switch this function to 32-bit operation. In order to add this parameter, however, the Fox team had to document a previously undocumented nSeed parameter. So, the updated syntax for SYS(2007) is:

```
nResult = SYS(2007, cString [, nSeed [, nFlags ] ] )
```

Ordinarily, you'll pass 0 or –1 for the nSeed parameter; that gives the same behavior as omitting it. Passing another value changes the results, but we're not exactly sure how. Pass 0 for the nFlags parameter for a 16-bit result value; pass 1 for a 32-bit result. Note that the nSeed value is ignored if you pass 1 for nFlags

Here are some examples:

```
? SYS(2007, "vfp")       && returns 31023
? SYS(2007, "vfp", 0)    && returns 31023
? SYS(2007, "vfp", 1)    && returns 34434
? SYS(2007, "vfp", 0, 0) && returns 31023
? SYS(2007, "vfp", 0, 1) && returns 3433001197
? SYS(2007, "vfp", 1, 1) && returns 3433001197
```

VFP also introduces a checksum function for records. SYS(2017) computes a checksum based on the data in the current record in the current work area. By default, all fields are included in the calculation except for memo and general fields, but you can pass a list of fields to omit. SYS(2017) also has the same nSeed and nFlags parameters as SYS(2007). The syntax is:

```
nResult = SYS(2017 [, cFieldsToOmit [, nSeed [, nFlags ] ] ] )
```

Here are some examples:

```
USE HOME(2) + "TasTrade\Data\Customer"
* Using original data
? SYS(2017)   && Returns 8310
? SYS(2017, "Region") && Returns 11204
? SYS(2017, "Region, Discount") && Returns 49624
? SYS(2017, "", 0, 1)   && Returns 841527743
? SYS(2017, "Region", 0, 1) && Returns 4047611504
```

```
* Now change a value
REPLACE Contact_Name WITH "John Smith"
? SYS(2017)   && Returns 10199
? SYS(2017, "Region") && Returns 60950
? SYS(2017, "Region, Discount") && Returns 30053
? SYS(2017, "", 0, 1)  && Returns 3617846100
? SYS(2017, "Region", 0, 1) && Returns 3844705268
```

One use for this function is to quickly check whether the data in a record has changed. If you store a checksum in the record, computed omitting the checksum field itself, then you can compare a new checksum for the record to the stored value to find changes. The code looks like this:

```
* At the time the record is created, do this:
REPLACE CheckSum WITH SYS(2017, "CheckSum")

* To check for changes:
IF SYS(2017, "CheckSum") <> CheckSum
    * Record has changed. Do whatever you need to
    * Update checksum
    REPLACE CheckSum WITH SYS(2017, "CheckSum")
ELSE
    * Unchanged
ENDIF
```

One area where this might be useful is with a table you're replicating across machines. In that case, you might put the checksum calculation in a trigger, so it's always up-to-date. Then compare the checksums from different versions of the table to find records that have changed.

When you call a function or procedure, VFP has a set of rules that determine where it looks for that routine. In one situation, the way it looks for the routine can be a resource hog. When a routine is bound into an APP or EXE file, that version is executed whether or not there's a copy of the same file along the search path. However, due to the search rules, VFP looks for the file on disk before it executes the one in the APP or EXE file.

The new SYS(2450) function lets you turn off this behavior. When you pass 1 as the second parameter, it tells VFP to search the APP or EXE before looking for a file on disk. When you pass 0 (the default), you get the old behavior. This function doesn't affect what version of the code actually executes, only how long it takes to find it. While it should speed up execution for pretty much any APP or EXE, it's most valuable in a WAN or other network situation, where the search can really slow things down.

Another new SYS() function, SYS(2060), seems to be one of those added for the convenience of the Fox team, which most of us will never use. Apparently, when the internal FoxPro engine receives a MouseWheel event from Windows, it checks the FoxPro event queue. If the last event on the queue was also a MouseWheel event, it updates a count of wheel rotations in the event rather than adding a new event to the queue. In some situations, handling MouseWheel events this way can cause problems. So, SYS(2060) lets you turn this behavior off and put each MouseWheel event on the queue separately.

There are several other new SYS() functions discussed elsewhere in the book.

Odds and Ends

The remaining language changes are not easily categorized, but they include several useful changes.

The CLEAR DEBUG command has been enhanced to clear all breakpoints as well as restoring the Debugger to the default position and emptying the windows.

The AGETCLASS() function lets you display the Open dialog specially configured for choosing a class and class library. It's the same dialog that appears when you issue MODIFY CLASS ?. There are two changes in VFP 8, one for the better and one for the worse. The better one is you can now use it on PRG files as well as VCX's. When the dialog appears, by default, it shows VCX files, but you can choose PRG in the Files of type drop-down list, as in **Figure 2**.

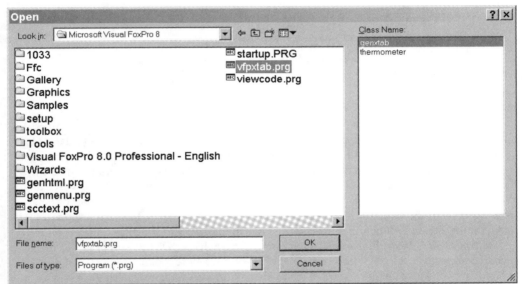

Figure 2. Choosing code-based classes. AGETCLASS() now allows you to choose either VCX-based or PRG-based classes.

The downside of this change is the function can no longer be used at runtime, only in the development environment. According to Help, that's because the code needed for parsing a PRG isn't included in the runtime environment. Because AGETCLASS() is used primarily for developer tools, we don't think this is a huge loss.

The QUARTER() function was added in VFP 7 to let you find out what quarter of the year a specified date falls in. However, it couldn't handle the empty date, firing error 11 when that value was passed. In VFP 8, QUARTER({}) returns 0, a condition you still need to test for, but it won't crash your applications.

Summary

In addition to the major items (described in other chapters), VFP 8 includes a number of relatively small changes to the programming language. In general, they're focused on fine-tuning those items that needed it.

Updates and corrections to this chapter can be found on Hentzenwerke's web site, **www.hentzenwerke.com**. Click on "Catalog" and navigate to the page for this book.

Chapter 14
Bits and Pieces

This is the "what's left over" chapter—it discusses changes in VFP 8 that don't fit into a specific category.

VFP 8 is considered by some to be the biggest upgrade to FoxPro since VFP 3 was released. The other chapters in this book have discussed language improvements, new and improved classes, enhancements to the database engine, IDE improvements, and a host of other changes in VFP 8. This chapter is devoted to things that fall into the "miscellaneous" category, such as what things have been removed from the box, what things have been added, and other items somewhat peripheral to the product.

What's out

One of the (minor) complaints some FoxPro developers have is the language gets more bloated with every version because obsolete commands and functions are never removed. While that's still true in VFP 8, some additional pieces have been removed.

The biggest item removed is support for Active Documents. In the security review of all applications Microsoft performed in early 2002, they found ActiveDoc support opened a potentially large security hole in VFP and Internet Explorer. Because of this, and helped by the fact that very few VFP developers used ActiveDocs, Microsoft decided to eliminate it from the product. The ActiveDoc class is still there (adding yet another item to the obsolete list) but it doesn't do anything, and the Fox team removed all references to it and its properties, events, and methods (PEMs) from the help file. If you rely on ActiveDocs, one problem you'll encounter after installing VFP 8 is not only will your ActiveDocs application not run under VFP 8, it'll no longer run under VFP 7 either because the install process removes some Registry entries needed by ActiveDocs. Fortunately, you can re-register those entries by creating and running a .REG file with the following contents:

```
Windows Registry Editor Version 5.00
[HKEY_CLASSES_ROOT\Visual.FoxPro.Application.8\shell\run]
@="&Run (VFP7 ActiveDoc)"
[HKEY_CLASSES_ROOT\Visual.FoxPro.Application.8\shell\run\command]
@="C:\\Program Files\\Common Files\\Microsoft Shared\\VFP\\vfp7run.exe \"%1\""
```

Specify the correct path for VFP7Run.EXE in the last line of this file.

The second biggest piece removed (or possibly the biggest, depending on your point-of-view) is the VFP ODBC driver and the VFPODBC.MSM merge module that installs the driver. Given that Microsoft has moved well past ODBC (first with ADO, now with ADO.NET) and the ODBC driver hasn't been updated for at least a couple of versions, doesn't support database events (added in VFP 7) or auto-incrementing fields (added in VFP 8; see Chapter 8, "Other Data-Related Changes"), and was removed from MDAC (Microsoft Data Access Components) several years ago, we can't say we're surprised by this. If your application still needs this driver, you can download it from the VFP Web site (**http://msdn.microsoft.com/vfoxpro**), at least as of this writing.

The other pieces removed are:

- Several sample applications and classes: the Client/Server sample application, the ActiveDocs solution sample, the Gopher Server application, the Pool Manager Server application, the TasTrade application (the TasTrade database, tables, and bitmaps are still provided), and the TypeLib sample class.

- Several tools: the Internet Search Wizard, CliReg32.EXE (which allowed you to register a VFP COM server remotely), and the Transformer (which helped translate fonts from one platform to another)

- Some ActiveX controls: FPOLE.OCX and DLL, which provide a means of running VFP commands from other applications, and FoxTLib.OCX, which retrieves type library information from files. The _TypeLib class in _Utility.VCX of the FFC was updated to use TLibInf32.DLL rather than FoxTLib.OCX.

Although it wasn't removed, the source code for the Converter, which converts older source code files such as screens and reports into the latest version, was moved from the Tools folder to XSource.ZIP in the Tools\XSource folder.

What's in

Balancing what Microsoft removed from VFP is what they added: many new samples, some new classes in the FFC (FoxPro Foundation Classes), and an old friend.

SQL Server and Access have both included a sample database called Northwind for years now. VFP has two sample databases similar, TestData and TasTrade, but not close enough for people who want to test how to switch between VFP and non-VFP data access (for example, using the new CursorAdapter class discussed in Chapter 6, "Improved Data Access"). Fortunately, VFP 8 includes a version of the Northwind database very similar to SQL Server's in structure and content. This database can be found in the HOME() + "Samples\Northwind" directory.

The Solution Samples pane of the Task Pane Manager (discussed in Chapter 4, "The Task Pane Manager") has an entire section, "New in Visual FoxPro 8.0", devoted to samples that demonstrate new features in VFP 8. (You can also get at these samples by running SOLUTION.APP in the HOME(2) + 'SOLUTION' folder.) Some of the features covered are event binding, CursorAdapter, XMLAdapter, grid improvements, and structured error handling.

The FFC has been a treasure trove of utility classes since its inception in Visual FoxPro 6. VFP 8 adds a few new classes. _PoolManager in _PoolManager.VCX provides a pool manager for objects. A sample that shows how this class works is provided under the Foundation Classes section in the Solution Samples pane of the Task Pane Manager. The other new classes in the FFC, in _WS3Client.VCX and _WS3Utils.VCX, provide the new Web Services classes and XML Web Services Builder described in Chapter 10, "COM and Web Services Enhancements".

Lastly, Puzzle is back! Although it doesn't appear in the VFP menu, you can bring it up programmatically with ACTIVATE WINDOW PUZZLE.

Configuration changes

There are two changes affecting the VFP configuration file (usually CONFIG.FPW). First, the maximum number of variables allowed, set with MVCOUNT, has been increased from 1,024 to 16,384.

The second change is you can now specify multiple configuration files by adding ALLOWEXTERNAL = ON to the CONFIG.FPW bound into an EXE (this setting is ignored for VFP COM servers). This tells VFP to either search for another CONFIG.FPW file or to use the file specified in any –C command line parameter. Because any settings in an external file override those in the internal one, this feature is handy when you need to tweak a few configuration settings at the client site, such as code page, the location of temp files, and so forth, but want to ensure certain items are set properly.

Improved error reporting

In an effort to improve their ability to track down serious application errors (sometimes called GPFs for their former name, General Protection Fault, or C5s for the C0000005 error number they display), Microsoft added the ability to send detailed information about the application at the time of the crash to the Windows error handler (sometimes called Dr. Watson). VFP now supports this enhanced error handling; this was actually added in VFP 7 Service Pack 1.

Figure 1 shows an example of the dialog you'll see when VFP crashes. To send an error report to Microsoft, click on the Send Error Report button; the Don't Send button closes the dialog without sending the report. If you want to see what information the error report contains, click on the provided hyperlink. The error report doesn't contain any personal or system information (such as your email address or processor serial number), only memory information about the crash. The Debug button likely serves to launch a Windows debugging tool, but we can't confirm this because it only causes more errors in VFP.

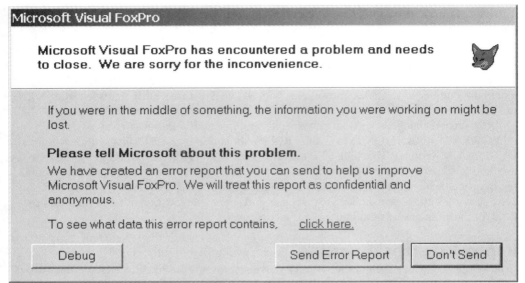

Figure 1. *VFP 7 Service Pack 1 added support for the enhanced Windows error reporting.*

VFP 8 also has better error messages than earlier versions. For example, if a VCX or SCX file is read-only at the operating system level, earlier versions of VFP display the error message "Cannot update cursor" when you try to build a project including that file. In a project containing hundreds of files, determining which one is the culprit can be a lot of work. Fortunately, VFP 8 shows the name of the file so you can change it to read-write and then try the build again.

Other changes

According to the VFP documentation, the only operating systems that support the development version of VFP are Windows 2000 Service Pack 2 or later and Windows XP. The supported operating systems for run-time applications are Windows 98, Windows ME, Windows 2000 Service Pack 2 or later, and Windows XP. The key word here is "support"; you may be able to get VFP to work on other operating systems (such as Windows NT), but Microsoft only supports the listed ones. Several developers have reported on the Universal Thread they had no problems running VFP 8 on a Windows 98 system as long as they copied GDIPLUS.DLL from C:\Program Files\Common Files\Microsoft Shared\VFP to C:\Windows\System. Our tech editor Jim Slater tested installing VFP 8 on Windows NT and found the Windows Component Update portion of the installation wouldn't work unless Service Pack 6 was installed; after that, VFP installed and worked without a hitch. We haven't tried it (because none of us has a system that old), but we suspect VFP won't run reliably on early versions of Windows 95 because several operating systems components VFP requires can't be installed on that version.

Windows XP supports 16-bit and 24-bit images for file icons, so the Fox team redesigned the icons for VFP-related files (such as tables, indexes, projects, and so forth) using higher color resolutions. **Figure 2** shows some of these icons as they appear in Windows XP. Even in earlier versions such as Windows 2000, the icon for VFP.EXE is more attractive. VFP 8 also allows you to attach high color images to an executable you create.

Figure 2. VFP 8 sports redesigned icons under Windows XP.

Because the new Web Services classes described in Chapter 10, "COM and Web Services Enhancements", use SOAP 3.0, this updated version is automatically installed on your system when you install VFP 8. The VFP CD also contains SOAP 3.0 samples.

Finally, Microsoft decided not to create localized versions of VFP 8. That means the IDE and help files will be available only in English. However, they do plan to provide a Localization Toolkit that will allow someone to create their own localized resource files.

Summary

VFP 8 is the most exciting new release of FoxPro in years. Unlike some earlier releases, this version has something new or improved for everyone. We hope this book has guided you through the discovery of the new and improved features and that you're as excited about VFP 8 as we are.

Updates and corrections to this chapter can be found on Hentzenwerke's web site, **www.hentzenwerke.com**. Click on "Catalog" and navigate to the page for this book.

Appendix

Appendix
Setting Up SQL Server 2000 XML Access

An add-on for SQL Server 2000 called SQLXML allows access to SQL Server over HTTP, with results returned as XML. This appendix describes how to set it up.

In order to access SQL Server 2000 using a URL in a browser or other HTTP client, or if you want to try the sample code shown in Chapter 6, "Improved Data Access", you have to do a few things. First, you need access to a machine with both SQL Server 2000 and Microsoft Internet Information Server (IIS) installed. Second, you need to download and install SQLXML 3.0 from the MSDN Web site (**http://msdn.microsoft.com**; do a search for "SQLXML", and then choose the download link).

> *These instructions can also be used if you have Microsoft Database Engine, or MSDE, installed instead of SQL Server.*

Next, you have to set up an IIS virtual directory. To do this, choose the Configure IIS Support shortcut in the SQLXML 3.0 folder under Start | Programs in your Windows Taskbar. Expand the node for your server, choose the Web site to work with, right-click, and choose New, Virtual Directory. In the General tab of the dialog that appears (see **Figure 1**), enter the name of the virtual directory and its physical path. For the samples in this book, use "Northwind" as the virtual directory name and "NorthwindTemplates" for the physical directory. Using Windows Explorer, create the physical directory somewhere on your system, and create a subdirectory of it called "Template" (we'll use that subdirectory in a moment).

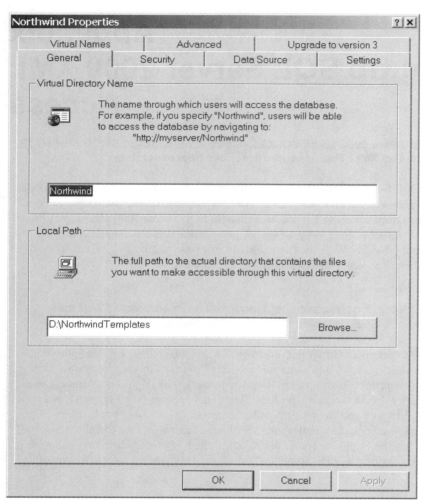

Figure 1. *Use the General tab to define an IIS virtual directory for a SQL Server database.*

In the Security tab, shown in **Figure 2**, enter the appropriate information to access SQL Server, such as the user name and password or the specific authentication mechanism you want to use.

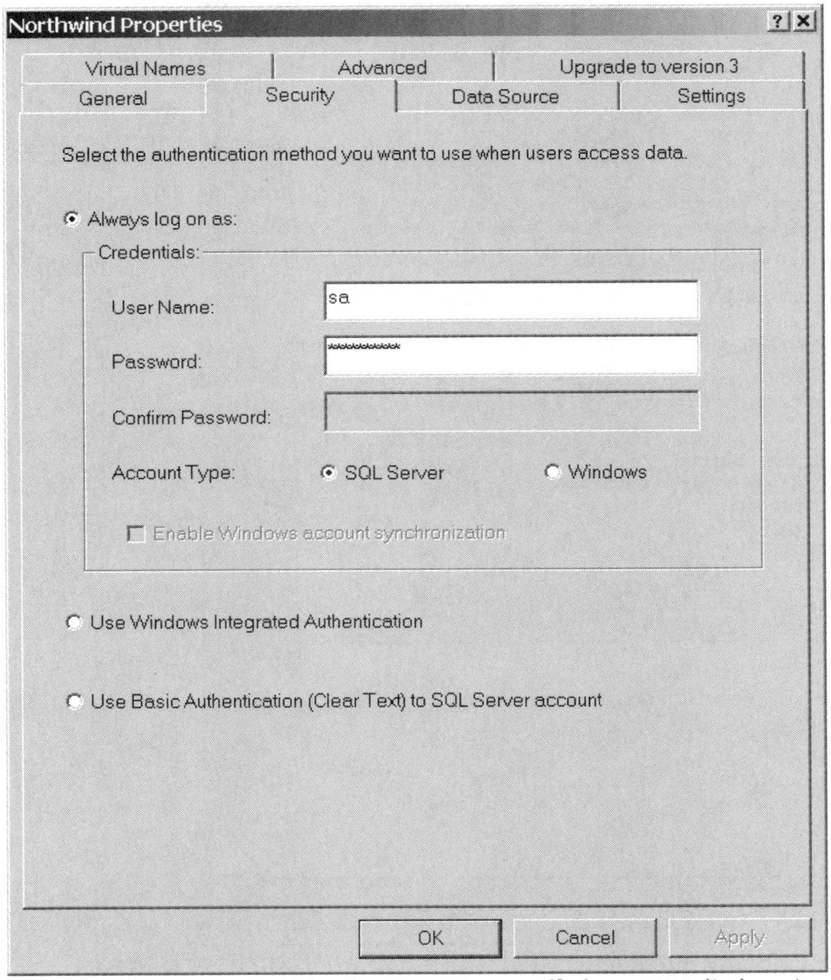

Figure 2. The Security tab allows you to specify how security is set up.

In the Data Source tab, shown in **Figure 3**, choose the server and, if desired, the database to use. For the examples in this book, choose the Northwind database.

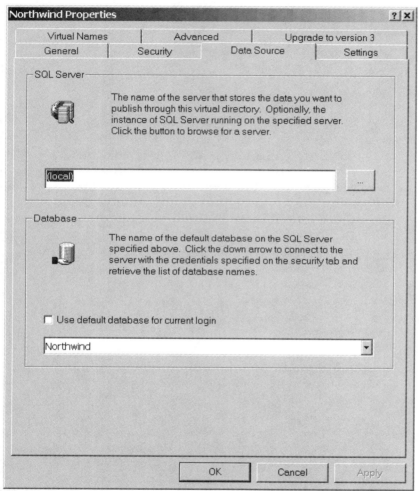

Figure 3. *The Data Source tab defines what server and what database is used.*

In the Settings tab (see **Figure 4**), choose the desired settings, but at a minimum, turn on Allow Template Queries and Allow POST.

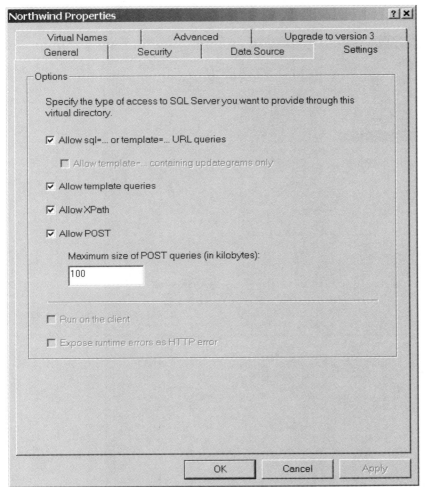

Figure 4. *Use the Settings tab to specify what types of access to SQL Server is allowed.*

In the Virtual Names tab, shown in **Figure 5**, choose "template" from the Type combo box and enter a virtual name (for this book, use "template") and physical path (which should be a subdirectory of the virtual directory; for this book, use "Template") to use for templates. Click OK.

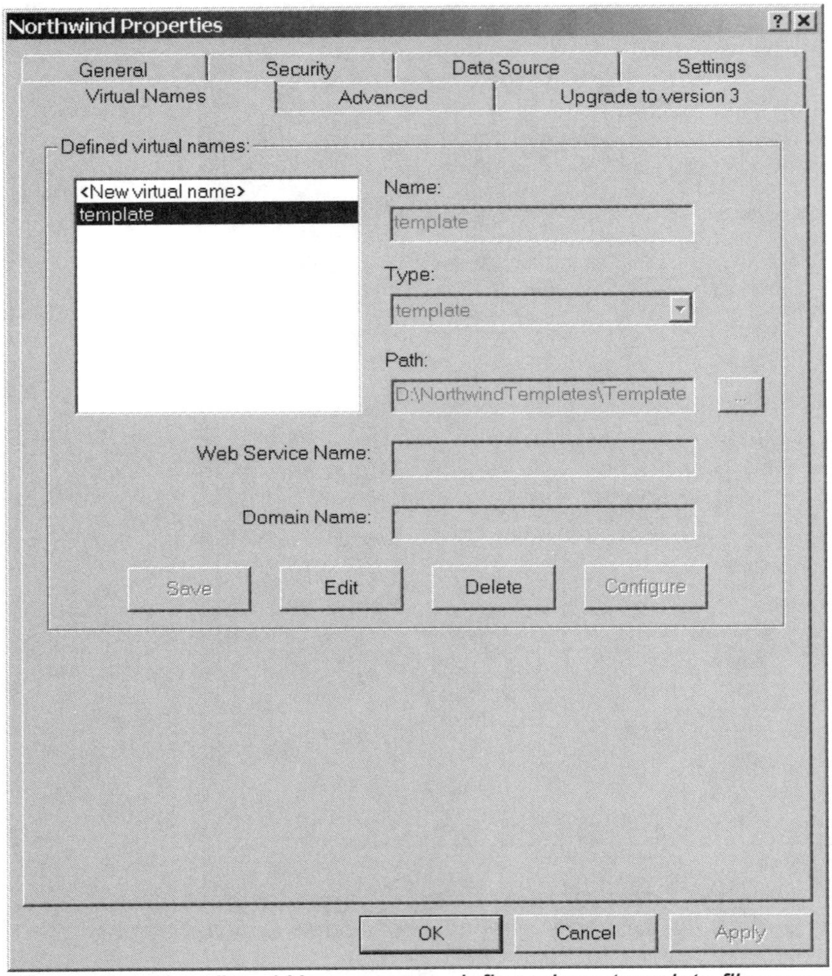

Figure 5. In the Virtual Names page, define where template files are stored.

To test this, put GetAllCustomers.XML (see note below) in the directory you specified for template files in the Virtual Names page. Then bring up your browser and type the following URL: **http://localhost/northwind/template/getallcustomers.xml**. You should see something like **Figure 6**.

*The Developer Download files at **www.hentzenwerke.com** includes GetAllCustomers.XML.*

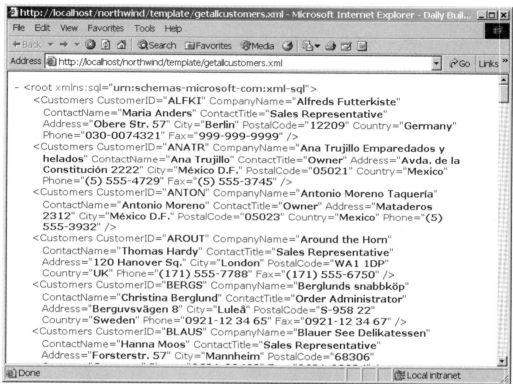

Figure 6. *If you've set things up properly, you should see an XML result from a query when you access SQL Server over HTTP in your browser.*

For more information on the Web server configuration process, see the Help file that comes with the SQLXML download.

Index

Note that you can download the PDF file for this book from **www.hentzenwerke.com** (see the section "How to download files" at the beginning of this book). The PDF is completely searchable and will provide additional keyword lookup capabilities not practical in an index.

Associated Projects page, Environment Manager pane, 69
Attach method, 137
auto-incrementing fields, 153–156, 170, 249
Auto-Update page, CursorAdapter Builder, 122–123
AUTOINCERROR OFF command, 155
AVG(), 158

— B —

BackColor property, 192
backup files, search results, 53
base class. *See also* CursorAdapters
    CursorAdapter, 118
    Exception, 222, 227
    features, 111
    OOP enhancements, 174–180
    viewing, 106
    XML-related, 135
Base class property, 21, 26
BatchUpdateCount property, 114, 164
Beautify option, 109
Before*(), 115–116
BindControl property, 181
BINDEVENT(), 207, 213, 214, 215, 216, 218–219
BindMe property, 209
bitmaps, 243–244, 250
Bookmark property, 126
borders. *See* VFP borders
BreakOnError property, 114
BSTR string type, 195
BufferModeOverride property, 114
Builder property, 26
built-in handler actions, 87
built-in VFP function, 114
button coloring, 192
byte arrays, 196

— C —

C5 errors, 251
captions
    adding in Report Designer, 103
    caption expressions, 160–161
Cartesian join, 96
Case checkbox, Filter page, 100
case-sensitive searches, 39

CASE statement, 222–223
CATCH statements, 222–223, 231–234
Category name property, 20
Category scroll speed spinner, 30
Category type property, 20
CD/CHDIR command, 237
CD command, 238
character sets, 242–243
character string, 239
Character type, 195–196
CHDIR command, 238
Check for New Internet Content section, Task Pane Options window, 77
checksum, 244
ChildTable property, 141
Class Designer. *See also* Toolbox; XML Web services
    controls, 17
    method editor changes, 106–107
    opening, 27, 108
    Property Sheet improvements, 107–108
    setting tab order, 108
    subclasses, 174
Class item, 21–22, 23, 24, 27, 30–32
class library
    adding, 21, 31
    FoxPane, 87–88
    managing, 34
    Member Class, 173–174
    specifying, 23
    specifying subclass, 88
    viewing, 106
Class library property, 20, 26
Class name property, 26
ClassLib field, 35
ClassName field, 35
ClassType field, 35
Cleanup Tables option, Task Pane Options window, 78
CLEAR ALL command, 77
CLEAR DEBUG command, 246
Client/Server sample application, 250
CliReg32.EXE file, 250
code-based classes, 246
code instantiating, example, 17
Code References